ONE
PARTICULAR
HARBOR

Janet Lee James

The Noble Press, Inc.

CHICAGO

Printed in the United States of America

Library of Congress Cataloguing-in-Publication Data

James, Janet Lee, 1951–
   One particular harbor / Janet Lee James
     p.   cm.
   ISBN 1-879360-30-6 : $13.95
     1. James, Janet Lee, 1951—Health.   2. Multiple sclerosis—
Patients—Alaska—Biography. 3. Alaska—Description and trav-
el.   I. Title.
RC377.J35   1993
362.1'96834'0092—dc20
[B]   93-33479
                                       CIP

Noble Press books are available in bulk at discount prices. Single copies are available prepaid direct from the publisher.

The Noble Press, Inc.
213 W. Institute Place, Suite 508
Chicago, Illinois 60610
(312) 642-1168

This book is lovingly dedicated to my parents
Richard and Anna Marie James
To my sister, Cindy, my brother, Richard
And to the tiniest, shiniest lights of my life
Matthew Joshua and Deborah Rose Brooks
And for Pooch

But there's this one particular harbour
So far but yet so near
Where I see the days as they fade away
And finally disappear . . .

Jimmy Buffett and Bobby Holcomb
"One Particular Harbour"

ACKNOWLEDGEMENTS

Since I'm nowhere near the writer I'd need to be to say how much she's meant to me all these years, I didn't even attempt it. Instead, I simply looked in my thesaurus under "Dollie Bucci, MS Patient," and wrote down a few of the words that came closest to describing how I feel about her. Among them are: loyal, strong, compassionate, intelligent, fragile, determined, funny, and above all else, *generous*. She is my friend for life, and beyond.

Much the same can be said about other old friends too, who have proven their worth in a thousand different ways. The Rosenblatts— Ira and Barb—never forgot and never stopped giving in any way. Carole Kunkle-Miller, Ph.D., my friend since we were seven, has been around for thirty-five years now, so I figure I can count on her for life.

It's important to me to say, also, that the dear and steadfast friends included in the pages of this book—such as Jane Hein, Cindy DuBois Rouse, Ryan Hixenbaugh, Ron Cash, Dave Gagnon, Tony Stone, and all the others—remain so today and are deeply loved and appreciated.

There are new friends, too, like Barbara Dockins and Bob Wellman, my dedicated and much-loved aides; and Laura Wallencheck, another writer whose depraved and deeply flawed character has helped me stay marginally sane throughout this entire process.

In addition to my immediate family, lots of love and support have come from my extended families, including the Lovetts and the entire Glavinic clan (especially my uncle Joe, who would have loved this).

On the medical front, my deepest gratitude must go to Benjamin J. Eidelman, M.D., Ph.D., of Presbyterian University Hospital in Pittsburgh. He has been my neurologist, my lifeline, and above all else, my friend. But were it not for his able assistants, Judy Webb and Fran

Brant, R.N., he'd be little more than just another garden-variety genius-physician.

And speaking of geniuses, there's my literary agent, Elizabeth Frost Knappman of New England Publishing Associates, and my editor at Noble Press, Doug Seibold. I don't quite know what to say here except that I love you both—and *thanks*.

Others whose friendship and willingness to help have meant so much include Jack Bogut, a radio legend in Pittsburgh; Bruce Van-Wyngarden, who single-handedly jump-started my writing career; and Mary Weyer and the entire faculty of the department of communications at Clarion University of Pennsylvania, Class of 1973.

Also, thanks to Ron Rukas, Chuck Blackburn, Georgie Conti Conroy and the others at Physician's Pharmacy in Tarentum, and to Deborah Yakunich of National Medical Care, Patty Harpel in Anchorage, Dawn A. Marcus, M.D., Mark Rauch, Sandy Koppler, Steve Wagner, Emily ("The Bug") Wellman, Judy Beck, Mark J. Grasak, Jr., and Colleen McGuire.

And finally, my appreciation to the agencies that have helped so much, including the Pittsburgh chapters of the Department of Aging; the Three Rivers Center for Independent Living; the National MS Society; and most notably, the Office of Vocational Rehabilitation. Bless them one and all.

AUTHOR'S NOTE

While preparing this manuscript for publication, it occurred to me that a few words ought to be said at the outset about the nature and intent of this work. First, it's important to note that the story told and opinions expressed in these pages are mine alone, and were never intended *in any way* to represent anyone else's circumstance or viewpoint.

Obviously there are as many different attitudes, beliefs, and convictions as there are severely disabled people in the world, and it would be ridiculous, if not completely libelous of me, to presume to speak for anyone other than myself.

In addition, I have to stress, in the strongest terms possible, that *as a profoundly disabled MS patient I represent a very small minority*. It remains abundantly true that the vast majority of MS patients experience relatively little difficulty with the disease and go on to lead active and productive lives for years and even decades. For those reasons alone, no one should be fearful of reading this book—the fact that *I* happened to draw the short straw, odds-wise, says absolutely nothing about anyone else's chances or expectations.

In conclusion, please understand that this story is true as I remember it, and forgive any details that may have grown fuzzy over time. Also note that some names and situations have been altered somewhat for reasons of privacy and respect.

ONE

Pittsburgh
Summer, 1973

IT WAS A LOUSY TIME to be looking for work as a disc-jockey. Pittsburgh was considered a top-ten radio market at the time and jobs in broadcasting were at a premium. The giants—powerhouse stations like KDKA, WDVE, and WTAE—attracted some of the best in talent from all over the country and were impenetrable fortresses to a beginner like me. These were the big leagues, and no one wanted to hear from you unless you had a solid reputation and years of experience behind you.

Problem was, I had neither. Fresh out of college, with little to recommend me beyond a brand-new degree in Communications and six short months of college radio experience, my job prospects were looking decidedly dim. And when you added to that the fact that I was a woman, the odds of my landing anything even remotely near an open microphone decreased exponentially, almost to the point of nonexistence.

However, so what? I'd beaten the odds lots of times before, and there was no reason to think it wouldn't happen again. All I needed was a little luck and a lot of perseverance, and sooner or later something would come along. I was perfectly sure of that. But until that happy day arrived, I still had to eat and pay the rent somehow. So taking the path of least resistance, I quickly landed a job tending bar full time, a skill I'd honed to perfection during my glory days at college. It was a lucrative arrangement, one that allowed me to maintain a decent standard of living while leaving my days free to search for something, *anything*, in my chosen field of broadcasting.

I started out optimistically enough, but the search proved increasingly futile and for eight long months I banged my head against studio doors without so much as a nibble. Finally, depressed and demoralized, I gave up the search altogether and decided to try another approach.

I reasoned that since advertising agencies produced commercials for radio stations, there had to be some sort of connection, jobwise, and that an agency might not be a bad place to start. It certainly couldn't hurt, I figured, so I quickly got down to business and began checking out possibilities in the ad world.

Typically, my first big break came as the result of a complete and total fluke. Late one Saturday night at the bar, an obnoxious, leisure-suited lounge-lizard named Al propped himself up on a barstool at my station and proceeded to offend everyone in sight. He had an annoying habit of insinuating himself into any conversation, invited or not, and anyone within earshot simply did their best to ignore him.

Eventually the talk turned to careers, and when I casually mentioned my lack of one, he boasted loudly that a buddy of his, some guy named Ron Cash, owned an ad agency in town and was currently looking for a new copywriter, a job for which I wasn't even remotely qualified.

"Hell, sugar," he leered as he coyly handed me Ron's phone number and address. "With those gams and a great set of headlights like yours, talent is the *last* thing you'll ever have to worry about—if you get my drift."

Spoken like a true invertebrate. I slipped the wrinkled piece of paper into my pocket and made a mental note to call this Mr. Cash of his first thing Monday morning to see about arranging for an interview.

I probably shouldn't have bothered. He was a good looking, nicely dressed man somewhere in his middle forties, but he had a sarcastic streak a mile wide and a tongue that could cut like a razor. Obviously someone had peed in *his* Cheerios that morning and he seemed determined to take it out on me. I couldn't imagine working for anyone more unpleasant, but I could see this was my ticket into the radio business and I really wanted the job. So, operating under the assumption that anything worth having was worth lying for, I jumped right in, determined to brazen my way through the interview.

Could he see some of the commercials I'd written recently? (*Commercials? What commercials?*) Uh, sorry, I hedged, empty-handed, but they were all on tape. No problem, he said—he had a tape recorder. Oh. Well. In that case all the tapes had been destroyed in a fire some time ago. They were excellent, though, and had won several major awards. Heh. Heh. I was on a roll. Could I type? Certainly. How fast? Oh, five or six thousand words a minute, somewhere in that neighborhood. Really? Would I care to demonstrate? Naturally I'd love to but, oddly enough, I'd somehow injured both wrists in a skydiving accident the day before . . .

I never blinked.

It is a measure of the man that he didn't have me arrested on the spot and instead only made me grovel for three hours before giving me the job. Later he told me he'd been so impressed by the level of deceit and effrontery I displayed that he would have happily made me a full partner right then, if only I'd thought to ask.

I came to love him dearly, and for all the reasons I so disliked him at first. His personality quirks were all manifestations of a rich intellect, and the sarcasm, once I tuned in to it, proved to be wit at its sharpest and a constant source of delight. He kept precious little to himself and in due course infected everyone around him with his own particular brand of madness.

Most seriously affected was his vice president and resident lunatic, Ryan Hixenbaugh. (Of the Pittsburgh Hixenbaughs, of course.) Ryan may have come from a well-to-do family, but he was really a bum at heart, and by the time I met him he'd already covered a lot of ground —there was a stint in the Merchant Marine, a Grand Tour of Europe, and hard as it was to believe, he'd once actually run away and joined the circus!

These were all qualities I highly prized in a person, and in no time at all we formed a solid bond of friendship that would last us all our lives. Ryan had a bizarre sense of humor, though, and it worried me a lot because I never knew when it was going to surface. We were standing on a street corner one afternoon, waiting for the light to change, when an elderly man came up to Ryan and tapped him on the shoulder. "Excuse me, sir," he asked politely. "Do the crosstown busses run all day?" Ryan never missed a beat as he spun around, slapped his thigh and sang out, "Doo dah! Doo dah!" It was an inspired bit of lunacy, vintage Ryan, and I still laugh out loud when I think of it.

Ryan and Ron quickly disabused me of any notions I had that advertising was simply a business, just like any other. It is the very essence of the enterprise that anything goes, and we did some of our best work in unconventional places. If you could think better standing on your head, well, then by all means please feel free—that's what the pillow in the corner was for.

Ryan worked best sitting on the john and it seemed like he was *always* in there, coffee and copybook in hand. Some days he wouldn't come out at all and I'd have to slide his mail, and even occasionally his lunch, under the door.

Ron, on the other hand, couldn't get anything at all done unless he had an audience, and he was forever holding court in his office, presiding over endless "creative meetings" on behalf of one client or another. These brainstorming sessions could often last until midnight or later, and to this day I have fond memories of the three of us rolling around on the floor, shrieking with laughter, unwilling and unable to stop until we'd come up with something good.

It was a quirky, happy little shop—just Ron, Ryan, me, and a free-lance artist named Jerry—and the four of us more than took advantage of our positions.

An ad agency works like this: clients would give us money to make commercials for them and then place them on the appropriate radio and TV stations. In some cases, these accounts could amount to hundreds of thousands of dollars a year and, naturally, every station wanted its fair share.

This is where the good part comes in.

Radio and TV stations were notorious for hiring young, good-looking men and women as sales reps, and whole platoons of them called on us daily. It was their job to bring us presents, buy us dinners, and see to it that our behinds were well and continually kissed. Inevitably our social lives merged with our professional lives, and Ryan and I, especially, played it to the hilt. It was like having access to a private, exclusive dating service, and life soon became an endless round of business lunches, dinners, parties, and celebrations.

But great social life aside, the very best part of the job for me was the free and immediate access I now had to every radio and TV station in town. Six short months before, I couldn't get past a receptionist's desk, and now I was welcome anywhere. I was happy as I could be, hobnobbing with the local stars and loving every minute of it. I thought it was the best of all possible worlds and I never wanted it to end.

* * * * * * * * * *

Over the past several months, however, I'd begun to sense that something strange was going on inside my body. There was nothing specific to it, certainly nothing I could put my finger on, but occasionally I'd feel a little bit off balance and disconnected, as though I was operating just a shade out of sync with the rest of the world. It was odd and mildly disconcerting, especially since I couldn't seem to find any reason to be feeling the way I did.

And there was more. Early one morning in June as I was drying off after a shower, I noticed an unusually peculiar sensation. The towel I was using was soft and fluffy, but against my skin it scratched and rasped as though it were made of sandpaper. And on top of that, my left leg felt vaguely numb and was burning and tingling at the same time, as though it had gone to sleep. I slapped it once or twice, hoping to wake it up and restore some normal sensation, but the strange feeling persisted.

It wasn't until a couple of hours later that the numbness wore off and I was able to go on about my business as though nothing had happened. But over the next several weeks half a dozen similar episodes occurred, and they were becoming increasingly hard to ignore. Once in a while I'd stumble against a piece of furniture, or clumsily trip over my own two feet for no apparent reason, and before long I began to feel like a real klutz. I know now that I should have told someone what was going on, but instead I kept my mouth shut and continued to hope that the problem would simply clear itself up and go away.

But it didn't, of course, and things came to a head early one October afternoon as I was returning from a recording session at KDKA, just a short walk across the park from our office. I was cruising along, enjoying the crisp autumn air, when suddenly my left leg gave out from under me and I hit the concrete—hard.

I lay there a moment, dazed and confused, trying to figure out what had happened. My stockings were torn, my knee was bleeding, and my shoulder hurt like crazy. I stood up, wincing, and tested my leg to see if it would bear any weight. It held, and I limped my way back to the office.

By the time I arrived, everyone had gone to lunch and the office was deserted. I checked the phone for messages, then went into the bathroom to clean myself up. After I bandaged my knee and changed into a new pair of nylons, I sat down to use the toilet, and that's when I *really* started to get worried. To put matters as delicately as possible, I could *hear* what was happening, but couldn't seem to *feel* anything at all. It was as though I'd gone completely numb inside.

Things were getting curiouser and curiouser. I made my way back to my desk and sat down shakily to try to think things through. Suddenly, without any warning at all, my left eye began to jerk back and forth uncontrollably and the whole room blurred and seemed to be spinning out of control. *What was happening to me?* As soon as my vision cleared and I regained my sense of balance, I decided that enough was enough and I picked up the phone to call our family doctor.

Luckily he was in his office, and I filled him in on what had been happening over the past couple of months. He listened carefully to what I was saying and agreed with me that it was most likely something harmless, like a pinched nerve or a simple spell of dizziness.

"You're probably right," he said, seemingly unconcerned. "But just the same, I want you to meet me at the hospital right away so I can have a look at you."

I explained that I was working until five but I guessed I could come by then if he really thought it was necessary.

"You're not listening to me," he said testily. "Five o'clock isn't soon enough. An hour from now isn't soon enough. I want you to drop whatever you're doing and get over here immediately. Right now."

"But—"

"I said *right now*."

Okay, okay. He could really get on my nerves sometimes.

I called my mom and told her what was happening, left a note for Ron, and inside ten minutes I was on my way to the hospital.

* * * * * * * * * *

We met at the emergency room and I climbed up on one of the tables so he could begin his examination. He was wearing his serious doctor face and didn't say much as he poked and prodded and jabbed at my leg with a pin. Could I feel that? Yes, dammit, I could feel that just fine. Could I wiggle my toes? Touch my nose? Make a fist? Yes, yes, a thousand times yes, I answered, annoyed. Everything was working perfectly and could I please go home now?

No, I couldn't. Everything did seem to be okay, but he wanted to keep me for a couple of days and run some tests just to be sure. *Sure of what?* Sure that everything was really okay. What kind of tests? Just tests, and quit asking so many questions. He told me to stay where I was and left to call Admitting to arrange for a bed.

I'd never checked into a hospital before and was surprised at how long it took. There were all sorts of forms and papers to fill out, and it wasn't until almost an hour later that an escort arrived to take me up to my room—a small, run-down cubicle that had definitely seen better days.

The bed was jammed between the door and a battered old nightstand, and was surrounded by stained yellow curtains that hung by chains from the ceiling. The walls were done in an institutional brown—muddy chocolate on the bottom and a dirty, peeling beige on top. Even the floor and ceiling were the same tired shade of brown. The windows were covered with heavy, faded drapes and looked out on the grimy facade of the psychiatric hospital across the street. All in all it was a great argument for socialized medicine.

The whole thing was depressing as hell and Mame, the head nurse, at least had the good sense to be embarrassed.

"Welcome to the Brown Hole of Calcutta," she sighed heavily. "Just put your things on the bed and someone will be in soon to help you get settled. Sorry about the room but we're short on beds and this is the only one available."

I said it looked as though it could have been the isolation ward in a madhouse once and she allowed as how that was probably the case. Once she was sure I had everything I needed, she wished me luck and made her way back to the nursing station. There wasn't much to do or see, so I sat down on the bed and thumbed idly through a magazine, waiting for the doctor and my parents to arrive.

My mom and dad got there first and were as confused as I was. Why was I in the hospital? And why hadn't I said anything about all this before? I told them everything I knew, explaining that the symptoms hadn't seemed important enough to mention before. As to why I was here, well, they'd have to ask the doctor that one because I sure as hell didn't know.

When he finally arrived he was as vague with them as he'd been with me. He explained again that it was probably nothing, but he wasn't one to take chances. Besides, he said, it wouldn't kill me to stay there for a couple of days while he ran some tests, would it? I had to admit he was right, but it didn't make the prospect of staying in that room any easier to take. He left then, saying we'd get started first thing in the morning.

* * * * * * * * *

The initial batch of tests wasn't too bad. I played Hurry-Up-and-Wait most of the day as the hospital took its pound of flesh in the form of X-rays, blood tests, EKGs, and the like. Nothing special, just the standard stuff everyone goes through. The hardest part for me was coming up with a urine specimen, and I wondered when we were going to get to the *real* tests. Surely he had something fancier than this in mind?

I got back to my room at five and was dumbfounded when I saw what was waiting for me there. Something like twenty-five baskets of flowers had been delivered and were stacked on windowsills, tables, trays, and even on the bed. I thought it was great—all this loot and I wasn't even sick! There were baskets from family and friends, of course, but most were from various radio and TV stations, and that's when I truly began to appreciate my job. The nurses were great about it all and even helped me to rearrange everything so I had room to get into bed and eat dinner.

Mom and dad arrived again at seven, along with my younger sister, Cindy, and my brother, Rich. We all had a good laugh over the flowers and sat around talking until some friends of mine dropped by to say hello. I was having a great time by then and had decided that this hospital business wasn't too bad as long as you didn't have anything wrong with you. To tell the truth, I was almost regretting the fact that I would be leaving it all the next day. But as it turned out, I wasn't.

Early the next morning the doctor sidled into the room and said that he'd ordered another test for me, something called a myelogram. However, Radiology was backed up and wouldn't be able to do it until the following day. It would mean another forty-eight hours in the hospital, but he really needed the test, so would I stay? I said it was okay with me, but what exactly was a myelogram? He explained that during the procedure, a small amount of dye would be injected into the fluid around my spinal cord, which would indicate if anything was wrong inside. It all sounded pretty heavy-duty to me and after he left I asked one of the nurses what it would be like.

She assured me that it was no big deal, almost routine in cases like mine, and certainly nothing to get worked up about. That was good enough for me, and I spent the rest of the day relaxing and talking to friends on the phone. More flowers arrived periodically and someone commented that my room was beginning to look like a funeral for some foreign head of state.

* * * * * * * * * * *

The myelogram should have been my first clue that something might actually be wrong with me. At seven-thirty the next morning a man from the Radiology department arrived with a clipboard and a whole sheaf of papers for me to sign. Since a myelogram is considered an invasive procedure, and since they would be doing a lumbar puncture, or spinal tap, at the same time, I would have to sign all the permission slips and waivers as though I were having surgery.

I signed everything without reading any of it, and tried not to listen while he told me in great detail what would happen later that morning. All I wanted to know was, would it hurt?

"No..," he said hesitantly, looking sideways out the window. "It won't hurt . . . much."

"Aw, shit," was all I could think of to say.

Just then a nurse came in carrying one of those backless hospital gowns and told me to slip into it. I put it on, then waited for an escort to arrive with the mandatory wheelchair for the long ride down to Radiology. I was beginning to get the routine down pat.

The X-ray room wasn't very big, and it was crammed full of all sorts of equipment, in addition to nurses, a doctor, and four or five technicians. A huge metal table stood in the center of the room and a heavy, ominous-looking machine was suspended overhead. I was starting to a feel a little uneasy. The doctor, a radiologist, came over to introduce himself, then asked me to climb up on the table and lie face-down. The table was cold and hard and uncomfortable, but there was nothing I could do about it except lie there quietly while everyone swung into action.

There was a vice-like contraption at the head of the table and while one nurse got my head secured in that, another began tying me down. Straps were stretched across my shoulders, hips, and knees, then pulled tight and anchored to the table. When they were finished I was completely immobilized.

I hated the feeling. It was as though all control had been taken away and I was trapped in an irreversible process which, once started, couldn't be stopped. I closed my eyes, took a couple of deep breaths, and tried to relax as they went on with their preparations. Someone scrubbed my back thoroughly with a disinfectant, then swabbed the entire area with Betadine. Finally, sterile drapes were put into place across my back and shoulders, leaving open only the small space in which the doctor would be working.

Next came the local anesthetic. I felt three or four sharp stabs and then a hot, burning sensation as the numbing agent took effect. Inside a few minutes I couldn't feel anything at all and I opened my eyes to see what the doctor was up to.

I knew it couldn't possibly be, but the needle he was holding looked like it was a foot-and-a-half long. He poured something carefully into the syringe, and when he turned and held it up to the light, I almost passed out. There was no way on earth he was putting that thing in my back, and I started hollering. Loud.

Paying absolutely no attention to my ranting, he moved to the side of the table and began feeling around on my spine.

"We're ready to begin now, Miss James. I'm going to insert the needle between two of your vertebrae and inject a little dye into the spinal fluid surrounding the cord. Please try and relax if you can. This won't hurt a bit."

The hell it wouldn't. Suddenly it felt like my whole back was caving in as he slowly pushed the needle home. I groaned involuntarily and a nurse reached for my hand and began to chant.

"It's okay now, the worst is over, don't move, don't move anything, take a deep breath and relax, the pressure is easing, don't move, don't move, don't move . . . "

She kept it up for the next half hour or so and it really was soothing. I still felt like a butterfly pinned to a board, but I made a conscious effort to relax and just get through it. Out of the corner of my eye I could see the fluoroscope, and although I knew I shouldn't be looking, I couldn't resist. After all, how often do you get to see your own insides?

It was hideous and fascinating at the same time. I could see the tip of the needle resting between two vertebrae and I watched, entranced, as the dye began to ooze into the clear cerebrospinal fluid. Soon the entire space was filled with the dye and gradually, clearly outlined on the screen, the spinal cord itself came into view. My actual spinal cord! All discomfort was forgotten as I stared, mesmerized, at the scope.

I heard a humming sound and slowly became aware that the table was moving. I was being tilted, head down, and I watched on the scope as the stream of dye slowly moved up my spine, exposing more and more of the spinal cord until it reached the base of my skull. The table stayed in that position for a couple of seconds while the X-ray machine clicked away, and then it started moving slowly in the opposite direction. Soon my head was above my feet and the dye was working its way back down my spine.

I watched the screen closely, looking for any obvious irregularities.

Everything looked fine to me, but then what did I know? As the table approached a vertical position I began to feel light-headed and a little dizzy. I must have blacked out for a few minutes because the next thing I remember, the table and I were back in our original, horizontal position. On the scope I saw the dye being drawn back into the syringe, and then watched as the needle was slowly, carefully withdrawn.

It was all over. The doctor congratulated me on my bravery, screaming fit aside, while the nurses cut loose the straps and freed my head. I asked him if he could tell anything from what he'd just seen and he said no, that I would have to discuss the results with my own doctor, once he'd read the films. I'd figured as much.

There was no wheelchair waiting for me this time. Instead, the nurses rolled me over on my back, then gently eased me onto a stretcher for the trip upstairs to my room. When I arrived, a team of nurses was waiting to move me from the stretcher into my bed. As soon as they were finished my parents and the doctor all crowded around me, eager to know how it had gone and how I felt.

"I feel okay, but my head hurts a little," I said groggily.

"That's fine. Perfectly normal," the doctor said happily. "You're going to have to lie completely flat without moving at all for the next eight hours or so until everything settles back to normal. If the headache gets any worse, just call the nurse and she'll give you something for it. I'll be back tomorrow to go over the test results with you, but remember now, lie still and no matter what, keep your head down."

Fifteen seconds later the freight train crashed into my skull. I shot six feet off the bed, screaming, and my mom ran for a nurse. I felt a quick, sharp jab and then moments later the sweet bliss of the Demerol took over, sending waves of relief coursing through my veins. My parents stayed by my side for the next eight hours until the worst of it was over and I finally fell asleep.

When the nurse woke me at eight the next morning I was feeling a lot better. The headache had settled down to a dull pounding and she assured me the pain medication would soon take care of that.

"But you'd better hurry up and get ready now. We just got a call from Rehabilitation and they want you down there right away."

This was great news. I'd heard wonderful stories about Rehab and its soothing massages and warm whirlpool baths. And now it looked like it was going to be my turn. Maybe this was the hospital's way of saying it was sorry about the myelogram. I quickly donned another hospital gown and waited eagerly for the escort to come and take me to my reward.

We passed several hydrotherapy rooms along the way, but instead of turning into any of those, she led me to a waiting area in the hallway and left me sitting alone facing a door with a sign that read "Electromyography." Before long the door opened and a doctor I'd never seen before beckoned me inside. Oh no, I thought to myself, what now? It was a tiny room, more of a closet really, and the only objects in it were a low, padded table and a complicated-looking machine sitting right beside it on a stand next to the wall. The doctor introduced himself and said that he would be administering the test, an electromyograph, or EMG.

"What about the whirlpool bath?" I asked.

He said he didn't know anything about any whirlpool bath, but if I would lie down on the table we could get started. He looked like a man who could be trusted, so I screwed up my courage and asked him the dreaded question.

"Is this going to hurt?" I asked, fingers crossed.

"Yes . . . " he said softly. "It will hurt."

I lay down on the table and stared hard at the ceiling, trying to dissociate myself from what was happening, hoping to reassure myself that nothing could be as bad as yesterday. The doctor was busy at the machine and neither of us spoke as he fiddled with a myriad of dials and switches. Several long minutes passed and when he turned to face me, his hands were full of what appeared to be electrodes. Each was connected to a long black wire which, in turn, was attached to the menacing machine itself.

Wordlessly he walked to the table and began attaching the large round patches to precise, carefully chosen points along my right arm —one each at my shoulder, elbow, and wrist. Electricity had always frightened me, and I was beginning to feel a little uneasy. But just as I opened my mouth to ask what was going on, he reached behind his back and quickly threw a switch.

For a few long seconds I held my breath and waited. The machine began to hum quietly and a soft, tingling sensation filled my arm. Then suddenly, like a white-hot bolt of lightning, my senses exploded as what felt like a hundred trillion volts of electricity crashed into my shoulder and shot in a searing arc straight down to the very ends of my fingertips. My head slammed against the table hard, and I bit down on my lip to keep from crying out as eleven times more the machine delivered its payload into my arm, each blast stronger than the one before.

By the time the last jolt ended, my lip was bleeding and I lay limp and whimpering, unable to resist even as I felt three more electrodes being attached to my groin, my knee, and my ankle. Before I had time to protest, the whole excruciating process began again, this time even more strongly. As the surges built in intensity, my leg began to jerk wildly on the table and my feet felt as though they were on fire. Desperate to do *something* to ease the pain, I grabbed for a pillow, pushed it hard against my mouth, and began to scream.

Then suddenly, mercifully, it was all over. When the last electrode was removed I sat up shakily and, refusing all offers of assistance, made my own way off the table and into the waiting wheelchair. I jerked the chair around, pulled the door open, and without a backward glance shot down the hall toward the elevator, not even bothering to wait for an escort.

As I rolled into my room I almost ran over Mame the nurse, who was just leaving. She must have seen the look on my face because for once she didn't say anything and kept on going. I pulled the curtains closed around my bed, climbed out of the wheelchair, and—finally giving in to the pain and the anger—fell sobbing into bed.

An hour later my doctor showed up with a sheepish look on his face.

"I'm sorry about the EMG," he said hesitantly. "I know it can be rough, but we had to do it."

I resisted the impulse to knock his head off and simply glared at him as I asked *why*.

"The EMG is a nerve-conduction test, and I had to know if your nerves are transmitting impulses properly."

"Well? Are they?"

"No."

Great. That was just what I needed to hear.

"Look," I said testily, "I think it's time you and I had a little talk." I was beginning to lose patience, with him in particular and the entire medical establishment in general.

"Not just yet," he hedged. "I've still got a few more test results to look at. I'm going to do that later this afternoon and I'll be in on Monday morning to go over everything with you then. In the meantime, please relax and try not to worry. I'll see you then."

And with that he was gone. It was going to be a long, long weekend.

* * * * * * * * *

True to his word, he was at the head of the procession that filed into my room first thing Monday morning. This was a teaching hospital, and everywhere he went, six or seven residents and medical students followed in a long white line. I'd gotten to know most of them pretty well over the previous seven days, and they were usually good for a laugh or two. But just then no one at all was speaking, and each was trying hard not to meet my eyes.

In the uneasy silence of the room my eyes focused closely on the doctor's hands as he made his way through the endless pages of my chart. Why hadn't I noticed them before? They were beautiful hands —gentle, caring, doctor's hands.

He closed the chart and sat down next to me on the bed while the residents moved in closer, forming a protective circle around me. Still no one spoke. He took my hand, cleared his throat, and then quickly, without preamble, said the words that would change everything forever.

"Our thoughts are now multiple sclerosis."

White. Everything is white and I can't see and I can't hear and if I don't start breathing soon I will surely die. Disoriented, disconnected, I fall forward, hoping it will hurt. Needing it to hurt. I have to feel something, anything. There's an arm around my shoulders. Good. It feels good. People are talking, going on and on and on, but it's all just words to me. Words like bubbles that float in the air above my head, never settling, never quite connecting. Someone touches my hand, my hair, my face, and finally, they are gone.

I sit alone in the quiet of the empty room, thinking. Is that it? Is that all there is? It was so simple. Six little words and nothing will ever be the same again. Wham, bam, you're a cripple, ma'am. So sorry but now there's the matter of the rest of your life. Have you given it any thought?

Thoughts? I can't think. I have to get away, just go. There's so much to do and maybe no time. What time is it? I have to know. I scream, WHAT TIME IS IT! and a nurse comes running. She catches me and I collapse, crying, against her body. Crying is good, she says, a good thing if only I can let it go, let it all come out.

It's okay, I say, I'm better now. It was all just a joke anyhow, nothing more than a silly, stupid prank—one of those practical jokes that doctors play on patients all the time to keep from getting bored.

No, she says softly, it's not a joke at all. It's honestly and truly for real and I'm sorry. Really, truly sorry.

Gears shift somewhere. *Sorry for what? So what if it's true? It's not going to change one single thing about my life. Doesn't she know who I am? Doesn't she know that I'm special? Hell, they can carve it on my forehead in big red letters for all the difference it's going to make to me. It's nothing really, no big deal at all.*

But where's my mom and dad? They must be on their way, but why didn't the doctor wait until they got here before he told me? Didn't he know I'd need them to hold onto? I'm getting scared now. My stomach hurts, my lips are numb, and I can feel my hands beginning to shake. Make them hurry, God, please, before I fall apart.

The phone rings and it's Ryan. I tell him what happened, but he can't understand what I'm saying. Says I'm crying too hard. *Crying? Me?* RYAN YOU CAN GO TO HELL. Slam. Gears shift again and I dial the phone. "Hey Ryan? It's me. Listen, the doctor was just in and told me I have MS. Pretty stupid, huh? But just a touch of it, nothing serious. Tell Ron I'll be back in the office in a couple of days. Hey, is the Miami trip still on for next week? Great! No . . . there's no need for you to come in tonight—I'm out of here tomorrow. See you then, babe. Yeah, I miss you too."

Here they are at last. Mom and dad and Cindy and Rich have come and everything's going to be okay now. But wait a minute—everyone's crying, even dad. What can I do to make them stop? And most of all, how can I tell them how sorry I am for all the pain I've caused? I must have done something terrible to have brought all this on, but I don't have any idea what it could have been. All I know for sure is that nothing will ever be the same again and that I'm sorry . . . so very, very sorry.

They stay with me all day and late into the evening. We pass the long hours talking quietly about what has happened and what it all might mean. None of us knows much about the disease except that it was commonly spoken of as "The Great Crippler of Young Adults." We wait patiently for the doctor or *someone* to arrive and explain it to us further. But no one comes. The facts, it seems, will have to wait.

At nine o'clock a voice comes over the intercom announcing the end of visiting hours—time for everyone to go home. Wearing our bravest smiles we hug and kiss and say goodnight, and I watch their backs as they walk slowly out the door. God, how I love them all.

Mame comes in later and asks if she can get me anything, or would I just like to sit and talk for a while? No thanks, I answer distractedly. I'm all talked out right now. But a sleeping pill would be great—I'm feeling kind of keyed up for some reason. She brings the pill and I swallow it gratefully, looking forward to the oblivion I know it soon will bring.

But three hours later I find myself lying back against the pillows, eyes closed, still wide awake. I hear a shuffling sound and look up to see Ryan standing at the foot of the bed, grinning. Maybe I really *am* asleep and dreaming. He can't possibly be here at midnight, can he?

Of course he can. He explains that while any fool can get into a hospital during visiting hours, only an actual genius could pull it off in the middle of the night. Anyhow, here he is, and aren't I glad to see him?

I tell him I'm *delighted* to see him, and I smile happily as he crawls into the tiny hospital bed with me and takes me in his arms. We lie talking quietly for a long time as gradually the reality of what has happened today finds its proper place in my heart. When there are no more words left to say, he holds me close as I cry softly onto his shoulder, never moving until, at last, I fall asleep.

* * * * * * * * * *

I really thought I'd be able to go home right away, but the doctors had other plans, and over the course of the next seven days I learned more than I ever wanted to know about multiple sclerosis. I was strangely uncurious about the whole subject, but I tried to pay attention to what they were saying and gradually some of it started to sink in.

While there were a lot of different theories, no one was really certain what caused the disease, and until someone discovered that, there was little hope for a cure. Everyone involved seemed quite optimistic, though, and I heard more than once that the researchers were closing in fast and that something big could happen within the next few years.

I found out that coming up with a diagnosis was no simple matter, either. Since no definitive tests for MS existed at that time, diagnosis was generally made on the basis of the process of elimination. Even if MS was initially suspected, everything else had to be ruled out first. In my case, for example, the myelogram was done in order to rule out the possibility of a spinal cord tumor, something the doctor had feared from the start.

Diagnosing MS is a little easier today due to the availability of more sophisticated testing procedures like CAT scans and MRIs, but mostly it's still a judgment call. Sometimes physicians are reluctant to pronounce a diagnosis of MS because of uncertainty, or an unwillingness to tell a patient that he or she hasn't much to offer in the way of treatment. And then, there's always the possibility that the diagnosis itself might be too much for a patient to cope with, and that hearing it could actually serve to worsen the condition.

But the consequences of *not* knowing can be devastating, too. If left in the dark, a person could wander around for years, terrified by the thought that what was happening to them was "all in their heads," a manifestation of some psychological disorder or—worse—

the result of a much more malignant or even deadly disease. I was glad my doctor and I had the same philosophy on this one.

Technically put, MS is classified as a "demyelinating" disease, one that affects nerve fibers in the brain and spinal cord. These fibers are the pathways for electrical signals sent from the brain to every part of the body. Each is covered with a sheath of myelin, a fatty substance that acts as an insulator, much like the insulation on an electrical wire. During an MS attack, or "exacerbation," parts of the myelin sheath are eaten away, exposing the fiber and slowing down or blocking altogether the electrical signal. As a result, important functions of the central nervous system, such as vision, mobility, or sensation, can be lost or diminished.

When this erosion of the myelin sheath occurs, other types of cells begin to proliferate and arrive at the site to form scar tissue, or "sclera." The term "multiple" indicates that this scarring can occur randomly, anywhere throughout the central nervous system, resulting in a wide variety of symptoms that vary from patient to patient.

There isn't anything predictable about MS, either. The classic pattern is one of attacks and remissions, but even these are different for everyone, and there's no way of telling what the reaction will be each time. In extremely rare cases the attacks are almost constant, and can result very quickly in total disability. Other people experience a much slower progression and enjoy relatively long periods of remission between attacks. A third group of people luckily don't experience much difficulty at all with the disease and can go on leading relatively normal, active lives for years and even decades.

As to treatment, well, the news here was disappointing. At that time there were no known agents that could halt or even alter the progress of the disease, and all treatment was strictly symptomatic. To that end, a wide variety of steroids and hormones were being used, such as cortisone, prednisone, and ACTH (adrenocorticotropic hormone), just to name a few. All had anti-inflammatory properties and, especially in the early stages of MS, could be very helpful in lessening the severity and duration of an acute attack.

That was why I was being kept the extra week. My original symptoms had worsened somewhat during my stay in the hospital, and I even began to notice some new ones. I'd developed a mild case of double vision, and my speech began to slur just slightly, as though I'd had a couple of beers too many. But it was my feet that for some reason bothered me the most. They felt as though someone had crushed all the bones inside, and the sensation was like that of walking barefoot over loose gravel. It didn't hurt, but it wasn't doing wonders for my sense of balance, either.

And so the decision was made to start me on my first course of ACTH—intravenously. Everyone has a long list of things they really hate, and IVs are right at the top of mine. I kicked and cursed for fifteen minutes while the poor phlebotomist tried to open a vein and push a needle inside, and by the time he finished I know he was considering a career change.

But damn if it didn't work.

It was almost miraculous. Literally overnight I noticed a lessening of the symptoms, and by the second day they were completely gone! I was ecstatic and convinced that we had found a cure. The doctors assured me that wasn't the case at all, and cautioned me about some of the side-effects I might soon be experiencing, like water retention, serious weight gain, and, in big capital letters, ANXIETY. These guys weren't fooling around.

On day three I began to bloat, and noticed my face was taking on the dimensions of a full moon in October. Athletes (stupidly) take steroids for a reason, and I remember telling one of the residents that if this kept up, I'd have to give serious thought to trying out for the NFL. He just laughed and said I could probably qualify.

On day four I received the first injection of Valium for my nerves. It helped, but there weren't enough tranquilizers in the world to calm me down, let alone put me to sleep. Overnight I turned into a strung-out bundle of raw nerve endings, snapping at everyone, pacing the halls night and day. Later one of the nurses told me she'd never seen anyone react quite so severely to the treatment, and she confessed that some of the other nurses were beginning to look at the idea of euthanasia from a whole new perspective.

On day five my appetite took on a life of its own. From morning to night I foraged for food, bribing nurses for extras on my dinner tray and pleading with friends and relatives for treats from home. Late at night I'd sneak off the floor and stage secret raids on the vending machines in the cafeteria. Ice cream sandwiches and cheese popcorn were what I craved most and I could never seem to get enough.

I wasn't above stealing, either. As dinnertime approached, I'd skulk around the halls, waiting for the food cart to arrive, and as soon as the coast was clear I'd dart out and snatch up all the dinner rolls and desserts I could carry. Then I'd race back to my room, pull the curtains closed around the bed, and sit stuffing rolls, cakes, and pies into my mouth as fast as I could swallow. It was sickening, but there wasn't a thing I could do to stop myself.

No one was happier (or fatter) than I when the IV was finally pulled and I was told I could go home. I had a long talk with the doctor, who said he thought I'd do splendidly but to call if I ran into any problems. He also cautioned me to guard against fatigue, stress, and especially heat, as any of the three could aggravate my condition. I promised, but told him not to worry because I was sure I wasn't going to have any problems at all. I just wasn't.

At last the great day arrived, and I discovered that getting out of a hospital is a whole lot easier than getting in. All I had to do was say goodbye to the nurses, pay my phone bill at the cashier's desk, and I was sprung. The fresh air tasted wonderful after two weeks of confinement, and while I stood waiting for my dad to bring the car around, I couldn't help feeling like a refugee. It had been a close call, but it was all over now and everything was going to be fine. We got the car loaded quickly, pulled out of the parking lot, and without so much as a backward glance, left the hospital and everything it represented behind.

TWO

Pittsburgh
Autumn, 1974

THE WORLD I CAME BACK TO was the same one I'd left only two short weeks ago. My apartment looked like it always had—messy, sprawling, and filled with things I loved. Huge stacks of books were piled up everywhere, dirty dishes filled the sink, and the cats were snoring loudly in the bathtub, just the way they always had. I dropped my bags in the hall and wandered around from room to room, happy to be back where I belonged. The place was old and beat-up, but it was mine and I loved everything about it.

Something was wrong that day, though. As I sat on the bed looking around, I sensed there had been a change. Instead of the happy homecoming I'd anticipated, I felt somehow distanced and detached from everything surrounding me. It just didn't feel like home anymore. My refuge had become an anonymous collection of rooms, an impersonal place filled with things I used to care about. It was disturbing; for some reason I felt tense, anxious, and deeply unsettled inside, and no matter how hard I tried, I couldn't seem to shake it. Even the cats seemed wary, and circled my feet a couple of times before jumping up on my lap in welcome.

Work became my salvation. When I first went back to the office Ron and Ryan treated me as though I were made of porcelain, each one scurrying to outdo the other in their efforts to see that I was comfortable and well taken care of. It was an unprecedented expression of friendship and kindness, and just as I was really starting to relax and enjoy all the extra attention, the two of them got bored and lost interest in me completely. Inside a month everything was back to normal and they reverted to type, just like the couple of renegades they were.

Outside the office, however, I remained the center of attention virtually everywhere I went. It seemed like everyone in town knew what had happened to me, and those who didn't, I told. I'd read somewhere that most people, when confronted with a serious illness, go through a common, predictable series of emotional responses, the first and strongest being denial. Of course I was far above all *that*.

Convinced that predictability was a virtue of the simple-minded and determined to beat the psychological odds, I talked about my diagnosis with anyone who would listen. I found I could work the fact that I had MS into the most casual of conversations, and before too long I was happily divulging the most intimate details of my condition to total strangers at bus stops and on street corners, eager to convince myself that *I* was in control and on top of the whole situation.

But any second-year psychology student could have seen what I was up to. By being so open and forthcoming on one level, I was able to kid myself into believing I had the denial problem licked. That, of course, made it possible for me to go on denying the new realities of my life on a much more dangerous, emotional level, and I went on happily talking and repressing for the better part of a year. It was such an obvious ploy, and it didn't stop there, either. Invariably at some point in the conversation, the person I was talking to would comment both on how brave I was to speak so frankly about my condition, and on how well I was doing, all things considered. Naturally this was the response I'd been angling for all along, and like a vain adolescent fishing for compliments, I milked the situation for all it was worth.

I found myself responding with something unspeakably arrogant like, "Oh, it's not so bad. It's really just a question of attitude." Or, "I believe in positive thinking. Everyone with MS doesn't have to wind up in a wheelchair, and I've already decided it's not going to happen to me," or something equally as offensive.

What I couldn't seem to understand at the time was that despite all my posturing and preening, I was nothing more than a very, *very* fortunate young lady. My MS was firmly in remission, and as far as anyone could tell I was symptom-free and healthy as a horse. But instead of acknowledging the fact and thanking God for my good luck, I was acting as though all of this was somehow a result of my own doing.

I had the market cornered on sanctimony and self-righteousness, and never once did I consider the unlucky ones—those who had been fighting the disease for years and who were already stuck in their wheelchairs. With every word I spoke I damned them all, implying smugly that their advanced states of disability were in some way their own fault—the result of a "weak will" and "negative thinking." These are all sentiments I heartily regret today, and even now I cringe a little when I think back on some of the really awful things I said.

Arrogance and pridefulness aside, however, the rest of that first year was given over mostly to humor and good-natured kidding. Typically, Ron and Ryan were the worst, daily scaling new heights of hilarity in their quest for the perfect cripple joke.

"Hey, JJ!" one of them would holler across the office. "What do you call a woman who's missing her right arm and leg?"

"I don't know," I'd answer warily, fearing the worst. "What?"

"Eileen! . . . Get it? . . . I LEAN! HAW! HAW! HAW!"

It got a lot worse before it got any better, and more than once I found myself wishing MS were contagious.

Overall, though, it was a happy time for me, and I was content to stay where I was for a while, surrounded by friends, tucked safely away in a cocoon of innocence and good intentions.

* * * * * * * * * *

But the following September brought some changes. With the coming of Autumn I noticed I was beginning to feel edgy, itching to do something different. I certainly wasn't unhappy where I was, and there was no place else I particularly wanted to be, but suddenly it seemed terribly important that I get a move on toward something fresh and new and exciting. I didn't know it then, but this vague restlessness was the beginning of an impulse that would come to dominate my life and act as the driving force behind everything I would ever do again. At the time, though, I just thought I wanted a new job.

"Warm and Wonderful" WLOA was close to the bottom of the heap in Pittsburgh, ratings-wise, and it was easy to see why. The station operated on a shoestring budget and the music mix ran the gamut from Perry Como and the Boston Pops to the very latest in disco—not a format to inspire much loyalty in anyone.

It's probably for that very reason that Bill Matta, the owner, decided to try something daring; he proposed to put a woman on the air in the demanding afternoon "drive-time" position from two to six each afternoon. Remember, this was 1975 and the idea of female radio announcers hadn't yet gained wide acceptance in broadcasting circles. Women *were* beginning to be hired as disc-jockeys, but they were mostly relegated to the less visible late-evening or all-night airshifts, and the thought of showcasing one during drive-time was considered risky business indeed.

Bill mentioned the idea to Ron Cash over lunch one day and asked if he could recommend someone who might be suitable. Ron told him he ought to talk to me, figuring correctly that I could screw it up as well as anyone else. Maybe even better.

I was ecstatic to say the least, and we quickly got together to discuss the possibilities. Even Bill seemed nervous about the whole idea at first, but he was determined to give it a shot and we spent the better part of an hour reassuring one another that it really could work.

But could it? The only on-air experience I had was in college radio, which at that time bore little resemblance to the real world of broadcasting. In fact, I didn't even have an aircheck or audition tape he could listen to. But Bill had come this far and wasn't going to let anything as inconsequential as my ineptitude and inexperience stop him, and we agreed I would start in two weeks. It was that simple. The salary would be substantially less than what I was already making, but to be perfectly honest, I would have paid *him* for a chance to work on the air of an honest-to-God, major-market Pittsburgh radio station, ratings or no ratings.

Ron and Ryan were wonderful, rallying around me with support and encouragement and offers of unlimited assistance. Ron, a former broadcaster himself, was especially helpful. He said I could call on him anytime for help and told me not to worry too much about screwing up since no one ever listened to WLOA anyhow. Friends can be such a comfort.

I still count the night before I went on the air as one of the worst of my young life. By nine o'clock I'd thrown up twice and by eleven I had called everyone I knew and begged them not to listen. Oddly enough, the idea that thousands of strangers would be listening didn't bother me at all. It was the thought that everyone who knew and loved me would hear me make a complete fool of myself the next day that had me so upset. As it turned out, I had every reason in the world to have been worried.

In the long, proud history of radio broadcasting, I don't think a worse performance was ever given than the one I gave that afternoon. I realize that's a sweeping statement, but I made a sweeping ass of myself and I have a tape to prove it.

By the time my shift ended and the evening announcer arrived to take over, I was near tears. I walked out of the studio without saying a word to anyone, afraid that if I did, I'd fall apart completely. People called me at home later that night, trying to be kind, but it was no use. I blew it, I knew it, and no amount of pretending was going to make me feel any better.

But somehow I found the courage to go back the next day and the day after that, and gradually I even began to improve a little. Phone calls and listener requests picked up, Bill started speaking to me again, and eventually I was able to relax a bit as I settled in and found my stride. Somewhere along the line I even began to enjoy myself.

* * * * * * * * * *

Like most people prone to excess, I've always operated on the assumption that anything done in moderation is a waste of time and that the middle of the road is a boring place to be. Why walk the straight and narrow when all the really fun stuff can be found off on the periphery somewhere? You just have to know where to look.

People who think this way tend to lead unconventional lives filled with highs and lows, peaks and valleys, and I was no exception. I lived always for the highs, tried to ignore the lows, and did my best to stay as far away from the middle as I could.

But nothing stays the way it is forever, and by the following April I began to notice some changes. All of a sudden the highs weren't so high anymore, and the lows began to take on some new and frightening dimensions. Something, somehow, had gotten all messed up inside.

The whole thing started out innocently enough as just another case of the blues. Everyone gets depressed once in a while, and at first I was sure that was all it was. I'd just stew in my bad mood for a while, use it as an excuse not to clean my apartment, then wait for it to pass. No sweat.

But this time it was different. It wasn't simply my time of the month, or a bad biorythmic phase, or anything quite so simple. MS, or more precisely my *awareness* of MS, was at the root of this one, and I was in for one hell of a siege.

I'd spent most of the past year doing a lot of talking and very little thinking, but now everything seemed to be completely turned around. Suddenly MS was *all* I could think about, twenty-four hours a day, awake and even asleep. It's hard to say for sure now, but I think the dreams were probably the worst part of it all. There were three of them, and they never varied.

In the first one I found myself inside an old-fashioned, hand-operated elevator—one of those old steel cages with wire mesh walls and a metal grate in place of a door. The building was dark and ominously quiet and there wasn't another soul in sight as I pulled the door shut and pushed the lever hard, locking myself securely in. I pushed the button marked "One" and waited as the elevator began its slow descent.

Moments later, almost imperceptibly, the car began to pick up speed. It was moving faster and faster, and when I realized what was happening I started to panic. I pushed the buttons frantically, desperately trying to stop the elevator. But it was no use. Suddenly there was the unearthly sound of metal shearing as the thick steel cables snapped and sent the car plummeting to the bottom of the shaft.

It was a long, long time to think about dying.

In the second dream I was standing all alone on a wide, empty beach as an immense tidal wave swept toward me from far out at sea—a deadly black wall of water towering higher and higher every second. I stood frozen in its path, unable to move as the boiling crest roared two hundred feet over my head, and as it came thundering down with all the power of heaven and hell, I woke up in an icy sweat, shaking and hysterical.

But the third dream was easily the most disturbing.

It was late at night and I was moving into a huge, dark house with five other women, all of them strangers. The first floor of the house, inexplicably, was an airline terminal, with living quarters for the six of us upstairs.

Our bedrooms were arranged in a row along a straight, narrow hallway that appeared to go on forever. As I passed all the other rooms, I stopped to take a quick look inside, noticing that each was done in a different shade of pastel and white. The rooms were light and airy, the beds looked virginal in their white lace coverlets, and sheer, frothy curtains billowed at the windows. They were lovely and I couldn't wait to see what mine looked like.

The hallway was deathly quiet, and as I stood facing the closed door to my room I was suddenly filled with a sense of dread, as though I knew something dark and evil was waiting for me on the other side.

I reached for the knob, turned it quietly, and with my hands shaking, walked slowly into a nightmare.

The walls and the carpeting were a deep, bloody red and in the center of the room, ominous and silent, stood a massive ebony bed. It was canopied and draped in heavy black velvet that was tied back with thick red cords to expose the base of the bed—an unspeakable horror of hideously carved figures and images too sick and depraved for words. Heavy velvet drapes covered the windows and the only light in the room came from a mass of ebony tapers blazing eerily at the foot of the bed.

Somehow I knew the room had always been there, waiting for me, and that this was the place I was meant to dwell in forever.

The air was thick and suffocating and I raced wildly from the room. The walls of the hallway closed in on me as I ran faster and faster across a thin rope bridge, down another empty corridor and out onto a wide, wooden balcony, where I stopped. I walked slowly to the bannister and looked down onto a dark, silent stage.

A small spotlight was shining and in its weak circle of dim yellow light I could see a cold, empty fireplace where three small stockings hung limply from the mantelpiece. Next to the fireplace stood a naked, lifeless Christmas tree and beside it on the floor was a child's wooden rocking horse. Riderless, it rocked gently back and forth, slowly, silently. Not a sound was made. The child who once owned it was dead.

It seemed that my incapacity for subtlety knew no bounds, and every time I had one of these dreams I carried the mood of it with me for days.

As my emotional state deteriorated I became obsessed with the concept of time. I remembered a story I'd once read about a man who felt the passage of time as a wind on his cheek. The unrelenting awareness of his own mortality became so debilitating that he eventually took to his bed, never to leave it again. I nearly, very nearly, got to that point myself.

Time had become my enemy. No longer could I afford the things I loved most, like long, quiet hours spent alone with a book or just my thoughts for company. Instead I felt a frantic sense of urgency about everything, a deep need to fill every second with some sort of activity, never mind what, never mind how trivial.

For a while, men took the place of everything else in my life. They were always available in inexhaustible numbers, but there never seemed to be enough to satisfy me. In and out of my life they moved, nameless and faceless, little more than a means to an end—an end I couldn't even imagine. All I knew for sure was that the deep, dark hours of nighttime and the dreams were more than I could face alone, and that as long as someone, *anyone*, was there with me, I could hold on tight and pretend for a little while that I was safe.

On nights when no one was there I'd run for miles, or exercise frantically, hoping that sheer physical exhaustion would be enough to get me through the night alone. But even at that, the dreams wouldn't let me sleep and I'd wake up agitated, feverish with the need to go in search of yet more men to help me forget the hellish red room and its terrible black bed.

I never want to know that kind of loneliness again.

I developed a morbid fascination with cripples and so-called freaks. I sought them out everywhere, in stores and on the streets, and I stared. I wanted to know, *had* to know, how it felt. Sometimes I asked—does it hurt? What does it feel like to be all twisted up and paralyzed? Do you ever want to die? I had to know because now I was sure, surer than morning itself, that one day I would find myself sitting there, too, all writhing and spastic and pathetic. The only thing I *didn't* know was when.

Time and disability had become a Damoclean sword, an ever-present threat hanging over me by a gossamer thread, and I was sure that when it finally fell it would cut cleanly. In one swift stroke all the things that gave my life meaning and purpose would be gone as if they'd never existed. There was nothing I could ever count on again, nothing was mine to keep.

I was only twenty-three years old when they told me I was damaged, and up until the moment those words were spoken, the whole of my life lay before me like a vast and empty canvas. But everything stopped still on that one gray morning in October. In the space of one short sentence everything I knew to be true and certain fell away, and I was left standing alone in a cold, dark place where no one else could ever dare to enter. The isolation I felt was all-encompassing and the loneliness almost unbearable.

My release took the form of tears, and once they started they never seemed to stop. Every morning I woke up crying, my eyes red and swollen, the pillows soaked. All day long at work I wept, alone in the studio, dreading the moment when I'd have to go home and face my empty apartment and the ceaseless dreams. I even cried in my sleep. I was beyond hope or solace, and nothing anyone said or did could make its way inside, to the place where all the tears began.

Ryan was the person I turned to most during that long and painful time. He was the best and closest friend I had, and he proved his worth a thousand times over merely by being there when I needed him. On nights when I couldn't sleep, or just needed someone to talk to, I'd make my way to his house, knowing I was always welcome. Far into the night he'd sit with me, listening carefully as I talked my way through whatever was troubling me. Other times he'd simply hold me closely as I cried out all the hurt and fear I was carrying deep inside. Without him, I'm not at all sure I would have made it through that spring and summer in one piece.

But without a doubt, my parents suffered the worst of it. It was only with them that I could really give full rein to everything I was feeling. It must have been a terrifying time for them, watching someone they loved go so completely to pieces. But they never caved in and they never once let me know how scared they were.

So much of the pain and guilt I was feeling was tied up in them. All their lives they had worked and sacrificed to make sure I had everything I needed, and now the reward they would receive for all their effort was a damaged child. The guilt I felt was unreasoning and overpowering. What had I done to the people I loved the most? I had let them down in the most profound way possible, and now and for the rest of their lives they would have to worry about me. I had put a sword over their heads, too.

As the months dragged on my depression deepened, like an ulcer that drained constantly but never healed. As a result, my physical condition worsened as the stress and exhaustion continued to build. Old symptoms like numbness and double vision reappeared, causing even more stress, which in turn brought on yet more symptoms. It was a vicious cycle I was powerless to break.

Eventually I began missing work. I'd call in sick and then spend the day in bed, huddled under the covers, hiding myself from everyone. When I couldn't stand to be alone any longer I went to my parents' house, where I sat for hours, trancelike, unable to speak or move.

I began to lose time. Hours would go by that I couldn't account for and suddenly I'd awake to find myself huddled in a corner of the room, sobbing and exhausted, with no idea how I'd gotten there. It was clearly time to do something serious, to get some kind of help for myself, but I didn't know what on earth it was I was supposed to do.

Then early one evening in June, Ryan came to tell me he was leaving. He'd been saving up for a long time and planned to drive across the country, stopping at every city he came to until he found a place to settle down. I'd always known that someday he would go, but I didn't know it would be so soon and I didn't know it would hurt so badly.

It wasn't so much that he was leaving—I was almost too far gone to care about that. It was merely the idea that my best friend was going off to start a whole new life somewhere else, while I was stuck forever, alone and unwell, in Pittsburgh. It just didn't seem fair somehow.

He was leaving the next day so we said our goodbyes quickly, mechanically, knowing it might be years before we saw each other again. Even now it still hurts to remember that night.

* * * * * * * * * *

And so Ryan was gone. But he'd left behind an idea that I couldn't seem to get out of my mind. Why couldn't I leave, too? Why not just run away to a place where no one knew me or anything about me? I could start all over there, forget everything that had happened and, somehow, get myself healthy again.

But where could I run to? And how could I do something like that to my parents? There weren't any answers, but the thought became an obsession, festering in my mind, exacerbating all the other problems I was having. Things got worse and worse over the next couple of weeks until they finally came to a head late one hot summer night in the middle of July.

I was on the phone with my friend, Judy, when it all began to fall apart. We were just chatting, talking about nothing in particular, when she said something funny and I started to laugh. I laughed and I laughed until it hurt to breathe, but still I couldn't stop. I felt all sense of control slip away as I dropped the receiver on the floor, rolled over on the bed, and began to scream. The phone was still on the floor when Judy got there. When she saw the shape I was in she called my mom and dad and, badly shaken, told them to come for me right away.

Something inside me shut down that night, some part of me that was able to think and feel and care too deeply about anything. It was as though all the pressure that had been building inside me for so long simply imploded, fell into itself like a collapsing star, leaving behind an emptiness that was cold and stark and quiet.

When my parents arrived they found me sitting up calmly in bed, the blankets arranged neatly around me, a look of firm determination on my face. I asked them please to sit down and to listen carefully to what it was I had to say.

They did as I asked and sat silently with worried looks on their faces, waiting for me to speak.

The year-long fever was broken, I said quietly, and now I needed to talk. I needed to put into words all the things we'd been so afraid to say to one another—to give voice to the fear inside me, and to say out loud at last how tired I was of pretending that everything was okay. Everything *wasn't* okay, and never would be again.

Intellectually, I explained carefully, we all knew that the chances of my ever ending up in a wheelchair were almost impossibly slim. All of the doctors we'd spoken to and every piece of literature we'd read had stressed over and over again that the vast majority of MS patients actually did quite well with the disease. In fact, relatively few of them ever faced the prospect of serious disability, and the chances of my being one of them were, again, very slim indeed. After all, I was young, strong, fit, and otherwise as healthy as I could be. Statistically, the odds were overwhelmingly in my favor. Those were the facts of the situation and there was no denying that they were encouraging, to say the very least.

But what I realized that night, I went on to say, was that the depression, the nightmares, and the paralyzing fear that had consumed me for so long had nothing whatsoever to do with the facts. Instead, it had all been about that one unspoken chance—that undeniable possibility, however slight or improbable, that I might turn out to be one of the rare, unlucky ones who got caught, regardless of the odds. Despite everything we'd been told and all that we wanted to believe, it was that one-in-a-million but ever-present chance that had been haunting me, and that would continue to haunt me forever.

I tried to tell them how it felt to live with the possibility that my time as a normal, functioning human being could be limited, and how frightening it was to think that I could wake up any morning of my life to find myself paralyzed and blinded, unable to move, see, or even speak. If it *did* happen, it could take years, I said, or it could happen overnight. But either way the result would be the same.

And because all of that was true, there was nothing left for me to do but to live my life in the present—in the here and never-ending now. Whatever the future held would have to be faced a day at a time. There could be no long-term plans made, no lifelong goals or aspirations. Above all, I stressed, there could be no more thoughts of marriage or a family of my own. How could I even *think* of allowing anyone to come too close now, knowing full well what it could cost all of us later?

The longer we talked that night, the clearer it became to me that I had to do *something*, and soon. There was a clock ticking inside my head now, counting out the hours, minutes, and seconds of a race that had already begun. I was late to the starting line and had no way of knowing where the race would end, but I knew then that I would run it alone, full out, never stopping to pace myself, and never once looking back.

But where would I run to? my father asked. And how would I know when I got there?

In the mere instant it took him to ask the question, the answer came to me.

Alaska.

I wanted to go to Alaska. Ever since the sixth grade, when my adored geography teacher, Carol Hill, first spoke to me of Alaska's mountains and vast, unexplored reaches, the place had held a special fascination for me. I'd studied its history and geography for years, and now, more than anything else, I wanted to go and see it all for myself. I'd never have another chance like this, I reasoned, and I was sure that once I got there I'd find a way to make it all work out.

Incredibly, it never occurred to either one of my parents to object, and we sat up the rest of the night making plans. I would give two weeks notice at the station, empty out my savings account, and as quickly as I could, get my brazen backside on the next plane headed north.

That's all there was to it, there was nothing more to discuss.

Bill didn't take the news quite so calmly the next day, but there wasn't much he could do about it. As soon as I got on the air that afternoon I announced to the world that I was leaving and moving to Alaska. The phones lit up immediately and it seemed like everyone who had ever listened to the station called in to wish me luck. It turned out most of them knew someone in Alaska, too, and that sparked an idea in my mind.

I opened the mike and said that if anyone cared to call and give me the names of their friends and relatives up north, I'd be glad to call them and say hello when I got there. It was a nice PR gesture and I figured it wouldn't hurt to have some built-in contacts in a place so far from home. The plan worked beautifully, and by the time I left I'd added over a hundred names to my list.

The next two weeks were busy ones. I had friends to say goodbye to, bags to pack, my car to sell, and my bank account to close. I was happy to find I had enough for a one-way ticket to Anchorage with a whole $600 left over. (Foolishly, I assumed that would be enough to get me through the first month or so in Anchorage, at least until I got set up somewhere.)

Early in August the big day finally arrived, and when we said goodbye at the airport there were dry eyes all around. It was a positive thing I was doing and everyone seemed to sense it. Besides, they were all convinced that this was going to end up as just a vacation, and they were pretty sure I'd be back home again in a matter of two or three weeks.

But I knew better. This was my chance and I was going to make the most of it. I waved at everyone from the window of the plane, then strapped myself into the seat as we taxied toward the runway.

This was it! I gripped the armrest tightly as the plane roared toward a takeoff. As the wheels left the ground I felt all the tension and pain of the past two years slip away, and I began to smile.

I would show that damned old Ryan.

THREE

Anchorage
August, 1976

IT HAD BEEN A MISERABLE flight. The big 747 lumbered down out of the sky and hit the runway hard, tires squealing, engines screaming. I felt my stomach turn inside-out as the pilot slammed the big jets into reverse and raced into the homestretch. Praying that we'd run out of speed before we ran out of runway, I closed my eyes and held my breath until the plane turned left and began taxiing toward the gate. Incredibly, we'd made it, and I gave silent thanks to God and the engineers at Boeing for getting us there in one piece.

The big sign on the side of the terminal read: WELCOME TO ANCHORAGE, AIR CROSSROADS OF THE WORLD. Judging by the size of the traffic jam on the runways, this was no idle boast; it looked as though everyone within a thousand miles of Anchorage had arrived all at once. Inside, the crowd at the baggage claim was frenzied. Hundreds of "slopers"—North Slope pipeline workers—were on their way into town for a little R&R, and each one seemed hell-bent on getting there first. They were a rough-looking bunch and I decided the safest thing to do was to get out of their way, so I elbowed my way up to the roundabout, grabbed my bag, and bolted for the exit doors upstairs at the far end of the terminal.

I sprinted past the big white polar bear in the lobby, ambushed a couple of Hare Krishnas who got in my way, and—badly as I could have used a drink—didn't even slow down as I passed the Upper 1 Lounge at a dead run. In ninety seconds flat I cleared the last hurdle and stepped outside into the bright, white sunlight of an early August morning in Alaska.

I don't know how long I stood there, gazing out over the scene I'd dreamed about for so many years. Everything was just the way I'd imagined it would be, all the colors intact. To the east the city was closely guarded by the mile-high crests of the Chugach Mountains, their sharp ridges gone soft now, furred over with a whole summer's growth of green and gold, while further south the brash young peaks of the Kenai Range still dazzled in their winter whites.

Cook Inlet was a silver streak against the western horizon and off to the northwest lay Mt. Susitna, the "Sleeping Lady," resplendent in her summer gown of fireweed and goldenrod. The opulence of it all was overwhelming and as I breathed in my first taste of that sweet, clean air I knew that finally, irrevocably, I had found the place where I belonged.

But I needed to get settled in somewhere, so I grabbed a cab and asked to go to the Holiday Inn downtown. The cabbie was a wiry little psychopath of undetermined origin who drove and swore like a native New Yorker, hurling a nonstop stream of invective at every pedestrian who got in his way.

"SOMBEECH NO GOOD FOKKING YANKEE! MOVE IT OR I FOKKING *KEEEL* YOU! GODDAM SOMBEECH!"

Jesus, buddy, I thought to myself—get a grip.

Somehow we made it to the hotel without killing anyone. I paid the fare with shaking hands and got the hell out of his way fast. Inside the lobby I spotted a clerk standing behind the counter and went over to see about arranging for a room. This was the time of the Alaskan oil-pipeline boom and I'd heard all the horror stories about the prices up here, but still I gasped when I got a look at the bill—one night's stay was going to cost just slightly less than an entire month's rent on my apartment in Pittsburgh! If this was any indication of things to come, my six hundred dollars wasn't going to buy me much time at all.

I didn't waste a minute of it hanging around the hotel. I tossed my suitcase on the bed, splashed some cold water on my face, and dashed back outside, eager to do some exploring.

To this day I can remember the overpowering sense of freedom and adventure I felt when I stepped out of the hotel on that bright, late-summer morning. I was five thousand miles from home and, for the first time in my life, totally, gloriously, on my own. Anything could happen, and I knew that when it did I would be ready—eager in fact—to test the limits of my new independence. I didn't have enough sense to be worried, and it was with no small measure of excitement that I walked out of the parking lot and turned east onto Fourth Avenue.

* * * * * * * * *

A lot has changed since then, but back in the mid-seventies much of Fourth Avenue was still a hard-drinking, end-of-the-line Gomorrah, the scaly underbelly of an otherwise invulnerable city. The sign in front of the downtown mission assured everyone that Jesus still Saves, but the drunked-up, passed-out bodies in front of the Montana Club raised some doubts. Following the local custom, I stepped as nonchalantly as I could over the sleeping men on the sidewalk, trying hard not to notice their open, urine-soaked trousers or the reeking vomit puddled around their faces. This was going to take some getting used to.

Further down the street some of the more respectable shops announced the fact that they were just that, by way of tastefully lettered signs that screamed NO WHORES ALLOWED! I grinned and wondered idly how they could tell who was and who wasn't. Maybe the ladies in question were required to carry some sort of identification, or maybe if you lived here long enough you just knew. I'd never seen an actual whore in person myself, so I wasn't sure what to look for, but I kept an eye out for signs of any as I continued on my journey.

I walked for hours that day, trying to learn for myself what it was that made this place so exciting.

At first glance, Anchorage itself appears to be a contradiction of all the natural glory that surrounds it—a non-sequitur on the grandest of scales. Ages-old, weatherbeaten log cabins butt up against sleek new office buildings of steel and tinted glass. Wild-west, shoot-'em-up saloons compete for customers with the trendy fern bars next door, and high-rise hotels reach for the sky, while just down the road the devastation of Earthquake Park lies sprawled in silent witness to the folly of standing too tall.

But the more I thought about it, the more I came to realize that Anchorage was exactly the way it had to be. It was a city built in fits and starts by people who didn't have time to waste. There was money to be made here—big money—but let's do it quick and damn the amenities. These people had no time for frills, for long-term planning, or even, it seemed, for simple human logic. Just get it up and get it running—that seemed to be the strategy. The result was a metropolis with most of the disadvantages of a big city, and very few of the advantages.

But strangely enough, an odd kind of fiercely protective civic pride has taken root among the citizenry here, as though the worse it gets, the better they like it. Sure, the rush-hour traffic jams are on a par with Los Angeles, and so what if our alcoholism rates are among the highest around? We *like* it that way, dammit, and if you don't, well, you can just shag your sorry ass right back to where it came from. No one invited you in the first place.

Lots of newcomers, or "cheechakos," took umbrage at this, but I thought it was just the right attitude to have under the circumstances. After all, didn't most people come to Alaska looking for a challenge in the first place? The prevailing theory was that if you somehow managed to survive Anchorage, the rest of the state would be a snap.

When I couldn't take another step I stopped for dinner at Peggy's Cafe, a little diner across the street from Merrill Field on Fifth Avenue. Merrill Field was the city's first airstrip, built back in the thirties, when bush pilots were the only link between Anchorage and the hundreds of small villages scattered throughout the state. Legends were born here, spawned by tall tales of those daring young pilots. They were giants by today's standards—By-God heroes who got the job done, never mind how, and who didn't expect no thanks, neither.

Crowded around the table next to me, deep in conversation, was a ragtag collection of what could only be described as colorful characters, throwbacks to another era. Half a dozen grizzled old prospectors and broken-down aviators were hunkered over enormous plates of flapjacks and bacon and thick white mugs of coffee, and all of them were talking at once. You sensed right away that this group met here on a regular basis to catch up on what was new in the world and to keep old memories alive. From the sounds of things, today's topic was going to be someone by the name of Crazy Angus Ferguson.

". . . Yessir, old Crazy Angus was a fool and a dangerous man. I can still see him clear as if he was sittin' right here . . ."

The old-timer looked like he was settling in for a good story, but

40

these things took time and a man had to get himself into the proper frame of mind. He'd just about sucked all the juice out of that particular wad of tobacco, so he reared back and hawked a soft brown bullet into the paper cup on the floor at his feet. He leaned over, grinning out of his one good eye, happy to see that his aim was still true. He wiped his mouth off on the back of his hand, then sucked half a cup of coffee in through the couple of decaying teeth he still had left, wincing a little when the hot of it jostled the rotten nerves.

Finally, with exquisite care and with two fingers delicately poised, he reached into his pouch for some fresh tobacco. He lovingly pushed a big plug of it into his cheek, then worked it around some until he got it set just right. Satisfied at last that everything was in its proper place, he leaned back in his chair and picked up the thread of the story of Crazy Angus Ferguson.

For the next two hours I listened, enthralled, as he spun endless yarns of life on the last frontier as lived by a man with a taste for adventure and, as one of the others put it, more balls than brains. Why, here was a fella who could track a polar bear clean across the Arctic in a blizzard, fire a bullet straight into his heart from a mile away, and pack him out singlehanded . . . all before breakfast!

There was no doubt in anyone's mind that Crazy Angus could do *anything*, and I felt a sense of sadness that he and all the others like him were gone forever now, part of a past that could never be recaptured.

But maybe that wasn't entirely true. This was still the Last Frontier after all, and maybe somewhere out there were those who still lived by their wits and the seat of their pants, determined to make a place for themselves in a land that demanded the best a person had to give. There was only one way to find out, and it was a lesson I would have to learn for myself.

The storytellers were still at it at the next table, but I was still on Pittsburgh time and it was getting late. Reluctantly I paid the check and stepped out into the cool, crisp evening air.

It had been a long day and I was exhausted by the time I got back to the hotel. As I was getting ready for bed, it occurred to me that I hadn't known a single moment of fear or sadness all day. In fact, from the moment I first set foot on Alaskan soil, the darkness that had surrounded me for so long seemed to have vanished completely. I felt as though I'd been given a second chance, and I made up my mind right then to do the very best I could not to screw it up.

I climbed into bed, turned out the light, and dreamed all night about Crazy Angus Ferguson.

* * * * * * * * * * *

I awoke the next morning with a vague sense of urgency. Time was ticking away and so was my money. I had to be out of the room by noon or else pay for another day, and I hadn't the slightest idea where I would go. I needed a place to live, a job, and a car, in that exact order, and the only lead I had was the caller list I'd brought with me from the radio station in Pittsburgh. I pulled it out of my suitcase, crossed my fingers for luck, and commenced to dial.

Remarkably, the very first person on the list brought results almost immediately. His name was Don and he was the great-great-nephew, or something, of one of the listeners who had called the last day I was on the air in Pittsburgh. He was tickled to hear from his long-lost relative, and soon we were chatting about other things. He asked what my plans were, and when I outlined my situation he immediately offered me the use of his apartment for a month while he was out of town. He was leaving that very evening, he said, so I could move in right away and use the time to get settled and find a job.

I was awestruck. People didn't behave like this where I came from and I couldn't understand such generosity from a total stranger.

"I appreciate the offer," I said hesitantly, "but why are you doing this? You don't even know me!"

"Don't need to," he answered happily. "When I first came to Alaska someone did a kindness for me, and this is a chance to pay back an old debt. So what do you say . . . do we have a deal?"

What the hell.

"We have a deal."

"Great! I'll be over to pick you up in fifteen minutes. Just be waiting in the lobby."

Don was an attractive man somewhere in his middle thirties and I liked him right away. We stopped by the apartment long enough to drop off my things, then spent the rest of the afternoon exploring Anchorage. He even bought me dinner, and by the time he left for the airport that evening we had become old friends. Later I would learn that Don was just a typical example of how warm and generous Alaskan people can be, and I think he'd be pleased to know that I, too, have since repaid the debt many times over.

The next pressing item on my list was a job, so early the next morning I dug out the Yellow Pages and looked under "Radio Stations" to see what was available. There were seven or eight stations listed and they were spread out all over town. Money was still the big consideration for me and I knew how expensive taxis could be, so I picked KBYR, the station closest to where I was staying, for my first attempt. I called and got an appointment that same afternoon with Bruce Kier, who was the station's program director.

Bruce was an iconoclastic sort with a sense of humor that bordered on treason, and right away I sensed we were going to get along just fine. I gave him a copy of my resume and I could see that he was visibly impressed by the fact that I had worked in Pittsburgh. So impressed, in fact, that he offered me a job on the spot.

"Don't you even want to listen to my aircheck?" I asked, stunned. Loose was loose, but this was really pushing it.

"Nah, I never fool around with that stuff," he said offhandedly. "Besides, this place can't afford to be too choosy."

I could see what he meant. The studios were a mess, the floors littered with papers, overflowing ashtrays, and the greasy remains of someone's week-old lunch. Every available surface was covered with dusty, unjacketed records waiting to be played—if, indeed, they were still playable. Chaos reigned and no one seemed to care.

But, so what? It was a job and it paid a whole lot more than what I'd been earning in Pittsburgh. Besides, it would buy me some time while I decided what it was I really wanted to do. For that reason alone I was happy to accept Bruce's offer. I wasn't scheduled to start for a few days, but that was okay too, since I still had a few things to accomplish in the interim.

First thing the next morning I was faced with the prospect of securing some form of transportation. This would be a tough one, considering the state of my financial affairs, but—ever the optimist—I grabbed a cab and headed for East Fifth Avenue, the automotive capitol of the Far North.

New and used car lots stretched for miles in both directions and I walked for hours without the first idea of where to begin. I didn't know a Buick from a Bentley or a Cadillac from a Camaro, so ultimately I did the only intelligent thing and chose the dealership with the best-looking salesman.

"Smiling Jack" Lovett from Texas was so handsome he made my knees weak. He worked for one of the biggest dealerships in town and he sounded like he knew what he was talking about, so I happily put myself into his very capable hands. We found the car I wanted almost immediately. It was a tiny, shiny, sexy little Fiat roadster, and I fell in love with it at first sight. But I sensed the hard part was yet to come—namely, how I proposed to pay for it. I took a deep breath and told him where I stood, moneywise, fully expecting him to boot me into the next time zone.

But he just laughed and told me to stay put while he went off to pull a few strings. Half an hour later he reappeared and, after accepting a down-payment in the sum of *five dollars*, smilingly presented me with a contract and a brand-new set of keys to the car!

I didn't believe it then and I don't believe it now, but I had done it. It was the financial coup of the century, and I signed the papers hurriedly, before anyone had time to change their minds. Money would never be that easy to come by again, but this was boom-town Anchorage and miracles were happening every day.

Later, as I drove happily off the lot in my new (to me) Italian sports car, I couldn't help reflecting on the events of the past few days. I'd been in Alaska exactly seventy-two hours and already I had: a) a place to live, b) a job, c) a car, and d) a date with Smiling Jack Lovett from Texas.

Things were looking better by the minute.

* * * * * * * * * *

I had the rest of the afternoon to kill, and being in a go-to-hell frame of mind anyhow, I turned the car around and headed north on the Glenn Highway, eager to see what lay in that direction.

The sun was warm and high in the sky, its long, late-summer rays firing bold streaks of silver across the broad, craggy shoulders of the Chugach Mountains. Ahead in the distance the sharp, steep peaks of the Alaska Range knifed thousands of feet into the sky, their ice-sheathed ridges magnifying the sunlight into an incandescent blaze of blue and white that spilled down the mountainsides and lit up everything in the valley below. The whole world seemed to be glowing that day and I sped through the first thirty miles of the trip in a happy daze, content just to have a look around.

That late in the season the fireweed was at its most dazzling—a blazing carpet of red that raced off in every direction like a prairie fire, its hot breath searing everything in its path. Here and there a bright splash of aquamarine flashed in the distance—a deep, cool oasis of blue. The perfect stillness of the water was a soothing presence in this otherwise wild and violent landscape. Mile after mile the spectacle went on, each new bend in the road revealing a scene more overwhelming than the one before, and before too long I became convinced it was never going to end.

Then abruptly, like clumsily arranged slides out of sync, the scenery changed. Suddenly I found myself in a rich, Wyeth-like landscape of rolling hills and lush, green pastures. The mountains moved back and opened up onto a wide panorama of farmland, meadows, and orchards that stretched all the way to the horizon in ever-deepening shades of green and blue and gray. The sense of quiet and tranquility was so complete that I was sure this was what the entire world must have looked like on that very first day, when everything was new.

I knew where I was now.

This was the legendary Matanuska Valley, Alaska's own Fertile Crescent. It was here that most of the state's farming and dairy industry was concentrated, and I'd already heard stories of fruits and vegetables grown here that rivaled in size anything Ripley could ever have imagined. It all has something to do with the angle of the sun and ultraviolet rays and the endless hours of summer sunshine, but it's not uncommon for a Matanuska cabbage to tip the scales at close to a hundred pounds! Imagine squash the size of watermelons, baseball-sized strawberries, and a zucchini you could use to feed the Seventh Fleet. "Big" just seemed to be the word for everything up here.

I felt like stretching my legs a little, so I stopped the car, got out, and began walking toward a thick, broad stand of hemlock and spruce at the edge of a small forest. I couldn't see it yet, but from somewhere deep within I could hear the sound of rushing water. I walked more quickly, hoping to find its source.

It was cool and dark in the little woods and before too long I came upon a tiny stream. A bright wedge of sunlight streaked down through the trees and sparkled off the water, which bubbled and danced across the rocks. I sat down by the edge of the brook and watched happily as a small brown rabbit bounced away, zig-zagging through the trees. Thoreau, I thought, would have liked this place.

I took off my shoes and socks and slid my toes into the cold, clear water. The only sound to be heard was the gurgling of the stream and as I sat there, lost in the quiet, I began to think of all the things that had led me to where I was at that very moment—alone and free, and in a place I wanted to be more than anywhere else in the world.

Would I even *be* here, I wondered, if it hadn't been for the diagnosis and all the changes proceeding from it? If no doctor had ever said those words to me, would I still be back in Pittsburgh, a third-rate deejay, ego-driven and happy to think I was making it? Probably. Maybe.

Or had I been destined all along for something more? As far back as I could remember, I'd sensed that my life would be different from everyone else's. Even as a child, while all the other little girls were dressing up their Barbie dolls and playing house with one another, I was curled up alone in my room with an atlas and a wall-sized map of the world, dreaming of adventures in exotic faraway places.

Was I preparing even then for a life outside the bounds of convention? And would I have found my own way here somehow, even if stronger forces hadn't stepped in and accelerated the process? There was simply no way of knowing. One thing was certain, though. The diagnosis had changed my life forever and had marked me in a way that no one else could ever know or understand. I would never be free of the threat of what might yet come, but I understood then that by coming here I had at least given myself a chance to become a part of life's great adventure, and to live a life so extraordinarily my own that nothing—not even an incurable disease—could ever take it away.

My heart was full at the prospect, and in answer all I could do was cry. I cried for everyone who wasn't there with me, and for all the people who would never know the wonder of simply letting go and giving themselves up to the world. I cried for all the time I'd wasted and for all the stops on the road ahead. But mostly I cried because I'd come so close to missing it all myself. I understood then that I didn't have any more time to waste and that I had a whole lot more to do before it was time to call it quits.

* * * * * * * * * *

The job turned out to be just about what I expected. I drew the early-evening airshift, a time when nothing much happens at a radio station, so I had no trouble at all adjusting to the format, such as it was. The only thing that was even mildly tricky was the idea of actually playing records on the air. By 1976 most radio stations had switched from records to tape, an infinitely more manageable medium, but KBYR had yet to make that leap of faith, so we muddled along in the dark ages of technology. Surprisingly, it was actually kind of fun.

Most evenings were spent with newly made friends at one bar or another. My personal favorite was the Pastime, a hard-bitten, rough-and-ready local saloon with little to recommend it beyond a great countrified jukebox and the grizzled old-timers who visited with dogged regularity. There was a younger crowd, too, who mostly came for the weekly dart tournaments.

The Pastime's dart team had advanced to the semifinals earlier that month and by way of celebration, a "raid" was being planned—in this case a fishing trip to the Kenai (KEE-nigh) Peninsula. I was invited to come along, and since I was anxious to see a little more of the countryside, I accepted eagerly.

Friday night was spent in preparation for the big trip the next day: food and car assignments were made; the boat was checked for leaks; and tents, sleeping bags, and fishing gear were inspected and pronounced fit and ready for action. I was assigned to ride with "Trader Rick" Berkheiser, the resident dart pro, so he and I made arrangements to meet the following morning at the bar and leave from there.

It promised to be one hell of a weekend.

The sun was shining, the sky was clear, and by the time we passed the outskirts of Anchorage, everyone was in a holiday mood. I was deep in conversation with Rick as we rounded Potter Marsh just outside of town, and when I looked up to see where we were, my first look at Turnagain Arm took me completely by surprise.

I'd often heard people say jokingly that the nicest thing about Anchorage was its close proximity to Alaska, and now I understood what they meant. In fifteen minutes we had gone from a busy urban scene to this one of pure, untouched wilderness. Immense snow-covered mountains rose thousands of feet straight up out of the sea to form an impenetrable wall of rock and ice that stretched as far as the eye could see, and beyond. For untold millions of years they had stood here, silent sentinels, magnificent in their bleak, forbidding presence.

Turnagain Arm was an ominous shade of gray that morning, a deadly, churning mass of water that cut its raw way fifty miles back into the mountains. A dangerous place, the tides here are among the highest in the world, averaging nearly thirty feet and often cresting much higher. It was an awesome thing to contemplate, terrifying in its power and enormity.

And it was all too much for this little city girl. Before long everything around me began to take on an air of unreality, as though I'd dreamed it all, and I was afraid that if I so much as blinked, it would suddenly disappear. I had become a victim of the phenomenon known as "scenic overdose."

It's difficult to describe the feelings that surface when you come face-to-face with the power and majesty of a place like this. It's as though Mother Nature had opened wide her treasure chest and spilled it all out here, and you find yourself feeling sorry for the rest of the world because there can't possibly be anything left. And just when you think you've seen the best and the most she has to offer, she'll lift her skirts one more time to reveal some new glory not even hinted at a moment before.

Sounds mushy, I know, but Alaska will do that to you.

The road wound and curved its way along the Arm, and as we journeyed on we came upon places with names like Rainbow and Indian and Bird Creek, each a tiny little outpost with no visible means of support save for a roadhouse or cafe to mark its existence. Because it's mandatory for all newcomers to the area, we stopped at the Bird House Bar in Bird Creek for a beer and for what Rick promised would be a uniquely Alaskan experience.

The first thing you notice about the Bird House is the huge blue bird leaning drunkenly out of the front window. Most things in Alaska tend to be bigger than life, but an eight-foot parakeet sipping a neon cocktail is really stretching the point, and makes for a jarring sight in this otherwise primitive setting.

The next thing you notice is the Bird House itself. At first glance it looks just like any other ancient, decaying log cabin (except for the bird, naturally), but if you look closer you'll notice that one end of the roof sits a little higher than the other. In fact, a part of the building has sunk almost completely into the ground, which makes for a rather awkward-looking appearance. As strange as it is (and it *is* strange) on the outside, it's actually worse inside.

The log walls and ceiling are absolutely buried under a century's worth of trash and trivia, each and every piece lovingly hung there by visitors from every corner of the world. Driver's licenses, blank checks, passports, jockstraps, and underpants cover every square inch of the interior, and you're welcome to contribute, too—just ask someone for the stapler. (The rule on the underpants, by the way, is that they have to be warm when you hang them, and for heaven's sake don't try to cheat.)

A dozen or so tree stumps serve as barstools, and the actual bar, like the building itself, slopes downhill at roughly a thirty-degree angle. It's obvious right away that the great earthquake of 1964 is responsible for the odd state of affairs here, but if you ask the bartender, he'll tell you that things were *really* bad before, and the quake just helped to straighten everything out.

The important thing, though, is to remember to hang onto your drink at all times. If you forget and let go, you get to watch it slide down the length of the bar and crash into the wall, at which point you owe the house a round. This can get pricey, too, depending on the size of the crowd.

We overstayed our welcome by about two hours (everyone does) and it was way past noon when we finally said goodbye and climbed back in the pickup.

Twenty-five miles later we came to the end of Turnagain Arm, the site of Portage Glacier. This is another mandatory stop, and nothing in the world could have prepared me for the sight of it.

The particular shade of blue that is the color of a glacier exists nowhere else in nature and is impossible to describe. All you can do is draw comparisons. Do you remember the snow scene in the movie *Dr. Zhivago*? Well, Portage looks like that, only bluer. An extraordinary river of ice, nearly a mile wide at its face, the glacier moves forward relentlessly and is constantly shearing off into massive blue icebergs that settle deep into the water and float majestically out onto Portage Lake. There the silent, frozen monoliths are carved by wind and water into fantastic, almost surreal shapes.

The effect was hypnotic, and if it hadn't been for the freezing wind that whipped across the face of the ice we could have stayed there all day. It was hard to believe it was the middle of August and we were just an hour outside of Anchorage.

A few miles past Portage the highway makes a wide left and swings off into the mountains to begin the long climb up to Turnagain Pass, elevation 988 feet. After a short stop to admire the view, we hit the road again and pushed on past Granite Creek, the Hope cutoff, and, finally, the dreaded 51 Mile Hill, a steep, scary climb. When we reached Upper Summit Lake Rick announced, with no small measure of excitement in his voice, that Cooper Landing was only seventeen miles away now, and just wait until I saw it!

Cooper Landing was where I gave up. I'd seen some wondrous sights in the past several hours, but as we came upon this perfect little village snuggled up on the shores of Kenai Lake, my senses finally went into overload and shut down altogether. To say that the lake was as blue as the sky at dawn, and that the mountains held the breathless aura of a moonscape, is to whistle in the wind. Words became utterly useless, and as we drove on in silence I gradually came to understand that some part of me had always lived here.

Everything was as familiar to me as my own name, and when we passed Bob's Kenai Lake Lodge I asked Rick to stop, knowing somehow that what I would find there would be important.

The cafe itself was full, so we walked through a pair of swinging saloon doors that led directly into the bar. It was dark inside, but it struck you right away that this was the kind of place that had inspired some of the great old country-western songs, including more than its fair share of third-rate romances. Cheap paneling lined the walls, a ragtag collection of mismatched glasses were stacked on the shelf behind the bar, and over the window a big red "Bud eis r" sign flashed on and off, proudly announcing the fact that the King of Beers—finestkind—could be had for only two dollars a bottle.

In the corner stood an old Wurlitzer featuring the very best in hardcore country music—twelve plays for a dollar—and over the door hung a ragged old moose head that stared, glassy-eyed, at the chewed-up dartboard that occupied the place of honor on the opposite wall. It was a faded, jaded oasis, a roadside reliquary where love was measured by the pint and nothing important ever happened. I thought it was absolutely beautiful.

The woman smiling up at us from behind the bar looked oddly out of place. Her soft blond hair was pulled into a loose bun at the back of her neck and when she smiled, the whole room seemed to brighten. She was the gentlest looking woman I'd ever seen and you could tell just by looking at her that she'd never done a wrong thing in her life. This was the woman you thought of when someone talked about their Sainted Mother.

Her name was Anne Poff and we struck up an easy conversation as she poured out our beers. She said that she and her husband had bought the lodge a couple of years ago and had been struggling ever since to make ends meet. Things were especially rough just then, she said, since they were short on help—it wasn't easy to find good workers out here in the middle of nowhere. My ears perked up immediately and I asked her what the job involved.

She said she needed someone who could cook, wait tables, and keep an eye on the bar when things got busy. They couldn't pay very much, she said, but meals were included and a small log cabin came with the job. Did I know anyone who might be interested?

Did I ever. Here was my chance, and if I could only convince her to hire me I could actually come to live here in Cooper Landing and, maybe someday, even to belong. I wanted it so badly it scared me.

I told her that I could do everything she needed—that in fact I'd do *anything*, if only she'd give me the chance. She seemed surprised, but she must have sensed how eager I was, and when she said I could have the job I almost collapsed with relief. We agreed that I would return to Anchorage, give a week's notice at the radio station, and report for work at the lodge the following Monday. I couldn't believe my good fortune.

I was flying high as we paid our check and walked back out to the truck. The last fifty miles of the trip went by in a blur and all I could think about was getting through the next seven days.

We caught up with the rest of the group in Soldotna and joined the caravan heading for Eagle Rock, a campsite on the Kenai River that was our final destination.

The weekend was a great success. There was plenty of food and beer, the fishing was great, and by the time we broke camp on Sunday night our bellies, bags, and coolers were stuffed with pounds and pounds of king salmon. Everyone agreed that this had been the best raid ever and plans were made to do it again real soon. It was dark by the time we left and I slept most of the way back to Anchorage. I didn't even wake up when we drove through Cooper Landing.

FOUR

Cooper Landing
Autumn, 1976

QUITTING MY JOB AT KBYR was a snap. Bruce thought it was hilarious that I would seriously consider leaving Anchorage and a "real" job to go sling hash in Cooper Landing, of all places.

"Just think, JJ," he quipped brightly, "if you ever get bored with Cooper Landing you can always head down to Moose Pass for a big night on the town! Or how about Clam Gulch?—now *there's* a thriving metropolis! HA HA HA HA HA HA!"

What a jerk. I told him he could fold it five ways and put it where the moon don't shine for all I cared, but I was going and I didn't want to hear any more about it. I left him chuckling in the studio.

Somehow I made it through the week, and when I went in to pick up my paycheck on Saturday morning, everyone wished me luck and congratulated me on my brilliant thirty-year career at KBYR. I was really going to miss this bunch of comedians.

I didn't see much sense in hanging around Anchorage any longer than I had to, so I decided to drive down to the lodge a day early and use the time to get settled in. I rushed back to the apartment and left a note for Don, thanking him for his generosity and inviting him to visit the next time he got down to Cooper Landing. Then I tossed everything I owned—some books and an armful of clothes—into the Fiat, gassed up at the Tesoro station, and inside fifteen minutes I was on the Old Seward Highway, headed south for the Kenai Peninsula and a future I could only begin to imagine.

You could tell fall was on its way that day by the bracing nip in the air and the soft dusting of snow on the mountaintops. Alaskans call this "termination dust," the result of an early high-altitude snowfall and an unmistakable sign of the approach of winter. The air was rich with the smell of the sea and I felt as free as the wind itself as it danced across the water and raced up the sides of the mountains.

The way I felt that afternoon was as close to a spiritual experience as I've ever come. As I drove on, a deep feeling of peace settled over me and I knew, in the place where people know such things, that I was exactly where I was supposed to be. For better or worse I was on my way, completely unafraid and joyful that at last my great adventure was beginning.

There were a lot of moose around that year and I had to stop several times and wait while whole herds of them crossed the road. There is *nothing* slower than a moose when it wants to be, but I learned early on that the last thing you want to do, ever, is honk your horn at them in frustration. They have a tendency to take it personally, and two thousand pounds of irritated moose can do some serious damage to your car, not to mention your person.

A hundred spectacular miles later I made the cutoff for the eight-mile drive into Cooper Landing, and when I passed "Our Point of View" lodge on the right, I knew I was getting close. Local legend had it that Walt Disney used to vacation there, and I could easily see why. Sitting halfway up the side of the mountain as it did, the lodge had an unmatched view of the surroundings and all the privacy a body could want. Old Walt could have hidden out here for weeks on end without a soul knowing he was around.

A mere fifteen minutes later I arrived at the lodge. I jumped out of the car and stood looking all around me, trying to take everything in at once.

The lake was deep and quiet and blue, a liquid prism that caught the light and splintered it into a thousand different colors, then threw it, dazzling, back up into the sky. All along its shoreline were thick green stands of spruce and hemlock, a dark and mysterious primeval forest. Above it all towered the sheer face of Mt. Stetson, a three-thousand-foot precipice with a crest as sharp and as black as obsidian. It was a scene from a dream, with a symmetry so perfect it bordered on cliche.

This was my home now. I was an official resident of Cooper Landing with a job, a place to live, and soon, I hoped, lots of brand-new friends. I turned and raced up the steps to the lodge, eager to see what was going on inside.

Once again the tiny cafe was filled to capacity, most of the customers being either tourists or truck drivers, as far as I could tell. In the midst of all the confusion I noticed a couple of waitresses scurrying around the room, their arms filled with huge platters of chicken-fried steak and big silver pots of coffee. I was anxious to talk to them but there wasn't an empty seat in the house, so I smiled briefly and wandered into the bar in search of Anne.

She was sitting on a tall stool talking to a couple of tourists, and when I walked in she jumped up and welcomed me with a big hug. She was especially happy to see me, she said, since another waitress had quit the day before, and would I be willing to start working that very night tending bar for a party some of the locals were throwing at the lodge? I said I'd be delighted.

Pretty soon the lunch crowd thinned out and Anne took me into the dining room to meet my three new co-workers, Pennie, Joanie, and Cherie. Pennie was rounder than most people, plump and funny, her soft brown hair frizzed softly around her face. She was one of the last members of the hippie generation and she looked the part, dressed as she was in a long, flowing batik skirt, a printed silk blouse, and layers of feathered and beaded jewelry. I hadn't seen anyone like her since the sixties and I found myself looking forward to spending time with her.

Joanie was a different story altogether. Her black, curly hair was piled high on her head in a towering beehive, and she came across as the sassy, brassy, road-wise career waitress that she was. I got the feeling that under that brittle veneer was someone I could care a lot about, but only time would tell.

Cherie was the little one. While technically not a dwarf or a midget, she just barely cleared four feet and was everyone's pet. I couldn't help wondering aloud how she ever got her job done, what with being so short and all. It was simple, she said. She kept overturned coffee cans at strategic points throughout the lodge, and anytime she had to use the cash register or the grill, she just hopped on up and went to town. Everyone else tripped over them constantly, but no one really minded because, well, they were there for Cherie.

Finally it was time to go inspect my cabin. It sat off to the left of the lodge, hidden in the trees about sixty feet up the side of the mountain, and to call it "rustic" would have been a serious understatement. As we climbed the hill, huffing and puffing, Anne warned me that the cabin was a little rough on the inside and she wasn't sure I would even want to live there.

I loved it. It was a little smaller than I'd imagined it would be and was truly in a sad state of disrepair. Most of the logs were split and peeling, the roof looked like it was about to cave in, and the heavy wooden door was hanging crookedly on its hinges. Anne explained that the cabin was about eighty years old and that the last person to live in it had been an old prospector and his billy-goat companion. Inside, it smelled like maybe the goat was still in residence, but I didn't care—this was *exactly* the kind of place I had dreamed about living in someday.

The front half of the cabin had a dirt floor and the back half was covered by thick wooden planks that had dozens of big bushy weeds growing up between them. Anne apologized for the weeds, but I thought they added character to the place and said I wouldn't dream of pulling them up.

In the corner opposite the window was a rickety old steel cot with a lumpy mattress, and next to that stood a beat-up, dented metal locker with a great big hole where the door used to be. The only other object in the room was a well-worn rusted woodstove that leaned like a tired old man against the far wall.

Conspicuous in their absence were any indications whatsoever of the presence of electricity, heat, or running water—omens I should have taken far more seriously than I did. But the view from the window was so breathtaking that it overshadowed all other considerations and I never gave the rest of it a second thought.

Anne offered to help me gather up some wood and lay a fire in the stove, but I wouldn't hear any of it.

"No, no, no," I said breezily, "there's absolutely no need for you to bother about that."

I told her I was a champion fire-builder and that I would take care of all that nonsense later. No problem.

At first she seemed reluctant to take me at my word, but I persisted and soon we were walking arm-in-arm back to the lodge, pioneer sisters under the skin.

Since I was to start out as cook at five the next morning, Anne wanted to show me around the kitchen and familiarize me with all the necessary procedures. Typically, I'd lied to her when I told her I'd worked as a cook before, but so far everything looked pretty straight-forward. Eggs, cheese, and milk were kept in the refrigerator by the stove, and bacon and sausage could be found in the big freezer out back. Nothing looked too worrisome, and I was feeling relaxed and confident when she dropped the bomb.

"I imagine with all your experience, you're a pretty good baker?" she asked offhandedly as she showed me where the flour and sugar were stored.

Oh God. I had a funny feeling she wasn't talking about frozen Crescent Rolls or Betty Crocker cake mixes, but I couldn't show any signs of weakness, so I lied yet again.

"Sure," I answered blithely, "nothing to it!"

"Good. Then I won't have to worry about training you. The list of what you'll need to do is taped to the side of the freezer by the door."

Once she was satisfied that I knew all I needed to know, she left for home saying she wouldn't be in the next day as she was making a run into Kenai for supplies.

"Now don't you worry about a thing," she said cheerfully as she headed for the door. "You'll do just fine. And remember, Pennie will be here in case you run into any problems. Bye now!"

The moment she was gone I raced back into the kitchen and grabbed the baking list off the freezer. I had to read it three times before the enormity of the task sunk into my addled brain. The lodge opened at six every morning and by then I was expected to have baked, *from scratch*, seven industrial-sized loaves of bread, eight large pies (two each of apple, cherry, blueberry, and banana-cream), and at least five *dozen* cinnamon rolls, each one the size of a small island.

I was in big, big trouble.

My hands were shaking as I put the list back in place and wandered out into the cafe in a daze. There were no customers just then so Pennie and Cherie were taking a break. I poured a cup of coffee and joined them and Joanie at the employees' table by the window. We started talking, and as gracefully as I could, I brought up the subject of baked goods.

"Oh yeah," Joanie said, grinning. "Welcome to Annie's Little House on the Prairie. She's a real fanatic about that stuff—wants everything done from scratch. It gets to be a real pain in the ass, too. Especially the mother-jumping cinnamon rolls." The lodge was widely renowned in the area for its fabulous cinnamon rolls and, almost without exception, every tourist who visited was eager to sample one of the delicacies they'd heard so much about. As a result, Joanie and the others had come to despise the rolls *and* the tourists with equal fervor.

"But that's crazy!" I wailed. "Hasn't anyone ever told her you can buy perfectly good bread and pies in the store nowadays? And Pepperidge Farm makes *wonderful* cinnamon rolls—all you have to do is thaw them out!"

Oh, but that would never do here, she explained, then excused herself as she left to make her point. She returned carrying a dinner plate that was completely dwarfed by the biggest, ugliest-looking cinnamon roll I'd ever seen. Thick, melting sugar-glaze oozed over the top and sides like toxic sludge, and on top of it all sat an enormous yellow glob of soft, hand-whipped synthetic butter. I started to gag.

"I know what you mean," said Pennie laughingly. "Each one of these babies weighs a pound and a half and, close as we can figure, is worth something like eight thousand calories apiece. My personal dream is to someday weigh ninety-three pounds and shove five or six of them down some fat tourist's throat."

It sounded like a reasonable goal to me.

"By the way . . ." Joanie asked casually as she strolled back into the kitchen, "you've never cooked or baked anything before in your life, have you?"

Bitch.

The party Anne had asked me to tend bar for that night was a huge success. Spike Edwards was the unofficial mayor of Cooper Landing, an honor bestowed largely because he knew absolutely everything that went on in this tiny community of less than a hundred. No one was really certain how he got his hands on so much information, but it was obvious that he had his sources, and everyone treated him accordingly.

This was intended to be a surprise party for Spike, but Spike already knew about it because, as stated previously, Spike already knew about *everything*, and something as simple as a surprise party was strictly small potatoes for him. Regardless, the cream of Cooper Landing society turned out for the occasion and by the end of the evening I had made some pretty important connections.

Sparky Green, the Landing's premier trombonist, invited me over anytime to examine his prize-winning outhouse. It had taken first place in the competition last year and everyone said it was really something to see—a two-holer with padded seats, recessed lighting, and piped-in Dixieland band music! I said I could hardly wait.

Bert and Woody Hobbs invited me to go with them to next week's town social, and a few of the younger members of the Romig clan said I could come and visit them at *their* cabin anytime I needed to get away from the "tight-assed Bible-thumpers" in town.

But the most tempting offer of all came from Wayne Kramer and his son, Nate. They invited me to join them anytime in their epic quest for the "rare and elusive" Gold-Finned Dolly Varden. They claimed to have exclusive rights to the best fishing holes in the area and promised to show me everything I needed to know. I was becoming well and truly plugged in.

Around midnight Pennie announced she was hitting the hay and suggested I do the same, "since mornings come awfully early in these parts." (I was beginning to love phrases like "these parts" and "just us folks," and was looking forward to the day when I, too, could comfortably wrap my tongue around a little of this homespun lingo.)

Pennie had the cabin up on the hill behind the lodge and I walked with her to the foot of the steep path.

"Are you sure you'll be okay up there tonight?" she asked skeptically. "I could come and help you get a fire started if you like."

I assured her that I was fully capable of building a fire and was, in fact, looking forward to it.

"Well, okay, if you're sure . . . but you'd better get a good one going since it's starting to get chilly at night now. I'll meet you at the lodge at five sharp, or four-thirty if you want a shower. G'night!"

Damn. I had completely forgotten about water—or rather the lack of it—in my cabin. Oh well, I thought to myself, clean teeth were the least of my worries that night. I hadn't walked fifty yards when Pennie stuck her head out the door and fired off a warning shot: "Be careful when you're walking around up there—there's been a black bear hanging around your cabin the past couple of nights!"

Oh. My. God.

* * * * * * * * * *

Inside, the cabin was pitch black. If you've never spent a night in the country, it's hard to imagine how utterly dark it can get, and I immediately began feeling around for the light switch. Only there *wasn't* any light switch, for the simple reason that there wasn't any light to be switched. I felt a momentary flash of panic, but I quickly pulled myself together, remembering that I'd seen an old kerosene lantern lying on the floor that afternoon. I kicked around a bit until I located it and was relieved to find it still contained some fuel. I fished around in my pocket for a pack of matches and soon the whole room was bathed in the soft, warm glow of the lantern. Believe it or not, it was actually kind of romantic.

Now that I had the first problem solved, it was time to tackle the woodstove. A quick check confirmed that there wasn't a stick of wood anywhere in the cabin, so it looked like I'd have to gather some outside. But what about the bear? I couldn't remember if light attracted or repelled them, so I did the only sensible thing and left the lantern sitting inside by the stove.

The moment I stepped outside I was overwhelmed by darkness again. I knew if I ventured too far into the woods I might never find my way back, and I certainly wasn't about to wander off alone into the impenetrable darkness, especially with that goddamn bear hanging around. While there wasn't much in the way of wood in the immediate vicinity of the cabin, I did spot a big bush growing nearby and began pulling wet, leafy branches off of that, deciding it would simply have to do. When I had an armful I hurried back inside, making a mental note to gather wood only in the daytime from that moment on.

The woodstove leaned menacingly against the wall, an inert mass of iron and rust, and I approached it with trepidation. "Go ahead," it seemed to dare me, "just try to warm my cold, cold heart." I opened the heavy firebox door and dumped the pile of branches inside, wet leaves and all.

I knew there was something you were supposed to do about kindling, but for the life of me I couldn't think of what it was. So, drawing on my experience as a backyard barbequer, I poured some of the kerosene from the lantern onto the branches, then tossed a match into the pile and jumped back as the fire roared to life. All *right*! I dove for the bed and crawled under the covers, luxuriating in the sudden warmth, and feeling a special kinship with pioneer women everywhere. There was *nothing* I couldn't do.

But soon I began to notice a burning sensation in my throat. It got steadily worse, and by the time I decided I'd better go investigate, the entire cabin was filled with thick, black smoke and I couldn't see a thing. Choking and gasping for air, I pried open the window by my cot, then fought my way across the room and somehow managed to pull open the door on the stove. When the air finally cleared a little, I peered cautiously into the firebox, only to find that my once-blazing inferno was now nothing more than a pathetic, smoldering heap of green wood and soggy, smoking leaves.

Infuriated, I grabbed a stick off the floor and began thrashing it around in the sorry remains of the fire, hoping somehow to beat it back to life. Suddenly a couple of sparks leapt out of the box, flew through the air and, with unerring accuracy, landed on some of the weeds growing up between the floorboards. These caught fire immediately, and in seconds the floor in front of the stove was ablaze.

I screamed and raced toward the bed. The mattress was thick and heavy, but I pulled it down and dragged it across the room to where the floorboards were now burning furiously. The flames were getting higher and higher and, panicky, I heaved the mattress into the middle of the conflagration, hoping against hope that the weight of it would snuff out the fire.

It worked. I had saved the day, but now I was without a bed *or* a fire, and the cabin was getting colder by the minute. Just then the lamp, having sucked up the last of the fuel, sputtered and died, leaving me once again in total darkness. It was going to be the longest, coldest night of my life.

I curled up on the mattress on the floor and pulled the blankets up over my head. It was too cold and too quiet to sleep, so I lay awake, shivering and miserable, thinking about my comfortable, undeniably warm apartment back in Pittsburgh, counting the seconds until four-thirty.

At last the magic hour arrived. I couldn't see a thing in the dark, so I left everything behind and hurried out of the cabin as fast as I could. Too tired to care about wild animals, I fought my way through the woods, stumbling and crashing into trees, and learning the hard way that bears do, indeed, shit in the woods.

Pennie had gotten to the lodge first and was already showered and dressed when I arrived.

"Hi! How did you sleep?"

"Fine. Just fine," I lied sullenly.

"I'm so glad. I was afraid you might have had some trouble with the woodstove." Was she putting me on?

"No. No trouble at all. The fire was wonderful, the cabin was toasty warm and I slept like a baby all night." It had become a question of pride now, and I wasn't giving an inch.

The shower felt delicious and did perk me up a little, but there was no way I could even begin to function without some coffee and a cigarette or two. I staggered into the kitchen and found Pennie standing in front of the grill, sipping a hot cup of coffee. She took one look at me, guessed my awful secret and, smiling, filled a second cup to the brim.

The rest of the morning went pretty much the way one would have expected it to. By eight o'clock the kitchen looked like Hitler's bunker the day after it was bombed, and by nine, seven customers had walked out, refusing to pay for their breakfasts. At nine-thirty Cherie was dispatched to Hamilton's Store to buy out their entire supply of bread, and for the first time in the history of the lodge, cinnamon rolls were absent from the menu. Joanie thought that was wonderful. I couldn't wait to have the whole damn thing over with.

She and Cherie took over for the evening shift at two and I generously volunteered to stay and clean up the mess I'd made in the kitchen. I was exhausted and near collapse, but I stayed until the bitter end, scraping, sanding, and scouring until the kitchen was repristinated and everyone was smiling again. Then I jumped in the Fiat and headed up the road, determined to find some help.

The Shrew's Nest was Cooper Landing's approximation of an all-purpose store, a small rustic cabin filled to the rafters with everything from galvanized washtubs to freshly ground coffee beans and ladies' gingham dresses. In the time-honored tradition of great general stores everywhere, a fat, pot bellied stove squatted happily in the corner, radiating warmth and good cheer, a friend to all who entered.

Joyce Olsen, the owner, was sitting beside the stove with a cup of coffee and her knitting, and she smiled kindly at me when I came into the shop. We had met the night before at Spike's surprise party, which by Cooper Landing standards qualified us as old friends, and we spent a cozy half-hour by the fire reminiscing over the good old days. When I mentioned that I was staying in the old log cabin up on the hill, she gave me a funny look and asked how I was making out.

Here we go again. I assured her that everything was fine, but there were a few items I could use, and I handed her a list I'd written out. She knew just where to find everything, and in no time at all the counter was piled high with all the things I would need to sustain life—assuming, of course, I would have a life worth sustaining by the next morning. There were two brand-new kerosene lamps, a five-gallon can of fuel, half a dozen candles "just in case," and, at Joyce's suggestion, a ten-gallon jug for carrying water. On impulse we added a big box of wooden matches and a brass tea kettle for heating water on the woodstove. I paid the bill, thanked her for her help, and loaded everything into the car.

The cabin looked a lot more manageable in the daylight. A quick look around reassured me that all the dry wood I would ever need was lying on the ground a short distance from the cabin, and I spent the better part of an hour picking it up and arranging it in orderly piles beside the stove. I was getting my second wind and worked without stopping.

When all the heavy work was done I carefully filled each of the lamps with kerosene, then hung one beside the door where I'd be sure to find it that night. I put the other one on the floor, right beside the bed. Next I placed the candles and matches in neat little piles at strategic points around the room and, finally satisfied that I was fully prepared, picked up my big new water jug and went down to the lodge for a fill-up and something to eat for supper.

Most of the tourists were gone by then and the only customers left in the cafe were seven or eight truckers, a fact not lost on Joanie, whose disposition had sweetened considerably. I went into the kitchen to say hi to Cherie, who was standing on her coffee can in front of the grill. Angel that she was, she happily fixed me up with a cheeseburger and some fries. (The rule was that everyone cooked their own food when they were off duty, but Cherie, bless her little heart, wouldn't hear of it.)

I carried my dinner back out into the cafe and one of the truckers waved at me to come and join them at their table. Most were drivers for SeaLand or Weaver Brothers and I was pleased to recognize some of them from my first visit to the lodge just a week ago. They introduced themselves using not their real names but their CB "handles." There was Pappy, the Ditchhugger, the Frenchman, the Bluebird, and one wrinkled-up old geezer known simply as Pruneface. Then there was the Hippie from Bird Creek and the ever-popular, oh-so-sexy Silver Fox, a criminally handsome, prematurely gray "older" man of about forty.

Just as I was sitting down at the table, a nice-looking young driver excused himself and wandered off in the direction of the men's room. I asked Pruneface who he was.

"Oh, his real name's Bill something-or-other, I forget what. He's got so damn many handles though, no one can keep 'em straight, so we all just call him Joe Abernathy."

Go figure.

In addition to all their handles, I learned which type of rig each one drove—a not-insignificant detail, I might add. Most of the SeaLand guys drove GMC Astros, or "Jimmies" for short. These were the "cab-over" style of truck, meaning the cab sat directly over the engine and the windshield was flush with the face of the truck. The guys were all quick to point out that it took a certain amount of nerve to get behind the wheel of one of these—since there was nothing between the cab and the road but the windshield, the driver was *always* the first one at the scene of an accident.

The Weaver Brother trucks were mostly "conventional" Kenworths—long-nosed monsters that gave new meaning to the word "macho." The outstanding feature of the Kenworth, aside from its sheer power, was its sleeper, affectionately known as the "Kenworth Inn." The Kenworth sleeper was roomier than most and a lot quieter, owing to its relative position aft of the engine. The trucker who slept in a Kenworth sleeper was a well-rested trucker indeed.

But the classiest set of wheels by far, everyone agreed, was the fabulous Peterbilt. This was the Cadillac of the big rigs, a diesel-powered fantasy of chrome and steel, worthy of its status as King of the Road.

"Old truckers never die," Bluebird intoned solemnly, "they just get a new Peterbilt."

I was fascinated by all this roadman's lore, and anxious to learn all I could about truck drivers and the world they inhabited. But the men wanted to know about me, too, specifically how I was making out with the little cabin on the hill.

"What kind of a fire you runnin' up there, little lady?" one of them asked casually.

I was exasperated. What was so fascinating about a woman living alone in a cabin in Cooper Landing? And why was everyone so worried about whether or not I had the right kind of fire? Why? Why? Why?!

"Because you're from the city is why," Pappy spoke for the entire group, "and most city folks don't know diddly-shit about building a proper fire."

"'Course there ain't no shame in that all by itself," he continued wryly, "but it's the stupid ones with too much pride to ask for help that gets themselves in trouble and wind up burnin' half the mountain down." He cast a skeptical eye in my direction.

Touche.

I buckled under the pressure and told them all the whole sorry story, fully expecting pointed accusations and recriminations all around. But they were a sympathetic bunch and inside five minutes the whole lot of them were marching single-file up the side of the mountain, hell-bent on setting that cabin to rights.

The Ditchhugger and the Frenchman laughed when they saw the pathetic pile of twigs and branches I had stacked beside the stove and went outside to gather me up a proper woodpile. Bluebird showed me how to trim the wicks on the lanterns so they wouldn't smoke up the chimneys, while Pappy gleefully demonstrated the correct procedure for laying a workable fire.

Surprisingly, there was a fair amount of technique involved. You had to have just the right proportion of logs to kindling (and they had to be *real* logs, incidentally, not these faggy little sticks I had laying around—"Jaysus, leave it to a woman to try and build a fire with *sticks!*" Pappy muttered disgustedly). And you couldn't just toss it in all willy-nilly, either. The important thing was to do the job right.

Once he had everything arranged exactly the way he wanted it, he struck a match, and with great delicacy and precision touched the flame to the kindling at the heart of the pile. The flame caught, hesitated a moment, then burst into a great conflagration that lit up the entire room. Now *this* was a fire a man could be proud of!

He tossed in a couple more logs for good measure, then showed me how to set the flue and the damper to make sure the fire would last all night long.

"No damn sense to building a fire that only burns a couple of hours, now, is there?"

I said I guessed there wasn't.

Once everyone was satisfied that I'd be safe for the next twenty-four hours at least, they filed back down the hill and climbed into their trucks for the long trip back to Anchorage. But before leaving, they made me promise that I would ask for help before doing anything that stupid again, *ever*. After all, pride is a silly thing and we all know what it goeth before, don't we?

Ten-four, good buddies, ten-four.

Things went a lot more smoothly at work the next morning, thanks to Annie's unflagging patience and Pennie's abundant good humor. Inside a week I was turning out bread, pies, and cinnamon rolls like a pro, and as far as I know, no one ever complained about his or her breakfast again.

Soon I could build a fire to rival Pappy's and life in the cabin became an unending source of joy. If there is any greater pleasure in the world than curling up in front of a roaring fire on a cold winter's night, I have yet to discover it. And for sheer perfection, can anything match a moonlit mountain lake at midnight, viewed through a window framed and overgrown with a glorious profusion of wildflowers? Not bloody likely.

As the weeks passed I settled into an easy camaraderie with the fifty or so drivers who were regular customers of the lodge. They were a hell of a nice bunch of guys, and I really looked forward to seeing them each day and sharing a couple of laughs. Eventually I even overcame my initial bashfulness about the CB radio and turned into a regular "ratchet jaw," just like everyone else, yammering happily to anyone and everyone who happened by and breakered in on my one-nine.

Pennie, who knew everything there was to know about the great outdoors, assumed responsibility for my education. Every afternoon after work we'd embark on long "nature walks" up the side of the mountain or around the lake, and Pennie would instruct me in the ways of the woodsman. I was a quick study for a city slicker and before long I could identify every tree, bush, and flower native to the area, and Pennie had every reason in the world to be proud of her new student. It was an idyllic life, quiet and undisturbed, one I wouldn't have traded for the world.

That is, until I met the Budman.

* * * * * * * * * *

"Code Nine at three!" Pennie shouted from the cafe.

By that I understood that there was a good-looking guy sitting at table three by the window. We had devised this little system so we could alert one another to interesting possibilities without causing undue embarrassment to ourselves or the gentleman in question, and it really worked quite well. I was busy at the grill just then and couldn't leave to go investigate, so I waited for Pennie to come into the kitchen and elaborate.

She was smiling and there was a twinkle in her eye. "It's the Budman," she said softly, waiting to see what my reaction would be.

Okay, fine, I thought to myself. At last I was about to meet the man I had come to dislike most in the world. His real name was Dave Gagnon, but no one ever called him that. Instead, it was "Budman" this and "Budman" that, until I couldn't stand to hear the sound of his name. He was on the order of a legend around here (to hear the women tell it, anyhow), and since the day I'd first arrived in Cooper Landing I'd done nothing but listen to stories about him.

He was the "nicest guy on earth" or an "arrogant son-of-a-bitch." Depending on who you talked to, he was either handsome or rugged, shy or overbearing, a flirt or a woman-hater, or all of the above. The only thing anyone could agree on—and the consensus was over-whelming—was that he was devastatingly sexy.

It seemed that whenever two or more women got together, the con-versation inevitably came around to the subject of the Budman, and one day I'd had all I could take.

"Aw, c'mon you guys, this is getting sickening. Can't we talk about something else for a change? Besides, this 'Budman' person sounds like a real jerk to me."

"But JJ, you've never seen him!" gushed one of the youngest and prettiest girls in town. "He's . . . he's . . . he's *French!*"

"So is escargot," I countered wearily, "and I turn green when I think about that, too. Now, if you'll excuse me, I have work to do." I stalked off haughtily into the kitchen, bored and disgusted.

But now here he was, live and in person, a Code Nine at table three by the window. I had to admit my curiosity was aroused, so I sidled over to the door and snuck a quick peek into the dining room.

God help me, he was beautiful.

Not in any conventional sense—his face had too much character for that—but in the way a panther is beautiful. Sleek and dark and menac-ing. His body was lean and compact, the muscles of his back and shoulders just hinted at through the soft wool shirt he wore. Black hair, brown eyes, and a perfect nose were all where they belonged, but it was his mouth that was making it hard for me to breathe. It was a hard, unyielding mouth with full lips that curved down at the corners in a frightening blend of cruelty and soft sensuality.

Suddenly I felt dizzy and confused. My mouth was dry, my hands were freezing, and my heart was pounding so hard inside my chest, I was sure everyone around me could hear. At that instant I *hated* him for the way I was feeling, and I turned to leave, quickly, before my eyes could give me away.

But before I had time to react, Pennie grabbed me firmly by the wrist, pulled me out to the table, and made the proper introductions.

"Hello, Dave," I smiled through clenched teeth, barely able to maintain my composure.

"You know my name. Use it." he said curtly, without looking up from his plate. This guy was really asking for it.

"But 'Budman' is a stupid name," I said in the most scathing tone I could muster.

The rest of the table fell silent.

"And you are a stupid woman."

Done. War had been declared, the battle lines drawn. I turned on my heel and walked back into the kitchen, seething, shaking, my face hot with rage. I leaned against the counter for support, breathing deeply, trying to regain control. It was fully five minutes before I was calm enough to go back to work.

When Pennie finally returned to the kitchen I was standing at the grill, my back stiffly facing the door.

"I can't believe what just happened out there," she said wonderingly. "Who does that bastard think he is?" Pennie was the only woman I knew who wasn't the least bit affected by him.

"Of course, calling him stupid wasn't the most intelligent thing you've ever done, either. Especially in front of all those other guys." She was also completely logical, and honest to a fault.

"Oh, well," she sighed, "I guess I'd better get back to work. Mister Big-Shot wants a piece of pie."

"I'll get it."

"But—"

"I said I'll get it." I didn't leave her any room for argument.

"Okay, but you'll have to warm it up for him. Just be sure you don't leave it in the microwave for more than thirty seconds. Otherwise, the filling gets too hot."

Right.

I cut a big, fat slab of blueberry pie onto a plate, placed it inside the microwave, and set the timer for one and a half *minutes*.

The thick blue filling was actually bubbling as I carried the plate out and placed it on the table in front of him.

"Your pie, sir," I said, smiling politely, "with apologies for my rudeness."

He stared at me for several long seconds, then nodded curtly and picked up his fork. I turned and forced myself to walk slowly back to the kitchen. The instant the doors closed behind me I tore off my apron, tossed it across the room to Pennie, and ran for my life out the back door.

I was halfway up the hill when I heard him roar. He sounded like a bull in heat and I fell to my knees in the dirt and laughed until the tears came. It was a childish, dangerous stunt to have pulled, but God it felt wonderful. I hoped his mouth would burn all night.

It did, of course, and that one incident set the tone for our relationship from that point on. We became loyal adversaries, worthy opponents in a never-ending game of one-upmanship, much to the delight of the other drivers and regulars at the lodge. I wasn't bad at the game, but David was better and it seemed like he was the one who always came out on top. Naturally he had the home-court advantage —and that, without question, made all the difference in the world.

Early one evening in December he sent word over the CB radio that he had rolled his truck into a ditch in Kasilof, roughly sixty miles south of Cooper Landing. He would have to wait there for the next eight or nine hours until a wrecker arrived from Anchorage, so would someone please bring him some food and hot coffee if they were headed down that way?

I knew *exactly* where he was stuck and I seized the opportunity without a second's hesitation. I filled a huge wicker basket with half a dozen roast-beef sandwiches, an entire chocolate cake, and an over-sized silver thermos of piping hot coffee—strong and black, just the way he liked it. Then, encouraged by loud cheers and a round of high-fives, I loaded everything in the car and drove off into the night, ostensibly on a mission of mercy.

The weather had been miserable all day and the roads were a sheet of ice, so I crept along slowly, fighting to keep the car on the road. Traveling at that rate, I figured it would take me almost three hours to get to him, but that was fine with me—this would be the ultimate "gotcha" and I passed the time thinking about how it would go.

I'd pull up beside his disabled truck, roll up my windows, and lock all the doors securely. Then, with a look of pure pleasure on my face, I'd gorge myself on a veritable feast of sandwiches and chocolate cake, topping it all off with a hot, delicious cup of coffee, savoring its warmth and rich taste. Finally, as a last, deeply satisfying act of cruelty, I'd smilingly pour the last of the steaming coffee out on the road, then turn the car around and drive back to Cooper Landing, laughing all the way at the thought of him slowly starving to death in the cab of his truck. It was going to be just wonderful.

I was almost there. I could feel the adrenaline pumping as I approached the last bend in the road, knowing he was just on the other side, stuck in the ditch by the bridge. I swung into the curve and switched on my high beams. As the road straightened out I peered into the darkness and straight ahead, right there next to the bridge, I saw . . . I saw . . . nothing. The road was flat and dark and empty, and I realized I'd been had.

I was foaming at the mouth, rabid with rage and frustration as I turned the car around and began the long drive back to Cooper Landing. He would pay dearly for this one. Someday. Someway.

It was well after midnight when I rounded the bend at the Kenai River and my headlights picked out his big tractor-trailer parked in front of the lodge along with ten or eleven others. He was inside, relaxing over dinner with his cronies, no doubt, waiting for me to return so the humiliation would be complete. Well, not in this lifetime, sweetheart.

It was pitch dark outside as I pulled into the confusing maze of trucks in the parking lot and looked around to see if anyone was watching. As soon as the coast was clear I jumped out of the car and dug around in the trunk for my tool kit. Then, calmly and deliberately, I proceeded to disconnect every brake line, every piece of wiring, and every last cable connecting his truck to the huge, refrigerated van it was pulling. And when that was done, just for good measure I let the air out of six of his eighteen tires.

There. It would be morning before he got it all put back together.

I could hear him laughing inside the lodge as I climbed the hill to my cabin. I barricaded the door behind me, fell into bed, and slept the sleep of the angels, lulled by the sweet soporific of revenge.

It wasn't until the following morning before I learned that due to my haste, the surrounding darkness, and my blinding rage, I had accidentally dismantled the wrong truck. Once again, David had won by default.

Our war of wills escalated steadily over the next several months, but the time eventually came when I had to step back and ask myself exactly what it was I had gotten myself into. My initial preoccupation was by then bordering on obsession and I found that, almost literally, I couldn't think about anything except him. He was on my mind all day at work, and by the time he arrived each evening at seven I was half sick with anticipation and the fear that he wouldn't come at all.

The moment he walked through the door I went to pieces. My hands would begin to tremble, I'd stammer and stutter like a shy six-year-old, and if I looked too long at his eyes I would simply stop speaking in mid-sentence, lost and utterly confused. It was embarrassing, and it was getting worse every day.

The only thing that saved me publicly was the adversarial nature of our relationship. Anytime we got within ten feet of one another the show began, and we kept everyone entertained with our bickering and backbiting. As long as I could hide behind the facade I had created and pretend that I despised him, I was safe. It was only later, alone in my bed, that my true feelings took over and I lay awake all night, dreaming and fantasizing, on fire with passion and desire. I wanted him so badly I ached.

What *was* it about him that could turn me inside-out and cause me to forget my own name at the mere sight of him? To begin with, he was the direct opposite of everything I found attractive in a man. He was cold and unyielding, cruel and insensitive, and a chauvinist of the lowest order. He was married, and as far as I knew, happily so. He was, for heaven's sake, a *truck driver*.

Had my response to him been purely physical I might have understood it. After all, he was flat-out gorgeous, and I certainly wasn't the first woman to react to him in that way. But there was much more to it than a mere physical attraction. I was after his heart.

I wanted to marry him. I wanted to have his children, iron his shirts, butter his toast, and spend the next fifty years watching him grow old and wrinkled. I wanted to know all there was to know about him, to wrap him up and take him home and curl up inside of his mind. I wanted to own his soul.

But I was forgetting something. I was dangerously close to breaking the promise I'd made to myself before leaving Pittsburgh. I'd decided then, for a lot of very good reasons, that I could never allow myself to get too close to anyone, or to want anything too badly. There was too much at stake and I couldn't afford the losses that would surely come if I took a chance and let someone, anyone, too deeply into my life.

Health-wise, I was feeling just fine. I was happier and stronger than I'd been in a long time. But I was aware, as always, that underneath it all nothing had really changed. The sword was still there, waiting quietly to take everything away.

So ultimately, David became my safety net. As long as he was married and there was no chance of my ever having him, I was free to turn him into anyone I wanted him to be. In my mind, he became my lover, my friend, my protector. He became everything I ever wanted in a man, and because I could never truly have him, I would never have to give him up.

The idealized man I'd created in my imagination bore no resemblance at all to the person he really was, and that's the way it had to stay. I couldn't risk allowing him to become whole and real to me—a living, breathing person. He existed only as my hero, my fantasy, my dream.

But dreams have a way of coming true at times, and much later, long after he was divorced, we came together and made our peace with one another. In another tiny cabin, deep in another snowy wood, we spent a long, quiet evening together, talking, laughing, and even tentatively sharing a few of our private secrets. And when at last he touched my face and kissed my mouth, I fell into his arms and cried with relief. That one kiss seemed to settle things between us somehow, and it was only then that I let go of the passion and, finally and forever, became his friend.

But even now, more than seventeen years later, when the telephone rings and I hear his voice on the other end of the line, something inside me stirs and I find myself wondering what course our lives might have taken if only things had worked out differently.

FIVE

Kenai, Alaska
February, 1977

Two THINGS HAPPENED AT the end of January. Pennie announced she was leaving the lodge, and the radio station in Kenai called and offered me a job.

Pennie had decided some time ago that Cooper Landing (pop. approx. 96) was a little too big and too busy to suit her tastes, and a quick trip to Seldovia to visit a friend was all it took to convince her that this was where she wanted to settle down. Seldovia was a little fishing village across Kachemak Bay, which surrounded the southernmost tip of the Kenai Peninsula. The only way in was by boat or plane and that suited Pennie just fine. She could finally get away from tourists and cinnamon rolls for good.

I wasn't especially anxious to leave Cooper Landing *or* the lodge, but I was sure it wouldn't be the same without Pennie, and the radio station offer was really too tempting to pass up. It paid tons more money than the lodge and it would give me a chance to live in Kenai, something I'd wanted to do ever since I first visited there six months ago. Besides, Kenai was only an hour's drive from the lodge, so I could drive up and visit Anne and all the truckers any time I wanted to.

Pennie and I gave notice simultaneously, assuring Annie that we'd stick around until suitable replacements could be found. They were, and two weeks later we said goodbye to the lodge and all our friends and headed down south to see what awaited us there.

I felt at home in Kenai right away. It was a small coastal village supported mostly by commercial salmon fishing and oil. In fact, Kenai had grown up around oil—some of Alaska's earliest and richest strikes had occurred right there, in Cook Inlet, and nearly a dozen off-shore drilling platforms were visible from the North Road, just a few miles outside of town. Half a dozen canneries were strung out along the shore around the Port of Kenai and during salmon season they worked to capacity, twenty-four hours a day. It would be wonderful to live close to the sea, and I was anxious to dig in my heels and become a part of this new world.

I arrived in Kenai around eight that cold February morning and headed straight for the radio station, which was located on the outskirts of town. Right away I was struck by how pretty the place was. The studios were housed in a small, neat building that sat back off the road in a stand of snow-covered trees. What a nice place to work, I thought to myself as I parked the car and went inside. The station manager was waiting for me and he introduced me around, then invited me into his office to talk about the station and what it was I'd be doing there.

It wasn't until then I learned the station was owned by a born-again religious group called Solid Rock Ministries—thus the call-letters, KSRM. From six in the morning until six at night the station operated with a contemporary, easy-listening music format. But from six P.M. until sign-off at midnight, the airwaves were taken over by what was laughingly referred to by many locals as "The God Show."

Excessive religiosity in any form has always raised my hackles and if I hadn't already committed myself to the job, I probably would have left right then. But I really wanted to stay in Kenai, and I decided that if they could stand me, then I could stand them—as long as they stayed off my back and refrained from thumping any bibles on my head.

I was assigned to the afternoon-drive shift, from two to six, commencing that very afternoon. In addition, I would carry my share of commercial production and become the new daily host of something called "Tradio." Tradio is the equivalent of an on-air swap meet, and it is an abomination of the very worst tendencies of small-town broadcasting. God, how I would come to hate that show . . .

"Good afternoon, you're on Tradio."

"Uh, yes, hello . . ." an anonymous voice would drawl. "I have for sale a steering wheel from a '74 Bronco, in like-new condition. I also have a slightly used nursing brassiere, size 44 double D, and six pairs of men's long underwear, only worn once. If anyone is interested, they can call me at . . . ."

It was a humiliating way to make a living, and I resolved to get out of it as soon as I possibly could.

The first thing on the schedule that day, though, was an on-air interview with the morning announcer. The idea was to introduce me to the community and let everyone know I'd be starting that after-noon.

But I had other plans for the interview. My first priority was find-ing a place to live and I used the opportunity to put the word out around town. I said I'd be happy to consider anything, but that I pre-ferred a small cabin somewhere off the beaten path. I was already homesick for my place in Cooper Landing and eager to find another one like it if I could.

The response was immediate and overwhelming. Inside an hour, eleven people had called with offers of rooms and small apartments for rent, and one woman, a Helen Keppel by name, even had a cabin that wasn't being used. "It's not much," she cautioned. "There's no running water or anything like that, and no one would ever want to live there permanently, but you're sure welcome to stay until you find something else."

It sounded perfect. I got directions to her place and made a date to go see her as soon as I got off the air.

Whether in a big city or a small town, one's very first airshift at any new radio station is never without its share of trauma, and this one proved to be no exception. From a technical standpoint, KSRM was a breeze. The station was beautifully equipped and I didn't have any trouble whatsoever on that end. Instead, it was my first live newscast that almost got me fired.

The wire-service teletype was kept in a soundproof booth just off the main studio, and a couple of minutes before newstime I had to run in, tear off an hour's worth of copy, pull out what was pertinent, and put it in some kind of logical order. This arrangement didn't allow any time for proofreading, so I went into the first newscast cold. Now, any rookie knows that it's a good idea, when going to work in a new area for the first time, to familiarize oneself with the proper pronunciation of local places and names. I learned the hard way that this was doubly true in Alaska.

The very first sentence of the very first story started off exactly like this: "Today in the villages of Naknek, Konigiganak, Aleknagik and Igiugig . . ."

I didn't see it until I was right on top of it and I realized immediately that the teletype had gone berserk. I panicked, not knowing what to do next. I was already into the story and there was no graceful way out, so I did the one thing I never should have done. I started to giggle.

For some reason I couldn't stop, and before I knew it I was out of control and in the middle of a full-blown laughing jag. I made a huge effort to pull myself together, but I could see it was no use so I gave up, closed the mike, and punched up a song. I was still laughing hysterically when the station manager burst into the studio, ranting and raving, furiously demanding to know what was going on. He was so mad I thought he was going to burst a blood vessel.

"Aw, c'mon John," I sputtered, waving the news story in the air. "The damn teletype screwed up. Look what it did to these names!"

He grabbed the piece of paper from my hand and as he read what was printed on it, his face got even redder and his hands began to shake.

"There's not a thing wrong with the teletype," he hissed. "But I'm not *at all* sure about you!"

Oops. Typically, I did the worst possible thing once again, and started laughing like a hyena. The madder he got, the harder I laughed, until finally he stormed out of the studio, muttering under his breath about broads and broadcasting and the futility of life in general. I wrote him off as an old sorehead and got through the rest of the afternoon as best I could.

So much for Christian forbearance.

As soon as I signed off at six I jumped into the car and headed out to Helen Keppel's place to have a look at the cabin. Her directions were kind of vague: "Just head out the North Road past Eadie's and make a right on Melody Lane. You can't miss it."

Melody Lane? She had to be kidding.

"What's Eadie's?" I asked, suddenly curious.

"Oh, it's just an old whorehouse," she said offhandedly. "Don't give it a second thought."

That was good enough for me. I turned left off the bridge road onto Kenai's version of Main Street and drove slowly through the center of town. It was wintertime dark and the halos of the street lamps cast soft shadows on the snow drifts piled up along the road. Most of the shops were closed for the evening and the sign in front of the bank said the current temperature was twenty-five degrees below zero.

Mt. Redoubt was out in all her glory that night. Roughly ten thousand feet of recently active volcano, she maintained an uneasy truce with the town and all the people in it. Sure, she had a temper and everyone knew it, but just then she seemed harmless enough. Sheathed in white, her massive peaks shimmered ghostlike under the light of a full moon and cast a benevolent glow across the water. I was enchanted. She would be my talisman for as long as I lived in her shadow.

On the far end of town, where the North Road officially began, I passed Larry's Club, a sprawling, wooden roadhouse that looked like it had seen better days. People were arriving in a steady stream, and every time the door opened, the sorrowful wailing of a god-awful country band fractured the stillness of the night. Judging by the number of cars in the parking lot, this looked like the place to be if you were in the mood for a little action, and I made a mental note to check it out the first chance I got.

Five miles later I came to the place I was looking for. Just off the side of the road, hanging crookedly from a pole was a huge, pink, wooden heart. Painted across it in big, white, loopy letters were the words "Melody Lane," surrounded by dozens of fat little musical notes. It was easily the tackiest thing I'd ever seen, the ultimate in cornball art, and I laughed right out loud at the sight. Whoever had painted that sign was someone I knew I was going to like a *lot*.

Melody Lane, for all the name's romantic connotations, was nothing more than an unlit dirt path hacked through the woods, just barely wide enough for a car. In the utter darkness it appeared to go on forever with no signs of human life, and I made my way slowly, fearful of sliding into the ditch. Cooper Landing didn't have a thing on this place.

After what seemed like an eternity I came to a small clearing in the woods, and with a great sigh of relief turned to the right and pulled up directly in front of the Keppel homestead.

The "house" itself looked like something out of a Wild West picture show. It was a long, low, one-story log cabin, sort of like the Ponderosa only not nearly as nice. Most of it was buried under a magnificent fall of snow and the great white clouds of smoke billowing from the stone chimney lent an air of coziness to the scene. It was a frontiersman's dream, the kind of place John Wayne would have felt right at home in.

I knew the moment she opened the door that this was the woman who had painted the sign. Helen Keppel was, without a doubt, the grandest, most outrageous, most wonderfully overdone woman who had ever lived.

Helen was a big woman and I guessed her age to be close to seventy, but she bore no resemblance whatsoever to the stereotypes commonly attributed to the so-called "elderly." Not by a long shot. She was a vision, draped from head to toe in a neon-orange muu-muu that swept from her neck to the floor in a dramatic flourish that Mae West would have killed for. A big white ostrich boa was flung carelessly around her shoulders and every time she moved, hundreds of tiny feathers flew loose and floated in a puffy white cloud around her head. But the crowning glory, the highlight of the whole ensemble, was the enormous jiffy-pop wig she wore—without apology, and to such stunning effect. This, I thought to myself, is a woman who knows how to make an entrance.

Jocko, her asthmatic French poodle, was yapping hysterically at her feet as she ushered me in.

"Hello!" she welcomed me grandly. "I'm Helen Keppel, glad to know you! Come on in and watch out for the buckets, this old place is falling apart and now there's a hole in the roof. I listened to your show this afternoon and laughed all day, it's about time they got someone with a sense of humor over there, those goddamn Holy Rollers are a true pain in the ass if you want my opinion. Can I fix you a drink?"

Sure she could. I wasn't in a hurry to go anywhere.

"Go have a seat in the living room then while I mix 'em up—scotch

80

okay with you? I'll be there in a minute, careful you don't trip over Jocko!"

From where I was standing in the kitchen I could see down the entire length of the house, a span that looked to be close to eighty feet, and at first I had trouble comprehending it all. It was obvious that Helen was a woman for whom the phrase "less is more" held no significance whatsoever, and the gaudy excess everywhere was staggering.

"Like it?" she hollered from the kitchen. "It just doesn't seem like home unless I have a few of my favorite little things scattered around!"

A *few*? The log house was enormous, but it could barely contain everything she had crammed inside.

The living room alone was enough to stun me into a walking coma. It measured something like forty feet in length, was built entirely from massive, single-length logs, and was absolutely overwhelmed by what can only be described as the world's largest collection of knick-knacks and bric-a-brac, as well as half a dozen "one-of-a-kind" paint-by-number portraits of Jesus and Elvis Presley.

I counted seven sofas in all. Four of them were pushed together to form an immense "conversation pit" in the center of the room, where they surrounded a huge wooden coffee table. Upon said table I counted, among other things: seven ashtrays, four stacks of coasters from the Seattle Space Needle, two ceramic frogs, a large red bowl of poker chips, three plaster statues of the Virgin Mary, and a huge plastic bouquet of mums and roses done in an arresting shade of blue.

The main focus of the room was an enormous stone fireplace that dominated the far wall and was the largest of its kind on the peninsula, according to Helen. She once told me it could actually burn half a cord of wood at a time, a statistic I found hard to believe. But knowing Helen, anything was possible.

A large velvet painting of the Last Supper hung over the fireplace itself, and beside it on the wall was a magnificent black bearskin surrounded by rows of homemade plaques with sayings like "Bless Our Cabin" and "You Don't Have To Be Crazy To Live Here But It Helps." Great big ceramic ashtrays dangled from the ceiling on tasseled macrame cords, giant sprays of plastic ferns bloomed in every corner, and—oh, it's pointless to go on.

I was still standing, trying to take it all in, when she came into the room carrying our drinks and a plate of reindeer sausage and crackers. She cleared a spot on the big coffee table and we settled down for a long winter's chat.

I learned that she and her husband, Mel, had homesteaded the place back in the fifties, when Alaska was still a territory. They had built the main cabin first and the other rooms had been added gradually as their family grew.

Years later, after Mel died, Helen resumed her career as a registered nurse, and now she ran a small clinic in town, much to the pleasure of everyone concerned. She was greatly loved and respected in Kenai, owing to her big heart and ready willingness to lend a hand to anyone, anytime. It was obvious to both of us that we were going to become great friends, and we talked animatedly for hours that night before finally getting around to the subject of the cabin.

"It's nothing much," she warned me again. "Like I said before, there's no running water or anything, but you're welcome to use it until you find something else. C'mon, we might as well go take a look at it now."

The cabin stood in a small clearing in the woods and was barely visible under a huge snowdrift that had buried it almost to the roof. We dug our way up to the door, pushed it open, and stepped inside.

I couldn't believe how tiny it was. The entire cabin consisted of one small room that measured only eight feet by twelve and was empty save for a table, a steel cot, and a little propane heating stove in the corner. What a break—never again would I have to chop wood for heat! Of course, there was still the matter of a fire for cooking, but that was something I could handle easily. Pappy had taught me well.

The only thing I was even mildly concerned about was the lack of water, running or otherwise. I still had my big jug, so drinking water was no problem, but what about bathroom and shower facilities? I'd never worried about either in Cooper Landing since the lodge was right there and had both. But this was an entirely different story.

Typically, Helen had an answer for everything. She pointed to a decrepit old wooden outhouse sitting out behind the cabin, explaining how fortunate I was that she'd had the foresight to build it so it stood facing into the woods. That way, she said, I could leave the door open and enjoy a bit of nature while I performed my daily ritual. Here was a woman after my own heart.

The other problem required a little more thought. Helen herself showered daily at the clinic where she worked, but since I couldn't do that, she guessed I'd have to shower the same way everyone else did, at the laundromat.

"At the *what*?" I asked, puzzled. I couldn't believe I'd heard her right.

"Oh sure," she insisted. "Lots of people around here don't have water, so they go to the laundromat and rent a shower every day. You'll probably have to wait in line, so allow some extra time, but the showers are clean and there's plenty of hot water."

Now that she'd explained it, it made perfect sense. With that problem solved the deal was sealed, and I went out to the car to get my things while Helen fired up the stove.

Half an hour later we had everything put away, and after a cheery good-night from Helen I undressed and got ready for bed. The cabin was warm and dry, and as I snuggled cozily into my sleeping bag I couldn't help thinking how lucky I was. Two years ago I couldn't have envisioned anything remotely like the kind of life I was leading now. But there I was, strong and safe, and happier than anyone had a right to be.

So it had all worked out just fine. The good guys had won again, God was in his heaven, and all was right with the world. I blew out the lantern, fluffed up my pillow, and fell asleep in the "temporary" cabin that was to be my headquarters for the next four years.

I had found me a home.

I learned right away that life on the homestead was going to take some getting used to. Early the next morning I woke up, like most people do, with an urgent need to go to the bathroom. Only this time there wasn't any bathroom. There was just that miserable old outhouse and, never having used one before, I didn't have the vaguest idea how to proceed. I crawled out of my sleeping bag, wrapped a blanket around me, and opened the door onto a dark winter's morning in Kenai.

Jesus, it was cold. To make matters worse it had snowed again overnight, and what seemed like a mile of waist-high snow lay between me and the object of my desire. This was going to be just awful. I went back inside and put on my boots, jacket, and gloves, then left my warm little nest behind and began clawing my way toward the outhouse.

I soon discovered that it's no simple matter to move through snow that deep. With every step I took, more and more of the cold, wet stuff packed itself solidly up under my woolen nightgown until I was howling with pain and barely able to move. By the time I reached the outhouse, parts of me were frozen that should *never* be frozen, and I was beginning to despair of ever regaining feeling.

Things weren't much better once I got inside. It was obvious that structural repairs hadn't been attempted in years. Half the floorboards were missing, the walls were little more than a formality, and the hinges were so rusted that the door was jammed wide open and wouldn't budge. But there I was, and at last the time had come to do what I had come to do.

It was at that exact moment I saw the toilet seat. It looked just like any other toilet seat I'd ever seen, but with one horrible exception: this one was frozen solid under an inch of clear blue ice. My first instinct was to cry, but I quickly pulled myself together and asked myself what John Wayne would have done in a situation like this. Just as quickly I realized that this was a stupid question, since *he* could have done what I had to do standing up and wouldn't have considered it a problem in the first place.

By then my bladder was sending out strong signals, and since I was completely out of options I did the only thing left to do. I pulled up my nightgown, crossed my fingers, and sat down as quickly as I could. For a few blessed seconds I didn't feel a thing. Then, acting on the same principle as a tongue on a frozen pump handle, my rear end embedded itself solidly, deeply, firmly into the ice.

In the next instant a white-hot bolt of pain shot straight from my backside to my brain, propelling me up off the seat and, screaming, out into the wilderness. I left three layers of skin and a year's worth of growth behind and it would be a week before I could sit properly again. Adjustments would have to be made.

However, there was still the matter of a shower to be attended to, and I hurriedly stuffed everything I would need into my backpack. It was close to nine-thirty so I dressed quickly, then stepped back outside into the frosty early-morning air. The sun was just thinking about coming up and the sky was a deep, iridescent pink, streaked from horizon to horizon in shades of violet and blue, and a purple so intense it seemed to color the very air. The woods surrounding the cabin were dark and silent, and I smiled right out loud as I thought to myself—*this* was the Alaska I had dreamed of all my life.

I managed to pull myself out of the trance I'd fallen into and got everything loaded into the car. As soon as the engine was warmed up I turned on the heater, put the Fiat in gear, and took off in search of the laundromat.

There is a phenomenon unique to northern climates known as an "ice fog," which can produce some of the most spectacular effects nature has to offer. When conditions are just right and the temperature drops sufficiently, any moisture in the air will freeze into tiny crystals that hang in the air and collect on any available surface.

There had been an ice fog the night before, and my first glimpse of Melody Lane in the daylight was one I'll never forget. Every twig on every branch of every tree was thickly encrusted with lacy crystals of ice that caught the pink morning light and fractured it into a million sparkling rainbows. Even the trees lining the road were shimmering and heavy with ice, and high overhead they bowed to one another, almost touching. Stunned, I drove slowly, almost reverently, through a crystallized cathedral—a frozen canopy of light and air.

All things considered, it wasn't a bad way to start the day.

I found the laundromat without much trouble, and I was relieved to see that I was its only customer. The old man behind the counter was busy folding clothes and didn't look up as I approached and asked if I could get a shower.

"That'll be a dollar," he barked. "Buck and a quarter if you want a towel."

Luckily I'd remembered to bring a towel, so I gave him a dollar and received in exchange two faucet handles, one hot and one cold.

"What are these for?" I asked innocently.

"Said you wanted a shower didn't you?" he snarled. "Now get to it and don't use up all the hot water, either."

85

A real sweetheart, this one. I picked up the handles, guessing correctly that they served as some kind of sophisticated anti-theft device in case someone would actually *think* of stealing a shower from this man.

The shower felt wonderful and I indulged myself fully, reveling in the sheer luxury of it. I must have reveled a little too long, though, because the next thing I knew the old buzzard was pounding on the door, screaming about the hot water. I got out, dressed, and dried my hair as quickly as I could, then dropped the handles on the counter and left the laundromat without a backward glance. Our relationship never grew any warmer, and he never spoke a civil word to me as long as I lived in Kenai.

By the end of my second day at the radio station, work had become almost routine. I turned over the reins to the God People at six and hurried into town to stock up on things I would need for the cabin— food, paper plates, pots and pans, kerosene, a small axe, and some toilet paper. I loaded it all into the car and then headed out toward the cabin.

Helen was waiting for me when I got there, curious to see how I was making out. She helped me put away my things and then showed me how to dig a cache in the snow so I could store my food and keep it safe from wild animals. Typically, I hadn't even thought about that.

Since she was being so nice, I told her the whole sad story of my experience in the outhouse that morning, and begged her advice. That one had her rolling on the floor, but after she regained her composure she patiently told me of the value of keeping a "slop jar" inside the cabin with me (an empty coffee can would do nicely, and please don't forget the lid). That way, she said, I could empty it at my leisure and avoid the problem altogether.

But if a trip to the outdoor facility *did* become necessary—say I had a gentleman caller—there still needn't be any problem. All I had to do was hang the toilet seat over the stove and then of course it would be nice and warm when I carried it with me to the outhouse. What could be simpler? It was just a matter of using your head.

Finally, she made a gift to me of one of her best copper cowbells and told me to wear it around my neck anytime I ventured into the woods or even walked along the road, explaining that the noise it made would frighten away any moose or wolves that might be in the area. Come to think of it, she said, a rifle might not be a bad idea either, if I could get my hands on one. (We didn't have to worry so much about bears just then as it was winter, and with any kind of luck they were all still hibernating.)

When she was completely satisfied that I knew everything I had to know, she said she was planning to head down to Larry's Club later that evening to do a little dancing, and did I want to come along? You bet I did.

If the idea of a young woman in her twenties going out for a night on the town with an "older" woman pushing seventy seems strange, you have to remember that Helen Keppel was no ordinary senior citizen—a fact made abundantly clear to me that very night.

When we got to Larry's at about ten, things were just starting to warm up and we made our way quickly to one of the tables near the dance floor. The band, strictly country, was as bad as I'd anticipated, but they were loud and enthusiastic and, hell, that's all anyone cared about anyhow.

Out on the dance floor a whole herd of skinny "cowboys" in pointy-toed boots, fancy western shirts, and enormous ten-gallon hats were leading their partners through the complexities of the Texas Two-Step and the Cotton-Eyed Joe. The women were dressed exactly like the men, the only distinction being that their hats were a little smaller—eight gallons at the most.

The whole thing confused me. Where had all these cowfolks come from? I'd seen a lot of strange people doing a lot of strange things since I'd come to Alaska, but bronco-busting had never been one of them.

"Hey Helen!" I shouted across the noisy table. "How come all these people look like they just rode in from Dodge City?"

She just nodded sadly and went back to stirring her drink.

By ten-thirty the place was crawling with men and it seemed like Helen knew each and every one of them. From the time we sat down until five the next morning she never missed a dance, and did her best to see to it that I didn't either.

"This is nothing!" she hollered as she waltzed by in the arms of one of her many partners. "Wait until summer when the fishermen are in town—you'll *really* see some action then!"

She didn't know the half of it. That first night at Larry's established a pattern I was to follow for most of the next several years. My days would be spent at work, my nights at Larry's Club looking for Code Nines, and every spare minute I had would be devoted to exploration. I was living in what I considered to be heaven on earth and I was determined, somehow, to see every square inch of it.

* * * * * * * * * *

One of the nicest things about working as a disc-jockey is that one usually becomes a desirable member of whatever community one happens to be in. A pillar of society, so to speak. Kenai was no different than most places in this respect, and shortly after I arrived all sorts of nice people began calling the station and offering their hospitality, each of them eager to show off what they liked best about the area.

There are more private planes per capita in Alaska than just about anywhere else in the world, and it seemed like everyone who called was a pilot of some kind. I made a point of not refusing anyone when it came to flying and at least three or four times a week I found myself airborne, a low-altitude eavesdropper on the rugged terrain and wildlife of the Kenai Peninsula.

My hosts and I flew everywhere that winter, from the spectacular Harding Ice Fields near Seward to the huge logging operations of Jakalof Bay off the southern tip of the Peninsula. From a thousand feet up I tracked the movements of huge pods of whales across the open stretches of Cook Inlet, and on days when the weather was especially clear I delighted in being flown low over the miles and miles of glaciers that carved their way deep into the mountains along the coast. The sight of the bottomless crevasses and the sharp, towering pinnacles of dazzling blue ice was enough to keep me pleasure-drunk for a week. It was a privileged view of the Alaskan wilderness, and to this day I carry those memories with me.

But there was plenty to do on the ground, too, and more than one way to get into a world of trouble. Dogsled racing has always been an important part of Alaskan culture and the tradition was kept very much alive in Kenai. Sled-building was a popular hobby and it wasn't unusual to find twenty or thirty sled-dogs tied up behind someone's cabin in preparation for the big races held almost every winter weekend. It looked like a lot of fun, and I was happy to accept when one of the local sledders, Al Primavera, phoned me at the station and invited me to join him the following weekend.

The sky was clear and the air was crisp when I arrived at the Primavera homestead on Saturday, and I was looking forward to getting out into the countryside. I'd seen every one of those old Sergeant Preston movies and I couldn't wait to yell "Mush, you huskies!" to a string of fifteen or twenty big dogs and watch them spring into action.

So naturally I was a little disappointed when I saw that the sled I would be riding was attached to only *two* dogs, who appeared to be on the small side and not very energetic to boot.

"Uh, Al," I asked as tactfully as I could, "is this it? Two dogs?"

"Well," he said, smiling, "you should be able to handle them. If not, we can always pull one off."

Of course he was kidding. Or so I thought. I couldn't see how those scrawny little things were going to pull me anywhere, but I swallowed my disappointment and pretended to listen as he gave me my instructions. He showed me how to get going (you really do yell "Mush!"), gave me the commands for left and right, and stressed the importance of staying loose and leaning into the curves, just like you would on a motorcycle. I'm sure he told me how to stop, too, but like I said, I wasn't really paying attention.

When everyone was ready, I climbed on board my sled and put my foot on the brake, a heavy steel claw that dug into the snow and kept the sled from moving. This was easier said than done, because the dogs were *really* eager to run. But I held on tight and waited for the command to go. Al was up front on his sled (he had six dogs, incidentally) and when he hollered "Mush!" I stepped off the brake and fought to stay upright while the dogs took off as if they'd been fired from a high-powered rifle.

For the first hundred yards or so I was okay—all I had to do was hang on and let the dogs do their thing. But then suddenly, dead ahead, the trail made a wide swing to the left and I realized instantly that I was in trouble. I remembered Al saying something about lean-ing, but for the life of me I couldn't remember which way, and now the dogs were approaching warp speed.

"Stop!" I screamed. "Freeze! Halt! . . . PLEASE!" But nothing had any effect. I was really scared. *What was the proper command?*

It didn't matter. It was too late to stop them anyhow. I closed my eyes and clutched the reins as the dogs raced into the curve. I was totally out of control, my mind a blank, and suddenly I felt the reins being ripped from my hands as I sailed through the air and slammed headlong into a wall of ice and frozen snow.

By the time Al got his team turned around and back to where I was lying in a crumpled heap on the ground, my shoulder was throbbing and I was checking to see if anything was broken.

"Are you okay!" he shouted, running frantically toward me.

"I guess so," I said angrily, fighting back the tears. "But why wouldn't the damn dogs stop?"

"Because you didn't give the proper command is why. I told you, all you had to say was 'Whoa'."

Oh. I guess I hadn't thought of that.

Al thought it would be best if we called it a day, but there was no way I was giving up then. I'd come here to ride a dogsled and that's exactly what we were going to do. And he wasn't going to take one of my dogs away, either. Once again my stubborn pride had taken over.

I climbed back on my sled and paid close attention to the new set of instructions he was reciting. My second attempt went much more smoothly than the first, and we went on to enjoy a splendid, twenty-mile ride through the backwoods country of the Kenai.

The dogsled-riding community in Kenai was a large one, and for the rest of the winter I spent most of my free time racing through the wilderness with one borrowed team or another. I never stopped carping, though, about the fact that no one would let me drive more than two dogs at a time. I must have gotten pretty obnoxious about it because, mostly to shut me up, the announcement was made that I would be racing *four* dogs at the big final race of the season at Arc Lake.

I was ecstatic. But there was just one catch: I would have to select the dogs I wanted to use all by myself, without any help from anyone. Fair enough. I was glad just to have the chance.

Race day dawned clear and cold, and when I arrived at Arc Lake, the scene was one of chaos. Hundreds of dogs and what seemed like thousands of people were barking at each other, trying to sort themselves into teams. It looked like it was going to be a great day.

I went and hung my number on the sled I would be using in the race, then started looking around for the dogs I needed to make up my team. The lead dogs were the critical component, and I wanted the biggest, strongest ones I could get my hands on.

Surprisingly, I found them rather quickly. They were fierce, powerful-looking beasts and they obviously wanted to run, straining as they were at their leads. I couldn't understand why no one else had snatched them up, and in all fairness I do have to say that their owners did try to talk me out of using them. But I paid absolutely no attention, firmly convinced that these were the dogs that would win the race for me.

I quickly selected two others and got busy securing them all in their traces, and when it was my turn to start I rode confidently up to the starting line. The race official gave the signal and, like the seasoned pros we were, the dogs and I streaked off across the frozen lake, operating as one, a well-greased racing machine. This is great, I thought to myself, and I couldn't help wondering what all the fuss had been about. Turned out four dogs were every bit as easy to handle as two.

At the far side of the lake the trail made a sharp left into the woods, and as soon as we were out of sight of the crowd I began to relax a little and settle into the rhythm of the race. The dogs were running hard and for the first couple of miles it looked like maybe we had a chance.

Then an unbelievable thing happened. As we approached the two-mile marker, the dogs gradually began to slow down. No amount of screaming and cursing on my part had any effect, and before long they simply stopped running altogether, dead in their tracks, to coin a phrase. I couldn't understand what was happening, but as I leapt off the sled and ran up to the front of the line, it all became perfectly clear.

Oh no. Oh no, no, no. It couldn't possibly be happening. But it *was* happening and all I could do was stare, shocked and stunned into silence, as right in front of my unbelieving eyes the four of them assumed the position and began a ritual that can most delicately be described as the Doggie Dance of Love.

I was dumbfounded, and as I stood there like some kind of "Wild Kingdom" peeping-tom, the realization of what I had done slowly worked its way into my brain.

Those two beautiful lead dogs, my prize catches, weren't sled dogs at all. They were someone's *pets*. Worse, they were females who had apparently just come into heat. Add to that the fact that my second string were males, and normal, healthy ones at that, and what you ended up with was this infuriating little canine *menage-a-quatre*.

Under any other circumstance I wouldn't have begrudged them their little indiscretion (I've been in heat a couple of times myself and could sympathize). But this was a race, dammit, and now all was hopelessly, irretrievably lost.

I sat down wearily in the snow and tried to look the other way while the four Hounds from Hell huffed and puffed and blew the house down. When it was finally over, all their passion and energy spent, I was left looking at four satiated, satisfied little balls of fur, sound asleep in the snow with no inclination whatsoever of finishing the race.

It was getting colder and darker by the minute and I was left with only one option: I picked up each of the sleeping dogs and piled them on the back of the sled, then pulled the reins up over my shoulders and began the long, miserable hike back to camp. Suddenly vivisection didn't seem like all that bad an idea.

When we finally arrived back at the starting line (an hour behind the last finisher, incidentally), my humiliation was complete. Everyone knew what had happened and, deservedly, I became the butt of endless sick jokes and leering innuendos.

It took a while, but eventually even I began to see the humor of it all. When the race chairman presented me with a special trophy for last place, I even managed to squeeze off a few rounds about the sexual proclivities of a group of men who spent more time with a pack of horny Malamutes than they did with their own wives.

Luckily for *all* of us it was the last race of the season.

* * * * * * * * * *

The approach of spring brought with it, as it always does for me, a deep feeling of melancholy and a vague sense of loneliness. While most people rejoiced at winter's end and looked forward to the time of reawakening and growth, I always tended to look at spring as an ending in itself. I *liked* winter, especially in Alaska, and I hated to see it go.

As the weather grew warmer and winter's icy landscape began to melt away, I found myself almost constantly drawn to the rocky coastline that bordered the town and was its fragile defense against the fury and the turbulence of the sea.

I had a special, secret place that no one else knew about, and late every afternoon I made my way down to the windy beach and climbed up onto a big, flat boulder sitting at the base of a cliff. There, huddled deep into the warmth of my parka, I sat for hours, gazing out over the cold, gray reaches of the sea, my eyes fixed on a point just beyond the horizon. It was out there somewhere that all the answers lay.

But what was the question? I couldn't seem to shake the feeling that something was coming, and that if I could only learn what it was, then maybe I could fix it and make it come out all right. It bothered me, this restless malaise, and increasingly I found myself torn between anger at the way I was feeling and the deepening need to discover its source.

My self-imposed isolation and utter lack of any meaningful male relationships had left me desperately lonely, and for the first time ever I was beginning to sense that there ought to be something more to my life than simply living from day to day, as I had been doing since coming to Alaska. I'd covered a lot of ground in the past few years, but I had little notion of having accomplished anything, and absolutely no idea of where I was headed next.

I felt as though I were being carried away helplessly by forces beyond my control. I seemed to be without purpose or direction, a detached being moving haphazardly through the world, merely reacting to all that was happening around me. I'd lost the reins somewhere, forgetting for a time that for as long as it was possible, the important choices were still mine to make.

But in what context? And what role should the MS play, if any, in the choices I would make? I'd been symptom-free for almost two years by then, and it was starting to look as though I might stay that way for quite some time to come. But could I *count* on it? Could I dare to take the chance that I might be one of the lucky ones, after all?

I was beginning to think maybe I could. I'd come this far, hadn't I? And who was to say it had to stop here? Lots of people had fought worse illnesses than the one I had and gone on to lead long and productive lives filled with love, happiness, and the joy that comes from knowing that at least they'd given it their very best.

And I would, too. I decided at that moment that I would put it all behind me and go ahead on the conscious assumption that everything would work out for the best. God *was* still in his/her heaven, after all, and as long as God was on my side, I was sure I could overcome anything.

Once I'd made the decision, everything around me seemed changed. Springtime was suddenly the best time there was to be alive, and I began to look forward to the long, warm days ahead, and to the last untroubled summer I would ever know.

SIX

■ ■ ■

Homer, Alaska
Summer, 1977

THE FISHERMEN BEGAN ARRIVING in June. They came from all over the country—from Washington, Oregon, California, and even as far away as Louisiana. And every one of them came with a clear purpose in mind: to fish until they dropped, and maybe go home a little richer than when they started.

But that was easier said than done. When you consider that a commercial salmon fishing license could run upwards of $80,000—not to mention the price of the boat, the gear, insurance, payrolls, and physical maintenance for starters—you begin to realize that this is a deadly serious business. Break that cost down over a short, restricted fishing season and you've got yourself something like a $20,000-a-day habit. It's no wonder these guys were in a frenzy most of the time, since any number of factors from bad weather to boat trouble could spell disaster, and something was *always* going wrong.

But they knew how to party, too, and any time they weren't fishing or mending nets, you could find most of them in Larry's Club, boozing and brawling and spending money like there was no tomorrow. Helen's prediction came true with a vengeance and our social lives soared to heights never before imagined. I didn't get much sleep that summer, and I remember dozens of sorry, hung-over mornings at the radio station. But we all have to pay for our sins and that was debt I'd happily incur again, anytime.

On fishing days I loved to sit on the cannery docks in the evening and watch the boats come in, their gunwales awash under the weight of a full load of salmon, the crews exhausted but delirious over the day's catch. The unloading process went on all through the night with hundreds of boats lined up at the canneries, each awaiting their turn at the cranes. Huge rope baskets were lowered into the hold and then lifted out over and over again with thousands of pounds of flashing silver salmon. When the hold was empty, the catch was weighed and credited to the boat's account and then, at last, the crew could collapse into their bunks as the next boat took its place in line.

Meanwhile, the cannery was working to its limit, around the clock, processing the catch before it had a chance to spoil. It was fascinating to watch the salmon go in whole at one end and then, hours later, come out the other end in little silver tins, ready to be shipped all over the world. Very little of the fish was wasted. Head and tails were ground up for animal feed and fertilizer, and even some of the offal discharged into the harbor provided dinner for the seagulls and the beautiful white beluga whales who patrolled the area, hoping to get lucky. Kenai's own balance of nature was well preserved here.

The cannery workers, for my money, had absolutely the worst jobs in the world. The work was seasonal and it paid by the hour, so it wasn't unusual to find some of them working twenty-four hours at a clip, whacking off the heads and tails of the endless procession of stinking dead salmon.

But it was the herring-squeezers who were the unluckiest of them all. Their job was to squeeze the egg clumps out of dead herring so that the eggs could be processed and sent overseas where rumor had it that people actually ate the awful-looking little things. If the mere thought of it didn't turn your stomach, then one good whiff usually would.

I don't know which stunk worse, the herring or the squeezers, but by the end of a long shift it was a moot point. It's a good thing the canneries provided food for these poor people because they didn't have a prayer otherwise. All over town restaurants posted signs that read "HERRING SQUEEZERS KEEP OUT," and thank God they did. It was a brusque but necessary admonition to the "unclean," the new outcasts of an otherwise tolerant society.

If you're not prepared for it, summertime in Alaska can really take you by surprise. The days begin to lengthen as springtime gives way to summer, just like everywhere else, but owing to its extreme northerly location, the transition in Alaska is much more dramatic than in the "lower forty-eight." Summer days become extraordinarily long, and by the end of June nighttime is pretty much a memory. As a result, everyone—even the old-timers—finds themselves operating on the edge of nervous exhaustion. It's easy to forget how much energy you get from the sun until you're faced with the prospect of it nonstop, and by then it's too late. I never did get used to going to bed near midnight with the sunlight streaming in my window, or to leaving Larry's Club at four in the morning, to find the skies as bright as noontime.

But the long days offered almost unlimited time for adventure, and I had plans for every precious second of it.

There might be prettier places on earth than Homer, Alaska, but if you know of any, please spare me the details. It would only ruin it for me.

The town itself is situated on the shores of Kachemak Bay, near the southernmost tip of the Kenai Peninsula, and looks pretty much like any other tiny fishing village in Alaska. But the thing that makes Homer different—and which is, in fact, the main reason for its existence—is the long, narrow spit of land that reaches five miles out into the bay and supports the fishing industry for the entire area. This is where it all happens.

Canneries, ship's chandlers, and charter operations are strung out along the waterfront, and way, way out there, virtually on the very end of the spit, lies the Port of Homer itself.

I remember the first time I visited. I walked for hours up and down the long, wooden docks, lost to everything but the sights and sounds and smells of the place. There was no mistaking the fact that this was a working harbor: hundreds of big wooden crabbers, trawlers, and greasy tenders fought with each other for dock space, each one of them contributing to the faint blue haze of diesel that hovered overhead and came and went with the breeze.

Tied up to the end of Pier D was a battered old wooden fishing boat, and if it hadn't been for the old man I spotted puttering around on its deck, I might have assumed it was a derelict. The hull was patched and pocked, the brightwork wasn't (bright, that is), and the wheelhouse looked like it was held together with baling wire. The simple fact that it was actually floating defied every law of physics I could think of.

I called over to the old man and asked what he was fishing for.

"Crab, mostly!" he hollered back. "But shrimps is okay, too—shrimps is jes' as good!"

I walked to the stern of the boat, leaned over the gunwale and asked him if crab were in season.

"Yeah, but just them dungeness, which I hate worser'n shit," he spat angrily. "*Kings* is what I like, but they ain't legal 'til August. I figger it this way though—a man's got a right to eat whatever he likes, ain't he?"

I said I guessed he did, and asked when he was going out.

"Fixin' to leave right now. Got some pots soakin' out in the bay should be full by now. Mebbe get lucky."

I asked if I could go along.

"Ferget it," he answered curtly. "Any fool knows it's bad luck to have a woman on board. Besides, you'd only jes' get in the way."

Never one to be put off so easily, I whined and wheedled and finally wore him down.

"Well, come on then," he sighed heavily. "Jes' see that you stay out of my way, and keep your mouth shut about the Kings. And remember, any crabs we catch is *mine*."

Such a deal.

I climbed on board and sat down on a pile of coiled rope while he jumped into the wheelhouse and fired up the big diesel engines. As soon as we were under way I joined him in the wheelhouse and watched, amused, as he cursed and pounded on the throttle with a wrench, trying to coax another knot of speed out of the weary old "bucket of bolts."

He was a man of very few words, but I learned that his name was Jack and that he'd been fishing in these waters for over forty years. It wasn't a bad life, he said, just lonesome sometimes and damn cold in the winter. But, hell, a man's gotta eat, ain't he?

When we arrived at our destination, I was surprised to see the surface dotted with hundreds, maybe thousands, of big pink marker buoys, each attached by a long line to a wire, cage-like crab pot sitting on the ocean floor far below. I'll never know how Jack knew which was his, but inside a minute he had a hook around one of the buoys and was pulling it up alongside the boat. All he had to do then was wrap the line around a winch, throw a switch, and in moments the pot broke the surface "slicker'n snot on a doorknob," as he so sweetly put it.

What a sight. Crawling around inside the pot were four or five live Alaskan King crabs. They looked like huge, angry spiders, and I was so startled I dropped the line I was holding and jumped back across the deck, fearful of attack.

Jack threw me a disgusted look and hollered at me to come and help him with the pot. I approached with great trepidation and, being very careful about what I grabbed, helped him muscle the cage up onto the deck.

Now what? He pried open the rusted lid with a crowbar while I stood watching, ready to jump in case one of the crabs escaped and tried to make a run for it. Jack wasn't paying any attention to me at all as he reached into the pot and grabbed ahold of a long, spiny leg. He had to fight a little, but in a minute he had the crab out of the pot and was holding it at arm's length, careful to avoid the vise-like claws that were by then desperate to get a purchase on anything.

"Aw shit!" he cussed loudly. "This is jes' a friggin' baby—ain't even a keeper!"

Without a backwards glance he tossed the crab over his head into the water, then reached into the pot for another. Out of the five in the pot, only one turned out to be legal. You had to be careful about size since there were strict measurement guidelines, and Fish and Game could get really nasty if you didn't play by the rules.

"Jesus, I hate them bastards," Jack muttered under his breath. "Fuckers'd jes' as soon send you to jail as look at you."

I couldn't help wondering why he was so concerned about size when we were already fishing illegally. I held my tongue, though, not wanting to rattle him any further.

"Oh well," he decided as he threw the keeper into the hold, "this'n'll do okay, but we gotta go get some more."

We pulled six more pots that afternoon and wound up with four keepers in all—three for him and, surprisingly, one for me. Of course, I had to earn that crab, so while Jack pulled pots and sized the catch, I sat on deck and cut bait.

This involved hacking dead and rotting "garbage" fish into pieces so they could be hung inside the pots as an enticement to future victims. I count it as a personal victory that I only threw up twice all afternoon.

Several hours later we were safely back in port, and before I left Jack let me have the pick of the catch. He put the crab in a big cardboard box, taped up the lid and sides, and told me to hurry up where I was going, " 'cause crabs don't live too long out of water and they *gotta* be alive when you kill 'em!"

Made perfect sense to me.

The big crustacean managed to cling to life throughout the entire ninety-mile drive back to Kenai, and Helen and I feasted like royalty that evening. That first taste of crab and the process required to catch him whetted my appetite for more, and early the next morning I was back in Homer, prowling the docks, hoping for another chance to go fishing. Neither Jack nor his boat were anywhere in sight, but there were plenty of others, and when I went home to Kenai that night it was with a whole carful of crab and halibut, and a brand new mission in life: I was going to become a sailor.

I put the word out all over the peninsula that I was looking for a job on a boat, and every remaining summer weekend found me back in the harbor, hustling work like a junkie hustles his next fix. There weren't many permanent jobs to be had, but I always managed to wangle my way on board something, either as an extra hand or simply as a guest along for the ride (something known in nautical circles as "supercargo").

It didn't matter what kind of a boat it was, either—sailboat or workboat, tender or trawler—if it floated, I wanted to be on it. The days were long and the work was hard, but I was learning and that was all that mattered. I loved the way I felt and even the way I smelled by the end of the day when my fellow crewmates and I tied up to the dock, iced down the catch, and, along with all the other harbor rats, headed up to the Salty Dawg Saloon for a beer and an evening's conversation.

Like all the world's great waterfront bars, the Salty Dawg is an anachronism, a relic of another time and place with an ambience all it's own. "Nasty" is usually the first word that comes to mind when you open the door and step inside. An odious brown cloud of cheap cigar smoke rolls like a fog bank down the bar and the overall aroma is a fetid mix of oiled wool, decomposing fish, and human sweat. But it's a solid, honest smell, one you could lock your olfactories on and know you'd really been somewhere.

Piles of rusty harpoons, fish nets, and crab pots are stacked in the corners, and the ceiling and walls are hung with tattered signal flags and dozens of well-worn life rings from scores of long-forgotten sunken ships. Behind the bar is an old-time, hand-cranked cash register and on top of that sits an actual human skull. Taped to the skull is a sign that reads: "THIS IS THE LAST PERSON WHO GAVE US A BAD CHECK." People mostly pay cash nowadays.

The routine was always the same. We'd all crowd together around one of the old wooden tables by the wall, order up a round of beers, and sit into the wee hours, drinking and telling lies amid rousing choruses of the great old sea chanteys—a centuries-old tradition among seafarers everywhere.

Most nights I didn't even make it back to Kenai. There was always an empty berth on one of the boats and things worked out better that way anyhow, since it was important to get an early start in the morning. By five o'clock we'd be up and at it again, pushing and pulling, sweating and swearing, happy to be back at sea.

* * * * * * * * * *

If God himself were to step down from heaven and tell me I could pick, out of all the days of my life, one single day to live over and over again, there's no question I'd choose the day that summer that we sailed away on a schooner named *Mariah*.

It was early on a Saturday morning and I was making my rounds of the harbor, hoping to latch onto a boat for the day. By that time I was pretty familiar with most of the vessels in the fleet, at least by sight, and so I was totally unprepared for the shock of the discovery I was about to make.

Normally, the slip at the end of Pier F was reserved for one of the big tenders—an old, rusted hulk of a workboat, so bad that even I wouldn't go near it. But for some reason it wasn't there that day. In its place was an extraordinary sight—a magnificent, two-masted, gaff-rig schooner of a style I didn't think existed anymore. She was a dream ship, a floating apparition, and quite simply the most beautiful thing I'd ever seen. Her name was *Mariah* and she measured an unbelievable eighty-five feet from her bowsprit to her transom in one long, unbroken sweep of graceful lines and curves.

A boat of those proportions would stand out in any harbor in the world, but here in Homer she dominated everything else in the water, her massive Sitka-spruce masts soaring up to a height of sixty feet and more, reducing all the other boats around her to mere toys.

Awestruck, I sat down on the wooden pier and quickly lost myself in daydreams. I imagined her as a pirate ship back in the 1600s, pillaging and plundering, her decks running red with blood. The images in my mind were so vivid I could almost see the old skull and crossbones snapping at her masthead as she made her deadly way up the Barbary Coast under cover of night. I probably have a tendency to overdramatize at times, but this one was really special.

I guess I'd been there an hour or two when I heard a voice calling out to me and I looked up to see a short, wiry little man standing on the foredeck by the bowsprit. Miraculously, he was inviting me to come on board!

I couldn't believe my luck as I scampered like a rat up the side of her hull and climbed nimbly over the rail. Standing on her deck, I felt like I'd stepped back into another century: heavy iron belaying pins lined the starboard rail; thick black ratlines, heavy with baggywrinkle, streaked skyward toward the crow's nest; and in the stern, in the place of honor, gleamed a fat, shiny brass binnacle. You just don't *see* stuff like that every day.

I learned the captain's name was Gary Donatelli, and I accepted eagerly when he invited me below for a cup of coffee and a look around. The main saloon was gorgeous, all fitted out in teak and brass, and as he led me from cabin to cabin I came to appreciate just how big a boat *Mariah* really was. Something like eighteen people could sleep comfortably below decks—more even, depending on the closeness of their relationships. In the chart room I stared enviously at the navigator's table, piled high with all the paraphernalia necessary to get safely and accurately from point A to point B. There were maps, compasses, charts, and even an ancient, battered brass sextant. It was all so damned *nautical*.

Gary explained that *Mariah* was a hand-built, one-of-a-kind "character" boat, an exact replica of the old coastal schooners that used to ply the waters of the Caribbean. Turned out she could have been a pirate ship after all. The nicest thing about her, he stressed, was the fact that she didn't carry an ounce of plastic, aluminum, or nylon anywhere on board. Outside of the big diesel engines (a necessity when chartering), everything was exactly the way it used to be: sails were made of canvas; the heavy, coiled lines were genuine hemp; and everything else was brass, cork, or wood. Of course, the absence of any modern conveniences, like, say, winches, made her a real bitch to sail, but she was worth it.

Gary must have sensed what was going on inside me, because next thing I knew, he was inviting me to go sailing with him the very next day! He said he'd put together a pickup crew of about ten friends and they were going to spend the day poking around Kachemak Bay and Cook Inlet and—who knew?—maybe even pull a couple of crab pots for dinner. Not trusting myself to speak, I could only nod my acceptance.

By six the following morning we were all assembled on deck, hard at work readying the ship for sail. Within half an hour we had everything stowed and secured, and Gary began issuing orders and passing out assignments to every member of the crew.

Under full sail, *Mariah* would fly an incredible three headsails at once and I was assigned to one of those. After memorizing exactly what chores I would be responsible for, I took my place up in the bows as we motored out of the harbor, happily in search of a breeze.

As soon as we were safely clear of the rocky quay, Gary cut the engines and called for the first sail-set of the day. The big canvas sails were heavy and clumsy, but we got them up without too much trouble. As soon as we were all secured, I climbed out to the end of the long wooden bowsprit, hoping to get a better view of things. From that outpost I watched breathlessly as the first strong gust of wind filled the huge square sails and sixty tons of schooner heeled over on her side and knifed her way out into the bay.

The breeze held and we sailed all day under a full spread of canvas, nosing our way carefully up the silent, mysterious fjords that cut deep into the mountains surrounding the bay. High overhead, immense blue glaciers sparkled in the sunlight like raw, uncut sapphires and all around us the wide platinum sweep of the sea shimmered, mirror-like, a ghostly reflection of billowing sails and towering spars.

We worked like galley slaves all morning and afternoon, and by dinnertime we were starved and threatening mutiny if Gary didn't stop and pull a couple of crab pots *right that very minute*. Luckily the catch was a good one, and we ended up with a dozen giant crabs— one for every person on board. Someone started a big pot of water boiling and in no time at all the feast was ready. We must have eaten our weight in crabmeat that day, lolling around on deck with butter dripping down our chins while Jimmy Buffett sang to us of wind and waves, sand and stars, and life on a warmer sea. Someday, someway, I hope to find him and thank him properly.

When it was finally time to head back, we were all too stuffed to do anything more than sit on deck daydreaming while Gary groused about his lazy crew and lectured on the finer points of celestial navigation. A school of dolphins were splashing and leaping at the bows and as I watched them play I became aware that this was one of the moments I would have to hold onto forever.

The wonder of that day is still with me, and every now and then I'll put an old Jimmy Buffett tape on the stereo and drink a toast to *Mariah*, that proud and elegant queen of the sea. I don't know where she's sailing now or how many other lives she's touched over the years, but for me there will always be that one particular harbor . . .

How I hated to see that summer end. It had been a time of wonder and freedom and discovery, and as the long, wild season wound itself down, all I could say was so long and thanks for all the fish. Winter would be coming soon, and it was time to go back to the real world.

* * * * * * * * * *

One morning in December I woke up late for work, and as I jumped out of my sleeping bag and stood up to dress, my left leg skidded out from under me and I fell over sideways to the floor, hitting my hip on the sharp edge of the cot. Damn. Of all the times for my foot to go to sleep on me. I sat on the floor for a moment, rubbing where it hurt, waiting for my foot to wake up.

But the numbness hung on, and when I opened my eyes the room was a blur, all the edges fuzzy and unfocused. Suddenly there were two of everything, double images that floated and faded and chased each other across the room.

It was back.

God help me it was back, and I didn't know what it was I should do. I closed my eyes and leaned against the bed, breathing deeply, trying to fight the tears and the nausea welling up inside me.

What had gone wrong? And why now? Was this the way it was supposed to happen? With no warning?—just a jolt and a crash and a fractured morning, and now everything I'd counted on was gone?

I felt like someone had kicked me in the stomach. It didn't make sense that the disease would come back now, just when everything was going so well. Nothing had happened to cause it—no crisis, no emotional distress, and no physical problem of any kind. It was just there again, a dreaded adversary that never seemed to tire of the fight.

I thought back to that bright spring morning by the sea, and the pact I'd made with God. I'd been so sure of myself then, sure that the worst was over, and confident that I could move ahead with my life knowing that God was watching over me. But that pact was broken now. I was all alone again, beyond help, beyond faith, and beyond any comprehension of what it was that had happened to me that morning.

I don't know how long I sat there on the floor, numbed and silent, enveloped in a dense fog of anger and disbelief. What seemed like hours passed, and gradually the awareness of what had happened began to settle in. I slowly came to understand that if the MS really *was* back, it was back only in the sense that it had never gone away. It had always been there, quiescent, dormant, silently awaiting a secret signal that would trigger the malevolence and bring it back to life.

Instead it was *I* who had gone away, who'd left it all behind, a memory of a fever passed. And the further I'd gone, the dimmer the memory had grown. Up until that very morning, I really thought I'd gotten away with it.

But I hadn't, of course, and I understood then that no matter how things might look on the outside, no matter how strong or healthy I might appear to be, the reality of my life would always be buried deep inside me somewhere, waiting. The worst *would* come, but slowly.

The gleaming sword hanging over me no longer shone with the swift, sure promise of a quick cut. It was rusted now, dulled and diseased, and when it fell it would only wound clumsily, hacking out small pieces of me, leaving no clean edge to heal. This is how my end would come—not with a bang, but a whimper.

When I opened my eyes again, the room had settled down somewhat and I could feel sensation returning to my foot. I stood up cautiously, careful not to make any sudden moves. When I was certain that everything was going to hold, I got myself dressed, walked slowly out to the car, and left like I did every morning for work. I still had a job to do. Nothing had really changed.

All day long I felt a little off-balance. Something—and I couldn't quite put my finger on it—was just a shade off, not quite right. It was disorienting; I felt like I was operating half a beat behind the rest of the world—a small lag to be sure, but enough to be annoying. I had no energy, no enthusiasm, and no desire to be anywhere but back in bed.

And on top of everything else, I noticed for the first time that my left foot had begun to drag a little, and that I was walking somewhat awkwardly, like a drunkard shuffling from one barstool to another.

It was embarrassing to say the least, and I stopped on my way home from work that afternoon and bought myself a sturdy wooden cane. At first I felt a little foolish carrying it, but it really did help and, more than that, it provided a visual signal to the world that there was a slight problem here, and excused me from having to walk perfectly all the time.

Even so, by the time I got into bed that night I was exhausted. Every muscle in my body ached and cried out for sleep, but instead of dozing off I lay awake for hours, worrying and wondering. I needed to talk to someone, but who? I'd long ago told Helen about the MS, but she was absolutely convinced that I'd been misdiagnosed and refused even to discuss the subject. The last thing I wanted to do was worry my parents long-distance, and it didn't seem to be the kind of thing I could bring up casually with any of my other friends. By the time I finally fell asleep, I'd decided I'd just keep it to myself for a while and wait and see what happened.

* * * * * * * * * *

When I woke up at six the next morning, I found a note from Helen taped to the windshield of my car. The note said she'd run into a Captain Bill O'Donnell in town the day before, and if I was still interested in working on a boat I should go see him first thing in the morning. He was skipper of the *Willie Allen*, an oceangoing tug currently moored in the harbor, and he was looking for a cook to replace the one who had just jumped ship. He had a deep and abiding hatred of women, her note warned, but what the hell, it might be worth checking out anyhow.

I let out a shriek of pure joy and pointed the car in the direction of the harbor. This was it! At last, an actual paying job on an actual oceangoing boat, and all I had to do was talk him into letting me on board! Then, if my luck held, I could really go to sea and become a sailor and earn my sea legs in that great old maritime tradition.

Sea legs? Was I crazy? I only had marginal control over my land legs at that point and I couldn't even imagine running around on a wet deck in a heaving sea. But wait a minute . . . he was looking for a cook, not a deckhand, and if I could stay below in the galley most of the time I just might be able to pull it off. I decided it was worth a try.

It was a twenty-below-zero morning when I finally arrived at the Port of Kenai and saw to my great dismay that the *Willie Allen* was nowhere to be found. Where could she be? I walked to the end of the long wooden pier, looked down over the side, and there she was— sixty feet of flaming yellow steel, fifteen feet straight down, the victim of an extreme low tide.

In order to get on board I had to crawl over the side of the pier, then climb hand-over-hand down a frozen steel ladder that was bolted flush against the pilings and covered with a thick, slippery coating of ice. As it turned out, that was the easy part.

The ship was floating about ten feet out from the dock, and someone had laid a wooden plank across the open stretch of water with one end resting on the bottom rung of the ladder and the other on the starboard rail of the ship. The idea, of course, was to step smartly across the plank and then hoist oneself gracefully down onto the deck. Simple.

But being neither smart *nor* graceful, I did the only thing I could think to do. Moving very slowly, I got down on all fours and straddled the plank, getting a death grip on it with all four limbs. Then, with my eyes tightly closed, I inched my way across, trying hard not to think about the churning, icy water below. When I reached the boat, I grabbed for a stanchion with both hands, threw myself over the gunwale, and landed in a clumsy heap on the cold steel deck. It looked like I'd have to work on my seamanlike swagger.

To my great surprise, I found I was still holding onto my cane, so I picked myself up and, carefully sidestepping the twisted cables on deck, made my way forward to the wheelhouse.

The skipper was slumped over in the captain's chair behind the big wooden ship's wheel and it was obvious he was nursing a hangover of epic proportions. His head was cradled in both his hands and he was moaning loudly, cursing in at least seven languages I'd never heard before. In front of him next to the radar screen was a plateful of cold, gray pork chops surrounded by a congealing pool of brown gravy. Next to that sat a cracked mug of greasy coffee so thick that the spoon stood upright in the middle of the cup. It was enough to take the shine right off the morning.

I tapped him gently on the shoulder and told him quietly who I was and why I'd come. It took a minute for my words to register, but slowly, painfully, he raised his head, and I could see his swollen red eyes try to focus. He started moaning again.

"Oh Sweet Jesus, oh shit, oh dear. It's bad enough I got this head on me, now I got a friggin' woman in the wheelhouse. There ain't no worse luck in the world. Get off my ship right now. Wait—you got any aspirin?"

I said I was sorry but, no.

"Shit, don't it figure. Get off my ship right now."

With that he buried his head in his hands and I sensed that my career at sea was over before it even had a chance to get started. But job or no job, I decided I wasn't leaving until this man had a decent meal, or at the very least a hot cup of coffee.

I left him to his misery and made my way below to the galley. The place was in such a state of disarray that it took a while to find everything I needed, but eventually I got a fresh pot of coffee going and some bacon and eggs frying in a pan.

He was still nearly comatose when I carried it all up to him, but he roused himself enough to take the plate and cup out of my hands. I sat and watched silently as he ate everything I'd prepared. After he'd mopped up the last of the eggs with a thick slice of bread, he took the steaming cup of coffee and drained it in one long, noisy gulp.

He was almost beginning to look human.

"Shit. You cook all that?"

I assured him that I had.

"You know how to cook lunch, too? And dinner?"

My time at the lodge in Cooper Landing definitely hadn't been wasted.

"Okay. You got the job," he made up his mind in a flash. "Pay's a thousand bucks a month, plus meals and bunk. You do all the cooking and cleaning and, for Christ's sake, stay the hell out of the wheelhouse. There ain't no worse luck in the world. Got it?"

Got it. I said I had some things to do in town, but not to worry, I'd be back in plenty of time to fix dinner.

"Hey!" he caught me with just as I was headed for the main hatch. "What's with the cane?"

Here it comes, I thought, the deal-breaker. I sat down and patiently explained my condition, then asked if he thought it would be a problem.

He thought about it for a minute.

"Hell no!" he announced at last, grinning happily. "Everyone walks stupid on a boat—no one'll even notice!"

Well, shiver me timbers.

It took me most of the day to put things in order. I had to quit my job, get word to Helen that I would be gone for a while, and pick up a few items I considered essential for life at sea—a Navy peacoat, a pair of Topsiders, an oiled-wool sweater and the regulation seaman's stocking cap. Who knew? If things worked out, I might just consider a career in the Merchant Marine.

It was after three by the time I made it back to the boat and the skipper was just beginning to stir. He took one look at me, all decked out in my finery, and almost choked on his coffee.

"Jesus!" he roared, laughing uncontrollably. "Where the hell do you think you are? *Annapolis?*"

Maybe not, I thought to myself, but if I ever got there, this was one sorry son-of-a-bitch who'd walk the plank for sure.

"Oh well," he chuckled, "gettin' close to suppertime. Come on . . . rest of the crew's below."

There were only two of them. Mack the engineer was a skinny, grumpy sea-rat of about forty, with the kind of face you see in old Errol Flynn swashbuckler movies—kind of swarthy and pinched-in around the cheeks.

He actually wouldn't have been bad looking if it hadn't been for the fact that every tooth in his head was either missing or in an advanced state of blackened decay. They must have hurt like hell, too, because he chewed aspirin like it was candy and bitched constantly about the pain. Luckily, he spent most of his time down in the engine room, so we were spared the worst of it.

Donnie, the deckhand, was a young kid in his early twenties, fresh-faced and eager, always ready with a quip and a healthy dose of adolescent sarcasm. He would become both my ally and my tormentor, a reassuring thorn in my side and, not least of all, the seasickest kid ever to set sail in this century.

They were both sitting at the table in the galley when we climbed through the hatch and each gave me a careful going-over as the skipper made the introductions. Mack was the first one to speak.

"Aw fuck, B.J.," he whined, "why'd you have to go and get us a goddamn *woman*? There ain't no worse luck in the world."

"Don't I know it," the old man sighed heavily. "But this one can cook, so keep your mouth shut and show her where everything's at if you want your supper. She'll be okay. Better'n nothing, anyhow."

The three of us watched silently as he turned and made his lonely way back up to the forbidden wheelhouse.

B.J.? I happened to know the captain's middle initial was "W" and I wondered out loud what the "J" stood for.

"Dunno," Mack answered dully. "Probably stands for 'Jackass,' knowing him."

Dinner was a huge success, and once everyone had stuffed himself full of spaghetti, garlic bread, and thick cuts of chocolate cake for dessert, barriers began to crumble and old resentments and superstitions slowly gave way to something approaching respect. After the dishes were washed and put away, the four of us gathered around a pot of coffee and the traditional seaman's cribbage board for a quiet evening's game. While we played, each of the men took turns filling me in on their particular version of life at sea.

I learned that the ship was under contract to one of the big oil companies operating in the area, and that we would be hauling bargeloads of equipment across Cook Inlet to one of the drilling rigs on the other side. The trip typically took about three hours each way, with a couple of hours required for loading and off-loading at either end. Pretty standard stuff. But since we could only set sail at high-tide, we had to be ready to go at any moment, twenty-four hours a day. And when you add to that the fact that someone had to be standing watch at all times, schedules could get pretty confusing.

That's where I came in. It would be up to me to see that there was always a hot meal ready for every one of them when it was their turn to eat, and to make sure that bunks were freshly made up at all times so that each retiring crew member could collapse as soon as he'd eaten. On top of all that I was assigned all the housekeeping duties, including scrubbing the head, a chore I would soon learn to despise.

I quickly settled into the routine of shipboard life, with all its pleasures and its perks. Anytime we were under way I stayed safely below in the galley, and I must say everyone seemed pleased with the high level of culinary proficiency I achieved there. Eventually B.J. eased up on the wheelhouse prohibition and actually let me sit in the pilot's seat during the long midnight-to-five watch. Once in a while he even let me take a turn at the wheel, an honor rarely bestowed on such a recent landlubber.

Morning was the time I liked best. As soon as the breakfast dishes were done I'd gather up all the leftovers and go out on deck to feed the big white beluga whales. A whole fleet of them lived in the harbor and

I delighted in watching them jump and play and leap out of the water, chasing after the tasty scraps of food I supplied. It was easy to get carried away and before long I found myself smuggling out whole loaves of bread and boxes of meat in an effort to keep them coming. I took a real ass-chewing from B.J. when he discovered that inside a month I had tossed half the ship's stores over the rail, but it was worth it. Lots better than Sea World.

But if the whales were loads of fun in the morning, it was an entirely different story at night. I don't know what kind of odd feeding schedule they were on, but every night around midnight they became extremely active and had an annoying habit of ramming themselves against the side of the ship in what I could only assume was a desperate plea for food. I know it *sounds* wonderful, but you have to remember that the *Willie Allen* was a steel ship, and when they really got going it was like trying to sleep inside the Liberty Bell.

It got so bad that I started sneaking whole buckets full of frozen fish into my bunk with me at night, so when the whales got too rambunctious I could toss a couple of salmon out through the porthole and try to fall asleep quickly before another one rammed us. The plan didn't work very well, though, and by the end of the first week I was actually considering depth charges. Don't get me wrong—I have a lot of respect for the folks at Greenpeace, but then none of them ever spent a night on the *Willie Allen*.

Someone once described life at sea as an endless series of long, empty hours of boredom, interrupted only by brief, horrifying moments of sheer terror. Well, I can't say as I agreed about the boredom—there was just too much to see and do. But I was soon to learn, in the starkest terms imaginable, all there was to know about the terror.

SEVEN

Cook Inlet, Alaska
December, 1977

W E ' D   J U S T   C O M P L E T E D   O U R eleventh trip across the Inlet and so far everything had gone off without a hitch. The trip over was uneventful, the sea as smooth as glass. While the men got busy unloading the barge, I began preparing dinner, a heavy meal of pork chops, yams, gravy, biscuits, and Boston cream pie—just the thing after a hard day's work. I wasn't particularly hungry, so while the crew sat down to eat, I went out on deck to relax and enjoy a cigarette.

It must have been close to thirty below that night. The air was so cold it hurt to breathe it and so clear that the distant, ice-capped mountains across the inlet seemed to be almost within arm's reach. Overhead, the sky was a deep, velvet black and the stars seemed so close it felt like you could scoop them up in your hands and scatter them, sparkling, like diamonds on the water. It was a breathless, silent night and I was alone on a wide, wide sea.

I heard a soft hissing overhead and looked up just in time to see the northern lights sweep across the heavens, a pyrotechnic blaze of blue and violet that swirled and shimmered and lit up the night with its fire. I was standing on a darkened stage, gazing up at a shining, phosphorescent curtain of pure light. It hung motionless from the sky in long icy folds, a frozen cyclorama so immense it seemed to eclipse even the vastness of the sea. Then, as an unseen hand brushed softly against the face of the night, the ghostly streaks of light began to glow brighter and brighter until, as if frightened by their own intensity, they raced away, only to form again in another part of the sky.

The incredible display lasted almost twenty minutes and when it was over I had to force myself to go below. While I busied myself with

113

the dishes the crew prepared to cast off, and as soon as we were safely out of the channel, Mack and Donnie joined me in the galley for our nightly game of cribbage. The mood was relaxed and everyone was looking forward to a pleasant crossing and a well-earned rest. But the sea gods had other plans for us.

We'd only been under way half an hour when the first huge wave thundered in from out of nowhere. There was an explosion of steel and glass as it slammed into us broadside and rolled the ship over, almost to the point of no return.

The galley erupted as everything that wasn't tied down sailed through the air and shattered on the steel deck. Debris was flying everywhere and suddenly, like a rogue torpedo, the coffeepot broke loose from its moorings and smashed against the bulkhead, scalding everyone with its contents.

But no one moved, or even breathed, as we hung suspended for what seemed like an eternity, not knowing which way it would go. It was probably only a matter of seconds, but as a wise man once said, some seconds last longer than others. Then slowly, miraculously, the ship began to right herself, and at that exact moment all hell broke loose.

"MAAACK!" roared the captain from the bridge. "For Christ's sake check the engine room—we're taking on water! Donnie! JJ! Get your asses up here on the double! OH SWEET JESUS, WE'RE ALL ABOUT TO DIE!!"

Everyone leapt into action at once. Mack raced down the gangway toward the engine room as Donnie and I sprinted up the stairs to the wheelhouse. The scene waiting for us there was one I'll never forget.

In the glare of the ship's searchlights it was clear that the sea had gone mad. Towering waves bore down on us from all directions, their crests boiling as the wind whipped them into a frenzy and flung huge sprays of spindrift up into the night. The wind was screaming like a tortured animal, forcing us to shout to be heard above it.

"What the hell's going on, skipper?!" Donnie was on the verge of panic.

"I'll be goddamned if I know! We was fine until I came around the Forelands and sailed right into this shit! Oh Jesus, here comes another one of them bastards now! HIT THE DECK!"

I grabbed for something to hold onto and stared, wild-eyed, out the window as a twenty-foot wall of black water rose up in front of us and exploded over the bows. The whole ship rocked with the impact and sent bodies flying from one end of the bridge to the other. For one terrible moment I thought I'd broken my neck. I was picking myself up off the deck when another wave plowed into us and I heard a mighty crash from below.

I flew down the steps to see what had happened. Oh God. I'd forgotten to latch the refrigerator shut and when the second wave struck, the big, heavy metal doors opened up, spilling everything out onto the steel deck. The main companionway had become a giant obstacle course, filled with broken glass, dozens of shattered eggs, and the slippery contents of twenty or thirty broken jars. It was a danger to everyone's safety and I searched around frantically for a mop. I *had* to get it cleaned up.

A moment later Mack crawled out of the engine room and raced past me up into the wheelhouse. I froze as I heard him tell the skipper that we were taking on far too much water and that he didn't know where it was coming from. What did that mean? Were we going to *sink*? I had to see for myself.

I dove for the hatch and lowered myself into the engine room. He hadn't been exaggerating—there was water everywhere and it was getting higher every second. I could see that it was now ominously close to the electrical panel mounted on the bulkhead, and I didn't even want to *think* about what would happen if it got any higher. The skipper was right. We were all about to die.

I turned to leave just as Mack was climbing back down through the hatch.

"Mack! What's going on!" I was really frightened.

"Out of my way!" he shouted as he shoved me back against the bulkhead. "I've got to get to the pumps!"

Oh thank God, we had pumps. Whatever the hell that meant.

The ship was pitching and rolling violently and I had to hang on to the railing as I made my way back up to the wheelhouse. The scene outside was even wilder than before. Donnie was grabbing charts out of the locker and B.J. was hunched over the radar screen, barking out orders.

"This motherfucker is more than we can take!" he shouted over the roaring of the wind. "And there ain't no way out but down, either—gimme that goddamn thing!"

He grabbed the chart out of Donnie's hand and began studying it intently. The idea, as far as I could tell, was to move in closer to shore where the storm wasn't blowing quite so hard. That was dangerous, though, because the coastline was extremely rocky and before we attempted anything we had to know exactly where we were. I was anxious to know how soon we were going to die so I could begin to prepare myself, but somehow this didn't seem like the right time to ask.

In a matter of minutes B.J. had our position figured out and slowly, carefully, we began nosing our way in out of the worst of the storm. It was remarkable. As soon as we were in the protective lee of the shore, the wind died down considerably, the sea calmed, and we could actually hear one another speak.

Mack climbed up into the wheelhouse and announced that it looked like the pumps were holding their own in the engine room, and he and Donnie ran out on deck and got busy lowering the anchor. "Might just as well sit right here 'til this bastard blows itself out," B.J. said disgustedly. "'Course we're piss out of luck if the anchor don't hold."

It held. We were secure for the moment and relieved to be out of harm's way. As soon as Mack and Donnie were safely back inside, I went below to start another pot of coffee and clean up the mess in the galley. Of course, none of us had any way of knowing it then, but the respite was only temporary and things were about to get a whole lot worse.

I was up to my elbows in broken glass when, suddenly, we were struck from below. There was an enormous crash, like two freight trains colliding, and every inch of the ship reverberated with the blast. I dropped the mop and clawed my way back up top. What had we hit?

B.J. was nearly hysterical. With one hand clutching the wheel, he was leaning out the open hatch, shouting orders to Mack and Donnie, who were up in the bows again wrestling with the anchor chain. I couldn't hear what he was saying because the wind was once again howling wildly and churning the sea into a seething cauldron.

"What happened!" I shouted to him. "What did we hit!"

"We hit BOTTOM is what we hit!" he screeched. "This godless whore of a storm is closing in and if we don't leave here *right now* she'll pile us up on the rocks, sure as shit!" He leaned back out into the wind. "What in the name of Christ are you two doing! GET THE ANCHOR UP! *NOW!!*"

They tried desperately, Donnie leaning on the heavy iron winch while Mack pulled and kicked at the windlass. But neither would budge. All at once the reason why became clear; somehow the anchor chain had slipped its track and wrapped itself around the winch the wrong way, jamming the whole system.

We were as good as dead. The full force of the storm was drawing closer every second and now we were helplessly chained to the bottom, caught like rats in a trap.

But B.J. would have none of it. "Take the wheel!" he screamed at me as he sprinted out on deck. He grabbed the winch lever and leaned the whole of his weight against it. I heard a high-pitched whine as the ship's hydraulic system strained to turn the heavy capstain and free the cursed anchor. The captain's whole body was shaking with the effort, and slowly, almost imperceptibly, the big steel drum began to turn. Then, suddenly, something broke loose with a loud boom and B.J. was thrown backwards against the gunwale as the winch spun wildly out of control. Seconds later, the empty anchor chain rattled up onto the deck.

I couldn't believe my eyes. The last heavy link was now just a mangled piece of steel. Our brand-new anchor was gone forever, far beyond anyone's reach at the bottom of the sea. It was a dangerous thing to have lost, and at the worst possible moment. But at least we were free, and that had to count for something.

"You did it, skipper!" I shouted as the three of them raced back into the wheelhouse, soaked and nearly frozen.

"Yeah, I did it all right," he spat angrily, "but now the fuckin' anchor's gone and so are the hydraulics!"

"So what?" I beamed, euphoric. "We're free and now we don't have to die!"

Mack grabbed me roughly by the arm and pulled me down into the galley. "Didn't you hear what the old man said?" he demanded, his hands shaking. "We burned out the goddamn *hydraulics!*"

"Is that bad?"

"Jesus Christ! How to you think we *steer* this thing?"

Oh shit oh dear. He went on to explain that our only option now was to head back out into open water where we'd be clear of the deadly rocks. And we could only pray that there was enough steering left to keep the ship on course and headed into the wind, because we'd sure as hell never survive another broadside like the first one.

The water in the engine room had been rising steadily over the past several hours and it must have picked that very moment to reach the electrical panel, because just then we heard a series of loud, sharp pops behind us. Those sounds could only mean one thing, and we spun around and watched in horror as every light fixture in the galley burst into flame.

There is *nothing* more dangerous than fire on board, and I screamed as Mack grabbed for the fire extinguisher, aimed the hose, and pulled the pin. A thick white cloud of foam shot from the nozzle, and one by one the deadly fires were brought under control. But as the last of the flames sputtered and died, something deep inside the maze of wires and switches in the engine room gave up the ghost, immediately plunging the entire ship into absolute darkness. We now had no electrical system at all.

I grabbed hold of Mack's arm and squeezed. Standing there in the dark with the ship tossing crazily, I could feel myself starting to crumble. "Oh Mack," I pleaded, on the verge of tears, "what else could possibly go wrong now?"

As it turned out, plenty.

We still had the big barge in tow, a fact that by now had everyone a little nervous. The demise of our electrical system meant that we were without running lights on both the ship *and* the barge, an extremely perilous situation. It was vital to our safety that we knew where the barge was at all times, and now that was impossible. Or so we thought.

As we stood there, not knowing what to do next, there came a loud roar from the wheelhouse. B.J. was raising six kinds of hell, pounding on the wheel like a mad Captain Ahab and calling for all hands. We took off at a dead run.

No one was prepared for what happened next. Not more than a

hundred yards off our starboard beam loomed the menacing barge itself. She was riding the crest of an immense wave and we stood, frozen in fear, as 110 feet of iron and steel barge bore down on us relentlessly, the now-certain instrument of all our deaths. Collision was imminent.

The skipper was the first to move. He kicked the throttle open, then swung the wheel over hard and waited. The rest of us held our breath and hoped against all reason that our lives might somehow be spared.

For a few terrible seconds nothing happened. The barge was so close we could almost read the numbers painted on her hull, and we knew that all the time we had left was only a matter of seconds. There wasn't even time to panic. All we could do was watch and wait. But then suddenly, at the last possible second, something caught and we started to move! Everyone began cheering and shouting at once as we slid out from under the barge's bows, crossed our own towline, and set a course for the open sea—right back out into the eye of the storm.

By the time we got clear of the rocks and back out into open water, the storm had lashed itself into a fury. And there we were, caught out in the middle of it, our once-proud ship now crippled and almost totally defenseless.

With our electrical system gone we had no interior lights, no running lights, no radar, no heat, and—scariest of all—no radio to call for help. Our steering was all but gone and it took everything we had just to keep the ship's nose pointed into the wind. We were in very deep trouble. It was clear that only God could save us now, and I wasn't sure he or she was even paying attention.

I learned something about sustained terror that night. I learned that panic only lasts just so long and eventually one of two things will happen: at some point you'll either die or your mind will shut down completely and switch over to automatic pilot, a state of near-unconsciousness. Either way, the panic stops.

But first you have to get through the hard part, and I lost control almost immediately. With the first strong rush of adrenaline I turned into a shrieking, hysterical madwoman completely out of touch with reality. I kicked and screamed and scratched, striking out at anyone who came near me, like a cornered rat with no thought for anything but my own survival. At one point I grabbed B.J. by the hair and pulled hard, screaming at him to radio the Coast Guard for help immediately. If he didn't do something *right that minute,* I swore I'd haul his fat white ass out on deck and feed his balls to the sharks. I meant it, too.

He reacted the only way he could. He tore my hand away, pushed me hard against the bulkhead and explained, loudly and firmly, that we were out of options and completely out of luck. The radio went the minute the electricity did, and anyway, even the Coast Guard wasn't coming out on a night like this. There would be no rescue at sea and the best we could hope for was to stay afloat until the storm blew itself out. Period.

Something inside me broke right then. My heart stopped pounding, the adrenaline stopped flowing and an eerie, almost supernatural calm settled over me. It was a calm born of the knowledge that there was nothing left to fight for anymore. Not even our lives. A moment ago I would have stormed the gates of hell itself for one more chance at survival, but now it was all utterly pointless. We were going to die, and nothing in the world could change that fact. The only questions were how and when.

The how became my main concern. I sat down quietly in the pilot's seat and focused my attention on the madness outside. My interest now was purely clinical. Death would come by drowning, I was sure of that, and I made up my mind to do it with as much dignity as I could muster. There would be no screaming or crying or clinging pitifully to the ship as she rolled over and began her long, final voyage into the abyss. No, I wasn't going to die like that. When the time came I would say one last quiet prayer, then walk calmly out on deck and step over the rail into the waiting black nothingness of the sea.

I remember at one point asking B.J. what the life expectancy was for someone in water that cold. Only thirty seconds? That's good. That's fine. I can stand anything for thirty seconds. But what will happen then? What will the actual dying be like? Will I go into shock and just fade away peacefully, or will I stay conscious to the very end, blind and sick with terror as I slip beneath the surface and take that last fatal breath? I wanted to know every detail.

And what about after? What will happen then? Wondering, I fell deep into a dreamlike state as I imagined my lifeless body sinking slowly into the bottomless void, eyes wide open in death, a sightless, drifting corpse spiraling slowly, slowly downward toward the unspeakable darkness below . . .

The shark comes up silently, a great white, his ghostly form rising like a specter from the depths, drawn unerringly to my last, desperate struggle, slowly his cavernous mouth opens as he draws near . . . circling, stalking, edging closer with every deadly pass.

Suddenly, with a blinding burst of speed, comes the horror of the final attack. Hundreds of razor-sharp teeth rip into skin and muscle as the huge, steely jaws lock down—a crushing, massive force unlike any other on earth. Thick, warm clouds of blood billow from the wound, an ancient signal triggering something deep inside his prehistoric brain, as the feeding frenzy begins and my heart and lungs explode in his mouth.

The terrible work is finished in a matter of seconds and I watch as the big fish glides away into the darkness, too stupid to know he's just eaten, his dull, lifeless eyes in search of yet another meal. Now and for all eternity I would be part of that shark, a mindless, silent predator, always searching, never sleeping . . .

As I came back slowly from the nightmare world of the deep, I sensed that everything around me had changed. A thick, pervasive silence had settled over the ship, and other than the wild howling of the wind and the heavy, distant pounding of the diesel engines, there wasn't a sound to be heard.

Donnie had gone below and crawled into his bunk. Having decided that dying alone in his bed was infinitely preferable to any of the other alternatives, there was really nothing else he could do. B.J. was slumped in the captain's chair, his sleepless eyes staring dully out the window at the insanity of the storm. The only visible sign of the tension he was under was the pale whiteness of his knuckles as they clutched tightly at the wheel.

Mack was sitting on the floor behind me, a solitary figure, silent and unresponsive and chilled to his very bones. He had wrapped himself up papoose-style in layers of jackets and blankets, but still he was shivering so hard I was afraid he was going to hurt himself.

We'd been without heat for many long hours by then and it was so cold inside the ship that our breath came out in rough, white clouds of frost that evaporated into a slimy sweat on the steel bulkheads and gave the wheelhouse the feel of a cold and clammy grave. I pushed my hands deep into the pockets of my parka and tried hard not to think about it.

The storm raged on all night, and it seemed that the worse it got, the less anyone cared. Once in a while Mack would grab a flashlight and stumble halfheartedly down to the engine room to check on the pumps, and occasionally we could hear Donnie retching in the head when the rolling of the ship got to be too much for him. But that was pretty much it.

At one point we did give serious thought to cutting the barge loose, thereby increasing our chances of survival, but even that seemed more of an effort than it was worth and the discussion was quickly dropped. Mostly we just sat and waited, each of us lost in our own thoughts. As the hours wore on, all I could think about was my family and how sorry I was to have done this to them. It was a lousy way to die, and now they wouldn't even have a body to bury.

The storm reached the peak of its fury in the hour just before dawn, as though it was determined to show us who was boss one last time before it pushed us under for good. The ship was pitching and rolling wildly as wave after wave hammered into us, and I sensed we were close to the end. There was nothing more to be done, so I said my prayers and whispered goodbye to everyone I loved. It was time to take that final walk across the deck.

Then all of a sudden, as the first cold rays of dawn streaked across the horizon, the skipper jumped up from his seat and began whooping and hollering for everyone to come and see! Mack and I leapt to our feet as Donnie raced up from below. What could be happening now? Was this *never* going to end?

Dead ahead, no more than half a mile away, lay the entrance to the harbor. *Our* harbor. The very one we'd left so confidently twenty-four long hours ago. No one could believe what had happened; all night long the storm had been blowing us home, a near-miraculous occurrence and an act of providence unequalled in my experience.

The wheelhouse exploded with cheers and shouts of joy. When I finally understood that we were really and truly going to live, I felt all the strength inside me ebb away as I collapsed on the floor in a cold sweat.

B.J. put the wheel over and headed for home as Mack and Donnie fell down beside me, limp and exhausted. Hardly a word was spoken as the weary old ship slogged her way through the tattered remnants of the storm, but every now and then B.J. would glance back over his shoulder and throw a disgusted look in our direction.

"If you three ain't the sorriest pack of assholes I ever saw . . ." he chuckled gleefully. "Two of you look like you seen a ghost for Chrissakes, and look at her—still scared shitless and sweatin' like a whore in church. I'd sure as hell hate to be stuck with the likes of you in a *real* storm!"

The old man came closer to dying right then than he had all night. Now that it was all over I guess he thought he could get away with pretending there had never been any real danger in the first place. It wasn't the smartest move he'd ever made and I could see that Mack and Donnie were on the verge of mutiny.

But what the hell. We never would have made it without him. He knew it, and we knew it, too. So we let him live another day, and did our best to ignore his maniacal raving as he drove the *Willie Allen* home.

Thirty minutes later we limped into port, and B.J. yelled for everyone to get out on deck and start securing the lines. Mack and Donnie jumped up and ran to help, but when I tried to stand I found that my legs wouldn't move. Not a muscle. Not a twitch. Everything was gone, and no matter what I did I couldn't get them to budge.

At first I didn't feel anything but surprise and confusion, like a drunkard who'd taken a punch to the head. I couldn't seem to make the connection between the fact that I couldn't stand and the two useless limbs crumpled underneath me on the deck. I shook my head, trying to clear away the dizziness.

Gradually the fog began to lift, and as it did the realization struck me that my legs had worked perfectly all night long. In all the excitement I hadn't even thought about them, and had taken for granted that they would be there when I needed them. And they *had* been. I couldn't remember using the cane once all night.

But now there was nothing left. And in the instant before fear and hysteria overwhelmed me, I remembered my doctor's warning about stress and exhaustion and the effect both of them could have on my legs. That was it! They were just reacting to what I'd been through in the last fifteen hours, and if I sat still and gave them a chance to rest, eventually they'd come back to life. They simply *had* to.

I concentrated on staying as calm as possible, and by the time the men came back inside I was able to stand. As long as I held onto something I looked perfectly normal and at first no one noticed anything was wrong. B.J. ducked below to do a quick damage assessment of the ship and came back looking a little shaken. I don't think he was prepared for what he found down there. But he must have been as tired as we were, because he sent everyone into town to clean up and get a little rest. He warned us all to be back on board by six, though, so we could get to work putting the ship to rights. I said I thought six o'clock was pushing it a little, all things considered, but he held firm.

We were all glad for the break, but when I turned to go, I felt my legs give way again and I collapsed in a heap at the skipper's feet. It looked like I was going to need a little help after all. Laughing like a couple of jackasses, Mack and Donnie picked me up bodily, then carried me out on deck, up the ladder, and across the dock to where my car was parked. Only after they had me settled safely inside did they stop with the wisecracking and let me know how concerned they really were. Was I going to be all right? Did I need some help getting home? Was there *anything* they could do?

No, no, I assured them repeatedly, everything was fine. I was just having a delayed reaction to all the stress was all, and as soon as I calmed down and got a little sleep, I'd be just fine. I urged them to do the same, and said I'd see them back on board at six.

I sat in the car until my legs came around enough to drive away, and as I did, I realized that I was leaving the *Willie Allen* for the last time. It simply wasn't possible or even fair to think about going back. I'd been given a warning, and now it was plain to see that I could never fully trust my legs again.

It was a lousy way to have to leave, though. I *loved* that rotten old ship and its rotten old crew, and in my own perverse way, I even loved the storm itself. Something wonderful happens when you put your life on the line, even in the most meaningless way. A sense of urgency and

124

a heightened awareness combine to add a certain zest to otherwise commonplace events. Colors seem a little brighter, the air smells a little sweeter, and even a battered old work scow can start to feel like home. I was going to miss it all terribly.

But as the old skipper had warned me all along, it just goes to show you what can happen when you let a woman in the wheelhouse.

There ain't no worse luck in the world.

* * * * * * * * * *

It took three full days for my legs to get back to normal and I spent the time alone in my cabin, pondering what my next move would be. Naturally I had to find a job right away, a prospect I didn't particularly relish. But at least this time I knew what I was looking for. The broadcast business was out, as I'd already walked out of a position at Kenai's only radio station. It was obvious that my body had experienced all the excitement it could handle for the time being, so I decided to seek out the most boring, stress-free job I could find, as long as it could be done on dry land and didn't involve the cleaning of floating bathrooms. As luck would have it, I found one almost immediately.

Oberts Insurance was a small, mom-and-pop-type agency in Kenai, and I learned from a friend that they were looking for a trainee to work in their personal-lines department. Since the word "trainee" is little more than a broad euphemism for "anyone can do it," and since the job sounded only a little less boring than watching grass grow, I went and applied that very afternoon.

The interview was a novel experience for me largely because, for the first time ever, I was reduced to telling the truth about my background and experience—or, more accurately, my total lack of either. I simply didn't know enough about the business to work up a convincing cover story, and naturally that took a lot of fun out of it for me. But at least this time I was hired on my own dubious merits, and I agreed to start right after the first of the year.

Something else that was new to me was the personnel arrangement at the agency. I'd never worked in an office with a dozen or so women (most of them single) before, and I was a little surprised at the social structure of the place. I thought I'd perfected the art of cattiness over the years myself, but this group was in a whole other league and I saw right away that I had some catching up to do.

The ringleader of the bunch was the office manager, Cindy DuBois (Doo-BWAH, if you please, and don't *ever* mispronounce it). She was just a kid in her early twenties, but a fighting spirit is something you're either born with or you aren't, and she came equipped with everything she needed to hold her own in the trenches: she had a mouth like a longshoreman, the reflexes of a prizefighter, and, most disarming of all, the eyes and the face of an angel. When pretty little Cindy put you in your place, you knew you'd really been put.

She also had, not insignificantly, two of the largest, firmest breasts this side of Amazonia. They were of legendary, almost mythical, proportions and had already become the objects of a great deal of civic pride. Members of the VFW were known to stand and salute when she walked by, and every year on her birthday one of the local dignitaries would climb up on stage at Larry's Club and sing a couple choruses of "Thanks for the Mammaries" in her honor.

It seemed like every man in town had a story to tell, or wished he did, of some magical encounter with her celebrated bosom, and those who didn't spent a lot of time daydreaming. Cindy, of course, professed to hate all the attention, but her extraordinary collection of bright, tight-fitting sweaters gave her away on an almost-daily basis. She was just my kind of woman, a funny, feisty little firebrand, and a friend who could always keep me laughing.

As soon as I'd read two or three manuals and passed a couple of tests, I was put to work hustling auto insurance, a cut-and-dried process if ever there was one. After only a few days I had the routine down pat and found I could do the job without really thinking about it, an occupational hazard which quickly led to some problems.

The mechanical nature of the job left me plenty of time to concentrate on other things, and increasingly I found my mind occupied with worries about my health. The shaky MS days I'd first experienced at the radio station were occurring much more frequently now, and I began to dread the occasional day-long bouts of double-vision, weakness, and exhaustion.

The hardest part was covering it up at work. Naturally everyone knew about my condition, but still I was reluctant to show any signs of weakness this early in the game. So once again I kept it all to myself and hoped no one would notice.

But before long it became impossible to hide what was happening. My left leg was growing weaker and more unresponsive all the time, and my cover was finally blown the day my cane skidded out from under me and I landed squarely on my face on the office floor. Right in front of everyone.

Cindy and I had a long talk over dinner that night. She proved my initial assessment of her to be true by the way she listened carefully to me, then offered some suggestions as to how we could make things a little easier for me at work, at least until I got myself back to normal. It helped a lot just to have someone to talk to and I went home to the cabin in a much-improved frame of mind that night.

Physically, however, things didn't improve much over the next few weeks, and it was during that time I began to notice a new and disturbing phenomenon. Like most people, I suppose, I'd always been pretty regular in my bowel habits and never really gave the subject much thought. But now that was beginning to change. Days, sometimes even a whole week, would go by with no signs of anything happening. At that point I didn't make any connection between my constipation and the disease, and quickly went to work on the problem with a bargeload of laxatives and bran muffins. They helped some, but not much, and I resigned myself to the fact that I was going to be uncomfortable for a while. If ignorance is bliss, then I was on top of the world.

But by the end of April the situation had gotten a lot more serious. Instead of improving as I'd hoped they would, my legs—especially the left one—had actually gotten worse; when I was finally forced to abandon the cane in favor of a pair of crutches, I knew I couldn't go on kidding myself much longer. For the first time in a long time, I was really scared.

I had gotten to a point where I realized that if I didn't get some help soon, I was in real danger of a total collapse. I needed to talk to someone who loved me, and that night when I called my parents in Pittsburgh, I broke down and told them everything. They listened carefully to what I was saying, then proceeded to give me holy hell for not having gone to see a doctor. Oddly enough, I hadn't even thought of that, but I promised to look for one right away, and by the time we hung up I felt a whole lot better.

Happily, though, my parents tend to overreact to calls like that, and the very next day my mom, God love her, arrived on the two o'clock plane from Pittsburgh. Good old Annabelle.

I was overjoyed to see her, and as soon as I made arrangements for some time off from work, we left for Anchorage in search of a doctor. In a stunning coincidence, the name we picked blindly out of the telephone book, a Dr. Bill Bowers, turned out to be one of the residents who had participated in my diagnosis almost four years ago in Pittsburgh! We had a good laugh over the turn of events, and then quickly got down to business.

There was no question, he said, that I was in the middle of a mild attack of MS, and that a short course of steroids—ACTH and prednisone, specifically—was clearly in order. As he was filling up the syringe I casually mentioned the problem I'd been having with constipation and how uncomfortable I was as a result of it. He gave me the injection, then sat down and explained that I was suffering from something known as a "neurogenic bowel" (the word "neurogenic" translates loosely from Latin as meaning "screwed up") and that it was definitely a function of the disease. It was the first time anyone had made that connection for me, and when I asked him how long it was going to last, he said there was no way of telling and wrote out a prescription for a killer laxative.

"Here, take some of this whenever you need it. And the next time someone tells you you're full of it, don't argue with them."

This guy was going to be all right. I thanked him for the medications, promised to call him in a week, and then Annabelle and I took our leave, relieved and somewhat optimistic.

Once again, the effects of the ACTH were almost miraculous and overnight my symptoms virtually disappeared. My vision cleared, my legs returned to normal, and I found I had more energy than I knew what to do with. By the third day I was feeling so terrific that I decided I'd treat my mom to a wild, white-water raft trip down the rapids of the Kenai River.

I know that sounds like an awful thing to do to your own mother,

128

but one of the things I like best about Annabelle is her sense of adventure and her willingness, eagerness even, to try anything once. Parts of the Kenai can be somewhat dangerous, and a couple of times the ferocity of the rapids really had me worried. But Annabelle had a ball, laughing and shrieking happily every time we crashed into one of the big standing waves in the canyon, and when we pulled the raft out of the river at the end of the run and I got a look at her face, I knew I'd done the right thing. I was really going to hate to see her leave.

By the time I went back to work, the ACTH had done its job completely and I was feeling better than ever. I'd put away the cane, broken out the high heels, and was ready to settle back into the mind-numbing process of selling car insurance. But I was certain this time around that this kind of work wasn't going to be enough of a challenge for me, and I decided that if I was going to stick with the business for a while I'd have to find a way to make it more interesting. The only way to do that, I reasoned, was to shoot for a commercial property/casualty agent's license and really give it all I had. It would mean an incredible amount of study and preparation, but so what? I'd done sillier things before.

I remember most of that spring and summer in vivid detail, and almost always with a touch of sadness. I don't know what it is inside of people, what mechanism exists that allows us to shut out the bad parts of our lives and move ahead confidently, joyfully even, in spite of all we know to be true. It could be we're only kidding ourselves, or maybe it's something deeper—a psychic shield we build against the demons as they howl and shriek their warnings through the dark back alleys of our subconscious minds.

All I know is that the instant the medication kicked in and I was back on my feet, I was able to forget, absolutely, the events of the past several months, almost as though they had never happened. Once again, nothing mattered but the present, and the only thing I was conscious of was a need to go and see and do everything I could, to live it all today and never mind about tomorrow.

I'd found a better friend in Cindy than I knew, and we spent all of that summer outdoors, laughing, exploring, and laying the foundations of a friendship that has lasted ever since. We fished for salmon on the Russian River, trolled for halibut in Homer, camped all over the Kenai, and—like the couple of fools we were—even risked our lives on a big blue glacier or two. If it was there and needed to be climbed, we climbed it.

And any time we weren't making new tracks in the wilderness, we could be found at Larry's Club, trolling for men. Cindy's two main assets came in handy on nights like those, and I found they worked almost as well for me as they did for her. From miles around, men were drawn to them like, well, like men to a great pair of assets, and all I had to do was stay close and catch the bodies as they fell. It was almost a little *too* easy, and before I knew it the summer was gone.

EIGHT

Manila, Philippines
September, 1978

BILL WERBER EXPLODED into my life with all the subtlety of a train wreck.

He was our agency's newest employee, and I can still remember in clearest detail the way he looked the first time he walked into the office. He was as handsome a man as I'd ever seen. He was tall and trim and perfectly groomed, a GQ kind of guy if ever there was one. He had the kind of white-blond hair that makes you think of surfboards and sunshine, and his eyes were a deep, cool shade of hazy summer-sky blue. God had been good to this one.

But there was more to him than just his good looks. He had a certain presence—a commanding, almost frightening air of authority—and from the moment he strode into the room I found it impossible to look anywhere else. Obviously, I was at a disadvantage from the start. As soon as the office introductions were made we struck up a conversation, and in no time at all I had him pegged as just another three-piece playboy—a sanctimonious, chauvinistic swine with no redeeming social value whatsoever. Sort of like Donald Trump, but without the money.

But all it took was one long lunch for me to discover that he was also one of the brightest, funniest men I'd come in contact with in years. He had a vicious, delicious sense of humor and he didn't give two consecutive goddamns whether anyone liked it or not. It didn't take long for me to get into the spirit of things, and by the time the dessert course was served we were bouncing each other off the walls, weak and choking with laughter.

From that moment on we were inseparable. I'll happily confess to a little romantic interest at the outset, and so would Bill, but that quickly gave way to something more substantial as we discovered in each other a mutual lust for blood. There was nothing we enjoyed more than a good fight, the dirtier the better, and never mind such stuff as diplomacy and tact. Winning was the only thing that counted.

Bill's mind, like mine, was an overflowing cesspool of useless and arcane information, and both of us were at our very best when we felt some cherished principle was at stake. Once we'd taken up our positions on opposite sides of an issue, we'd begin to argue. For hours we would hammer at one another, our faces getting redder and our voices growing louder, until we'd get to the point where we nearly came to blows. Then, just for fun, we'd switch sides and argue the other way, just to see who was cleverest. It was an exhausting exercise, but one we looked forward to night after night with mutual delight.

But afterward came the part we both liked best. Once we had the air cleared and all our ruffled feathers soothed, one of us would break out a bottle of scotch and we'd settle ourselves in for a long evening's chat. Far into the night we would talk: tentatively at first, but as time went by, with an openness and intimacy I'd never before known with a man. It was as though I'd found the other half of me in Bill, and he in me, and over the course of that winter we came to know one another as friends in a way equally new to both of us—wholly and without reservation.

I guess it was only natural that he would have an interest in my illness, but at first I resisted all his efforts to come to a better understanding of it. There was nothing to talk about, I insisted stubbornly. I was feeling fine and as long as that was the case, there was no sense in going over and over it. Besides, what was the point? I had MS, that was the fact, and no amount of talking was going to make it any less true.

But if I couldn't see how damaging all my denials were, Bill could, and slowly, carefully, he encouraged me to look deeper inside myself and talk about what it was I was feeling. It wasn't an easy thing to do, because I found that by admitting certain things to Bill, I was forced to admit them to myself, and that opened up a whole new world of disturbing possibilities.

But even at that he wouldn't let me off the hook, and little by little

I began to speak to him of things I'd never been able to say out loud to anyone before. I told him how frightened I was by the knowledge that someday I might wind up in a wheelchair, and how when I thought about the possibility my mind would freeze, unable to focus on the images it saw. I told him of the nightmares I used to have and how fearful I was of ever getting too close to anyone, or even of owning anything of value, because I was afraid that someday it would all be taken away. Gradually, as the long winter months wore on, I opened up completely and told him everything that was in my heart.

If Bill taught me anything, he taught me that burdens shared are burdens lightened and that once in a while it's okay to bleed a little, as long as someone with a bandage is standing close by. He, along with Ryan, was the surest friend I'd ever known, and the bonds of trust we built that winter would serve to hold us firmly together through all the pain and insanity of the years to come.

* * * * * * * * * *

Toward the middle of February things began to slide a little. The constipation was becoming more of a problem than ever, and at the same time I noticed my left leg had begun to weaken again. By the end of the month I was back on my cane, frustrated with the relapse. Bill had never experienced any of this with me before and I remember he was a little shaken at first. I explained to him that these annual bouts with the disease were becoming almost routine, and that a shot of steroids would fix me up as good as new. There was really nothing to worry about.

But this time there *was* and, oddly enough, Bill was the first to notice.

It was a Saturday night, and as usual we were at Larry's Club having a few beers. I'd just ordered my sixth or seventh when I noticed him looking at me with a strange expression on his face.

"Jesus, JJ, where are you putting it?" he asked wonderingly.

"What are you talking about?" I answered, surprised. "You've seen me drink beer before. Lots more than this, too. Besides, you sure as hell put away your share tonight."

"Agreed. But so far I've been to the bathroom four times and you have yet to get up off that barstool. A normal person can't drink that much beer without having to pee at least once."

He was right. Any other night I'd have been in and out of the bathroom half a dozen times myself, but for some strange reason I just didn't have to go. It didn't seem like anything worth worrying about, so I quickly changed the subject and went on to enjoy the rest of the evening.

But by six the next morning I was in agony. When I awoke my bladder was cramping violently, my abdomen was tight and distended, and it was clear that if I didn't get to the outhouse soon, something was going to explode. I managed to get out of bed and pull on a pair of boots, but by the time I made it to the outhouse I was doubled over, gasping out loud with the pain. I sat down hurriedly and waited. Seconds, then minutes went by with no signs of anything happening. My abdomen was hard as a rock and the pain was getting worse every second. I had to do something, and quickly.

I found that by pressing hard against my bladder with both hands I was able to release a small stream of urine. The relief I felt was indescribable and I repeated the process again and again for the better part of an hour. When it was finally over and my bladder was empty, all I could do was lean weakly against the wall, sweating and shaking.

What was happening now? I was completely mystified. I'd never experienced anything like this before and the only thing I could pin it on was the MS. I knew all about neurogenic bowels, but could there possibly be such a thing as a neurogenic bladder?

You bet there could. I went to Bill's and called Dr. Bowers right away. When I told him what had happened, he explained that this sort of thing was a symptom sometimes seen in MS patients. He said the problem was caused by interference with the nerve that was responsible for emptying the bladder. It didn't sound too serious yet, he said, but if it was left untreated for too long, all kinds of nasty things could happen. He didn't elaborate, but I could just imagine.

The safest thing to do, he urged, was to see a urologist as soon as possible. That way tests could be done to determine the extent of the damage and a course of treatment prescribed. I thanked him for the advice and promised to look into it right away.

134

The tests, three of them, were all to be done at once—the equivalent of a urological grand slam. But to spare me any undue discomfort, a general anesthetic would be administered so I could sleep through the whole procedure and never feel a thing. That was the best news I'd heard all week.

When I came out of the recovery room I was still a little groggy, but I managed to sit up and pay attention when the urologist came in to go over the results of the tests with me.

He explained that, as a result of nerve damage from the MS, my bladder had undergone some pretty radical changes over the past year or so. Since the proper impulses weren't getting through my nervous system any longer, the muscular walls of the bladder had lost their tone and were now stretched far beyond their normal capacity. In other words, where a normal bladder could only hold a pint or so of urine without causing discomfort, mine could tolerate well over a *quart* before I felt anything at all. That explained the episode in the outhouse.

The best way to treat the condition was medically, he said, with a special drug that would stimulate the nerve leading to the bladder, causing it to contract and empty itself completely. But just in case it didn't, he was going to prescribe something else, a long-term antiseptic that would act to suppress any infection that might start as a result of residual urine left in the bladder. Was all that clear and was I willing to take the necessary medication? I said it was fine with me. After all, if something could be fixed with just a pill, I was all for it.

So that was the end of that. As far as urologists go, he was okay I guess, but looking back now I have to wonder why he kept so much information from me. Had he bothered to warn me then of what might be waiting for me down the road, I might have done a few things differently and spared myself a lot of pain and humiliation. But he didn't, and for that reason I've never been able to forgive him. He knew, and he never said a word.

Since I was already in the hospital, the decision was made to start me on an IV course of ACTH in hopes of getting my legs back in shape. I was glad to hear it, and as soon as the IV was in place I relaxed and crossed my fingers, waiting for the magic to begin.

But for the first time since my diagnosis, the steroids failed to do the job completely. Instead of the overnight success I was anticipating, the results were only marginal; when I finally went back to work I was still leaning heavily on my cane for support.

* * * * * * * * * * *

It was about a month later that odd little stories began surfacing around town of people who had been to see the "psychic surgeons" in the Philippine Islands, and who had come back with incredible tales of miraculous cures effected at the hands of these so-called "healers." At first I couldn't believe what I was hearing; people with serious, sometimes life-threatening illnesses were traveling halfway around the world to have what was termed "surgery" performed on them by people with absolutely no medical training.

It all sounded like something out of "The Twilight Zone" to me. As closely as I could determine, these healers bare-handedly opened up the body, pulled out gobs of sick and diseased tissue, and then closed everything back up again, all without benefit of surgical instruments *or* anesthesia! As far as I was concerned the whole thing was ridiculous, and I said so—loudly—to anyone who would listen.

But there were a lot of people around Kenai, including Bill, who weren't anywhere near as skeptical as I was. In fact, a friend of Helen's, a young construction worker recently diagnosed with terminal brain cancer, had just returned from Manila claiming to be completely free of the disease. Even his doctor admitted to being stumped when a new set of x-rays showed the tumors to have completely disappeared.

I still wasn't convinced of anything, but Bill apparently *was* and immediately sprang into action. I was kept completely in the dark until several weeks later, when I was floored by one of the biggest surprises of my life: I was waiting at my desk for a hastily called after-work meeting when virtually everyone I knew, including Bill and our new boss, Phil Turkington, walked in as a group and gathered all around me. Then, giggling like a bunch of schoolkids with a secret too good to keep, they presented me with all the funds necessary to cover round-trip airfare, sixteen nights in Manila, meals, tips, and all the spending money I'd need while I was there! Even my parents had sent a check from Pittsburgh.

I was flabbergasted. It was an extraordinarily generous act, a complete surprise, and one I accepted with gratitude, wonder, and tears. I still hadn't changed my opinion of the healers, but in light of all that had been done for me, there was no way on earth I wasn't going to go. Stranger things *had* happened, as the saying goes, and who knew? Maybe there really was something special going on over there.

There was a lot to do before I left—passports, shots, and so on—but time and luck were on my side and within two weeks I was ready to go and meet my fellow travelers. (I would be joining a group of about thirty others, all of them strangers, who were making the same journey I was.) Everyone was smiling confidently as I waved goodbye at the small airport in Kenai, but all during the flight to Anchorage my nerves began to build. What could I possibly be thinking? Was I seriously planning to fly halfway around the world to take part in some bizarre wizard ritual? Hell, I was as crazy as a loon.

The nineteen-hour flight to Manila was torturous for me, and by the time we began our final descent I was exhausted and my legs were almost completely gone. It was obvious to everyone that I was going to need some help, and I was relieved when the flight captain radioed ahead and asked that a wheelchair be waiting for me when we finally landed.

Manila, always hot and humid, was experiencing an extraordinarily oppressive heat wave that April. The instant the flight attendant opened the big steel door at the front of the airplane, I felt every muscle in my body turn into jelly as I gasped for breath, trying to fill my lungs. I'd been warned about the weather this near the equator, and I guess I really should have known better, but *nothing* could have prepared me for this.

The temperature was close to 110 degrees and the heavy, woolly air was almost liquid—a humid, suffocating blanket that hung like a shroud, making it all but impossible to breathe. By the time I was carried down the steps to the tarmac and placed in the wheelchair, every inch of me was soaked and dripping with sweat, and I felt so light-headed I was afraid I was going to pass out.

But all of that was forgotten momentarily when I opened my eyes and got my first long look at the tropical wonderland that was Manila. I was surrounded by a wild kaleidoscope of colors that flashed and danced and swirled, a spinning palette of hues so bright and bold they defied description. Tens of thousands of Filipinos dressed in brightly colored costumes were crowded along the runway while dazzling, multicolored banners flew like huge exotic kites above the breezy, open-air terminal. Everywhere I looked, masses of brilliant tropical flowers bloomed in wild profusion in the hot jungle air. "Intense" is the only word that even comes close to describing the scene. It was completely overwhelming, and for the longest time all I could do was sit and stare.

The sun was setting over Manila Bay as we boarded the bus for the hotel, and all along Roxas Boulevard rows of stately coconut palms were silhouetted in black against the raw, incendiary streaks of red and orange that filled the evening sky. It was a blazing, glorious welcome, and we watched in silence as the last fiery glimpse of the sun slipped beneath the horizon and pulled the night down behind it like a shade. The sunset was over as quickly as it had begun.

* * * * * * * * * *

My first "surgery" was scheduled for eight the next morning, and when I climbed into the wheelchair and rolled into the waiting room I spotted five or six members of our group lined up in wooden chairs against the wall. Judging by the looks on their faces, they weren't any happier about being there than I was. We smiled weakly at one another, hoping to boost our courage a little for the ordeal that lay ahead.

Periodically, a young Filipino girl named Maria would emerge from the adjoining room, call out a name, and beckon the next "victim" inside. The person in question would rise, pale of face and weak of knees, and then disappear quietly into the "healing room" next door. The fact that none of them were ever seen or heard from again that morning didn't do anything to lower the anxiety level in the waiting room, and by the time my name was called I was a nervous wreck.

The treatment room was small and bare of any furnishings, except for a small leather "operating" table and a wooden stand that held three or four stainless steel basins and a stack of clean white towels. Crowded around the table were Maria and the "healers"—three small Filipino men dressed casually in short-sleeved shirts and slacks. One of the men spoke as I entered the room.

"Good morning, ma'am," he said softly. "I am Nino. What is the problem?" I assumed he was the head honcho.

"I have multiple sclerosis," I answered shakily, feeling more like a fool than anything else.

He merely smiled kindly as the four of them helped me out of the wheelchair and up onto the table. In a moment they had me positioned the way they wanted me—face down, arms at my sides. I watched out of the corner of my eye as they began their preparations.

Maria took a towel from the table, shook it out, and draped it loosely across my neck and shoulders, while Nino and his assistants dipped their hands in a pan of warm oil, and then wiped them off on a towel that smelled faintly of alcohol. It was as close to sterile technique as they ever came, and I found myself wondering what the AMA would have to say about the whole procedure.

When at last everything was ready, they approached the table as a group. The two assistants, Ramon and Luis, each took hold of one of my wrists and waited while Nino folded his hands in a prayerlike gesture, then placed them gently on my head.

"Everything is ready very well, ma'am," he intoned solemnly. "We begin with the brain."

The hell we do. I jerked my head up and tried to scramble off the table, but the three of them were too quick for me. Ramon and Luis pushed me back down and held me firmly, as Nino began gently massaging the back of my head.

Surprisingly, it wasn't too bad. If this was all there was to it, I thought to myself, they could keep it up all day. I settled down and tried to relax as the motion of his hands grew firmer and more insistent.

After about thirty seconds I heard a soft hissing sound and felt Nino's fingers dig deeper into my scalp. Too deep. It was almost as though I could feel them moving around *inside my head*. This was getting a little weirder than I'd anticipated, and I opened my mouth to protest.

But just then there were several loud squishing noises and I felt something warm and thick trickle slowly down my neck and across my shoulders. What in the name of God was going on? I tried to reach for my neck but found my hands still tightly pinned to the table. So, against all my better judgment, I screwed up my courage and opened my eyes.

It was the one thing I should never have done.

The blood was everywhere—a rich, red flood that covered my shoulders and dripped slowly from my neck in thick, crimson strands to form a viscous puddle around my head. It was human blood, *my blood*, and at the instant I realized where it was coming from, my mind streaked off into another dimension and I passed out cold.

When I came to, Luis was slapping my wrist gently and speaking to me in a soothing tone of voice. At the same time I could feel a tight, pulling sensation at the back of my head. Oh God, what was happening now? I didn't dare move.

Nino dropped something into one of the steel basins at his side, then handed it to Ramon, who carried it over to where I was lying on the table.

"Look ma'am," he said softly. "From the brain." As he spoke, he tipped the pan so I could see what was inside.

It was a sight I never expected to see on this earth. Floating in an inch or so of water was a large, rotting clump of tissue, sickly gray and thickly clotted with dark, black sacs of blood. It took a moment to register that this was *me*. This horrible, putrid mass was part of *my* body, pulled by human hands from deep within my brain. I felt the bile rise in my throat as my stomach heaved and I vomited all over the floor. That was it. I was gone again.

As I came around the second time, Maria was swabbing at my neck and shoulders with a clean towel and Nino was rubbing gently on my head.

"All finished operation, ma'am. You go now."

Go now? Didn't he know there was a *hole* in my head? I could never go anywhere again.

"No, no, no," he insisted, smiling, "hole all closed up now. Everything okay very fine."

I was still dizzy and faint, and too weak to protest as they eased me off the table and back into the wheelchair. One of the group leaders was summoned to help me back to my room, and on the way she explained in more detail how the entire "healing" process worked. She said that twenty-five or thirty more operations would be done on various parts of my body and that the procedure would be the same every time.

After I was positioned on the table, she said, the area to be worked on during that session would first be cleansed with rubbing alcohol, then swabbed with a sweet-smelling oil of some kind. Next, Nino would begin firmly massaging the area in question. After a minute or so I'd hear a soft hissing sound, then feel a warm sensation as the body opened up and blood began to flow from the wound. At that point I'd start to feel Nino's hands moving gently inside me as he carefully removed any sick or diseased tissue he encountered.

When the procedure was finished, she said, he would simply press his hands firmly over the wound for a few seconds while the skin closed, and that would be the end of it. After the blood was wiped away, all that would remain would be a small red area resembling a rash or a mild sunburn, and even that would fade away in an hour or so.

That's all there was to it, she said blithely as she opened the door to my room and helped me inside. "Oh, by the way," she added as she turned to leave, "you're welcome to have anyone you like in the room with you while you're being operated on. In fact, lots of people even take snapshots—they make *great* souvenirs!"

I realized then that I was in the presence of a madwoman and as soon as she was gone I fell into bed, crying and nearly hysterical. It had been a horrible mistake to have come to a place like this, expecting to be helped. Instead, I was worse off than ever before. I was sick, scared, and angry—and half a world away from anyone who cared.

I lay in bed all afternoon, going over and over the operation in my mind, trying to make some sense of it. But I couldn't. There was simply nothing in my frame of reference that could allow for what had happened, and no way to explain it either. I finally gave up and fell asleep.

By dinnertime I was feeling somewhat revived, so I got dressed, climbed back into my wheelchair, and went to join the rest of the group for dinner, curious to see how everyone else had fared. They all had pretty much the same story to tell as I did and, reassuringly, just as many questions. So when one of the group leaders stood up and announced that there would be an important lecture that evening on the principles of "psychic healing," we all agreed to go and see what we could learn.

At first I didn't have any trouble understanding what the lecturer was saying. He was a plump, elderly Filipino, the grandaddy of all the healers, and he reminded me a lot of Norman Vincent Peale as he yammered on and on about the power of positive thinking and all the amazing things the human mind was capable of doing. So far, so good.

But things took a turn for the bizarre as his talk expanded into the supernatural, and before long he was speaking to us of things like astral projection, spirit guides from the "other side," harmonic vibrations, and some strange new phenomenon known as "channeling." Shirley MacLaine would have felt right at home.

But it was all a little too cosmic for me and I left halfway through in disgust. I'd been right all along. The whole mess was nothing more than a lot of bullshit wizard crap and I wanted nothing more to do with it. I went to the bar and downed a couple of San Miguels (a thick, potent local beer), then rolled up to my room and got ready for bed. Since I was no longer planning to attend my scheduled operation the next morning, I decided I'd try to spend the day doing a little sightseeing. I dug out a couple of tour brochures provided by the hotel, then got into bed and thumbed through them lazily until I finally fell asleep.

I woke up a lot earlier than usual and, glad to have a jump on the day, reached for my robe and stood up. But I froze instantly when I realized what had happened; *I was standing up.* I wasn't standing erect, and I wasn't standing unsupported, but I was standing! I grabbed for my cane and slowly, carefully, took a few tentative steps toward the dresser. Everything held. I walked around the room a couple of times, then sat down on the edge of the bed, thoroughly bewildered.

Could it be possible that this was the result of just that one operation yesterday? Was there really something *to* all of this? Wizard crap or not, I decided I couldn't afford to ignore it and I rummaged around the room searching for my clothes. I didn't want to be late for my second operation.

This one went a lot more smoothly. Nino and the boys didn't seem the least bit surprised to see me up and out of the wheelchair, and once I was lying face-up on the table they went directly to work on my abdomen. The procedure went exactly the way it had been described to me the day before—there was a hiss, a couple of squishes, a warm rush of blood, and by the time I finally felt brave enough to open my eyes, Nino was up to his elbows in my intestines, happily yanking out all sorts of awful, bloody stuff. It wasn't any easier to watch this time around, but at least now I had a reason for being there, and that made all the difference.

For the remaining two weeks I was scheduled for two operations almost every day, one in the morning and one in the afternoon. To kill time between the first and second that day, I put on my bathing suit and headed for the roof, which is where the hotel's swimming pool was located. A dozen or so of the others apparently had the same idea and were already in the water when I arrived. A spontaneous round of applause went up as they spotted me walking with just the support of a cane, and I felt like a real celebrity as I eased myself into the pool.

I was amazed to see that every one of them seemed to be vastly improved over the night before, too, and we all started talking at once, eager to share our experiences. There were some serious cases here. Most of the people in the group had cancer of one form or another, and many of them were terminal. One young boy had cerebral palsy, another had muscular dystrophy, and two of the others were suffering from leukemia. It wasn't a group with much cause for optimism, but you wouldn't have known it that day. The mood was euphoric, the talk was animated, and little by little group of total strangers drew close and eventually became friends.

The operations got a lot easier to handle as time went on, and by the fourth day I had abandoned my cane altogether. My legs were working perfectly and I was feeling better than I had in more than a year. Most of the others in the group were, too, and several of us began taking advantage of some of the daily tours offered by the hotel. We spent one whole afternoon on the island of Corregidor, the much-bombed site of MacArthur's command post during World War II. We traveled the route of the Bataan Death March and placed a wreath at the memorial, then traveled by boat across Manila Bay. Best of all, we took an overnight trip to the spectacular open-air markets of Baguio, the summer capitol of the Islands.

But by the middle of the second week, some of the younger members of the group were getting hungry for a little more action, so we took our problem to the Filipino travel guide stationed in the lobby. He had several suggestions, but the one that sounded most tempting to all of us was a canoe trip down a wild jungle river. It seemed like the perfect way to see a little more of the area, and we made arrangements to leave early the following morning.

* * * * * * * * * *

Almost all of the island of Luzon is covered with thick, tropical vegetation, a situation no doubt brought on by its relative proximity to the equator and the fact that it receives about a zillion feet of rainfall a week. But even knowing all that, I was amazed at what we encountered that afternoon. The further we drove from Manila, the thicker the overgrowth got, and by the time we arrived at our destination the words "deepest, darkest jungle" were the only ones that applied.

Our guides and canoes were waiting for us at the bottom of the steep riverbank. In order to get down to them, we had to hack our way through a dense tangle of undergrowth made up mostly of mosses, fallen tree trunks, and thick, green, jungle vines. A machete would have helped, but as one of the guys quipped, "Gee, Dr. Livingston, we plumb forgot to bring one!"

There were three heavy wooden canoes and nine of us in all, including the guides, so we split up into teams of three and stashed our gear safely under the thick mahogany floorboards. Then we pushed off from the shore, dipped our paddles in the water and struck out boldly for the center of the stream.

The river was a steaming, fetid stream of sludgy brown water that wound itself lazily through steep, narrow canyons of green. The canyon walls rose hundreds of feet straight up and were covered with thick jungle foliage, completely impenetrable to the eye. In some places the walls were so close to one another that the tall palms and vines lining their crests grew together in a twisted, tangled mass to form a vast, domed canopy high overhead. Occasionally this "roof" was so dense that even sunlight couldn't penetrate, and the river took on the feel of a dark and gloomy underworld, silent and eerie in its stillness.

High above, though, the skies were anything but quiet. Flocks of gorgeous, wildly plumed tropical birds were screeching and squawking, filling the air with their raucous cries. Meanwhile, hidden deep within the jungle, scores of unseen monkeys called to one another shrilly, their harsh, insistent voices echoing loudly through the canyon. At first it was unsettling, like the soundtrack from a bad Tarzan film, but once I got used to the sound I found it almost comforting.

Life along the riverbank was a constantly changing panorama, filled with sights I'd never even imagined. Small, joyfully naked children splashed and danced in the water at the river's edge under the watchful eyes of the older women who were busily tending to the family laundry several yards upstream. Immense gray carabao, or water buffalo, were absolutely everywhere. They lumbered like four-legged boulders along the riverbank, grazing constantly, their sharp, pronged horns rooting around in the undergrowth in search of roots, leaves, and other tasty morsels. It was fascinating to watch them chew up the jungle on one end, while simultaneously expelling it out the other, each huge turd the size of a loaf of bread. With my own recent problems in mind, I grinned and wondered to myself what it would be like if one of *them* ever got constipated.

The trip upstream was a long, hot pull and before too long we could hear the roar of the rapids in the far channel of the river. We couldn't see them yet, but judging by the sound I guessed we were in for one hell of a ride back down. We were all relieved to reach the river's end, a deep, cool lagoon fed by an enormous white waterfall that plunged straight down from hundreds of feet above. The water had gone from brown to sparkling blue and we jumped in delightedly, laughing and shouting like children at play in a tropical Eden.

Afterward, refreshed and rejuvenated, we climbed aboard two

primitive bamboo rafts and held on tight as our guides pulled us, whooping and screaming with laughter, right through the center of the roaring waterfall into a cool, dark cave carved out of solid rock in the wall behind it. For an hour or more we stayed there, transfixed by the sight of a perfect prehistoric world of emerald green and silver, framed majestically by a frothy, pounding curtain of pure white.

The trip downstream was a fast, exhilarating ride, and all we had to do was hang on tight and hope the canoes stayed upright. We careened wildly through the rapids, narrowly escaping collision with dozens of midstream boulders and, once, almost rammed headlong into a hapless water buffalo who didn't recognize the urgency of the situation. He would have paid with his life, too, because we were clearly out of control.

Toward the end of the run, as the river's pace slowed down and the water turned once again to brown, I could sense that everyone was as sorry as I was to see the adventure come to a close.

Back in Manila the surgeries went on as scheduled, two a day for the rest of our stay, and by the night of the big farewell bash it was plain to see that everyone was feeling great. I remember thinking that the happy, smiling crowd of people gathered in the bar that night didn't even resemble the sorry group that had arrived just two short weeks ago. Those people had been sick and depressed, largely hopeless and, in some cases, frighteningly close to death. But now all of that had changed somehow, and as I joined the others on the dance floor I realized we'd all be going home with some amazing stories to tell, and maybe—just maybe—a bright ray of hope for the future.

Looking back over the whole episode now, it's hard for me to explain, even to myself, my feelings about what happened in Manila. *Intellectually* speaking, I know now that it was all a hoax, and not a very sophisticated one at that. I've since seen all the stories on "60 Minutes" and other news documentaries, debunking the healers as nothing more than well-practiced charlatans, deft at the art of sleight of hand. And *of course* all they ever pulled from my body was chicken blood and entrails.

But oddly enough, to this very day I don't regret having gone.

Something *did* happen over there—a psychic pep rally on a cosmic scale. And for the the first time in my life I saw demonstrated, in the most graphic possible terms, the incredibly powerful link between the mind and the human body.

Was I cured of multiple sclerosis by the healers? Not in any way imaginable. But there was a lot more to it than that; I was sick, scared, and sitting in a wheelchair when I arrived in Manila. By the time I left I had thrown away even my cane, and was feeling stronger and healthier than I had in quite some time. Furthermore, I stayed that way for an entire *year* after I returned to Alaska.

In and of itself that proves nothing, certainly—spontaneous remissions happen all the time with MS. But I'd learned a powerful lesson about the mind and the difference it can make in a person's life. Even now when I look at the photographs of some of the operations (yes, I did break down and have a few snapshots taken), I smile to myself and whisper my thanks to those who loved me enough to have given me such a gift.

NINE

▬▬ ▬ ▬▬

Anchorage, Alaska
September, 1979

IT WAS THE DAMNDEST thing. I'd been back from the Philippines since early May, and things couldn't possibly have been better. I was feeling terrific, my career was coming along just fine, and my social life was back to its usual frenetic level. On top of that, Bill and Cindy and I had grown closer than ever and, between the two of them, I had all the fun and companionship I could possibly want. As far as I could tell, my life was close to what most people would consider perfect.

So why did I feel so miserable inside? And why the lousy mood? I couldn't put my finger on what it was, but something had been building up inside me for the past couple of months—a dull, steady pressure that had no form and no real substance. It was just always there, a free-floating anxiety that kept me on edge and seemed to grow stronger every day. It didn't make sense to me at all to be feeling the way I was. After all, I'd gotten lucky again and it looked like I was going to be okay for awhile. I could take it easy, forget about my health, and enjoy some time filled with calm and peace and quiet.

But maybe that was the problem. Maybe my life had gotten a little too calm and settled, a condition I've never considered especially entertaining *or* productive. I'd always operated best with my back against the wall, when I was caught in a tight spot with nothing but my wits to pull me through. But just then there was none of that in my life, and I missed it.

Most days Bill and I would meet for a drink after work to relax and talk over the events of the day. Normally I was the first to arrive, but for some reason, one evening I felt especially tense and edgy. Instead of heading for the bar, I got in my car and drove around town aimlessly, trying to come to terms with what it was I was feeling.

But it was pointless. Instead of easing up, the mood I was fighting just seemed to grow stronger and more intense until I felt like I was going to explode. It was well after dark when I gave up the fight and dropped by Cindy's place for a shower, and maybe one of our cathartic, world-class bitching sessions. We were better at *that* than we were at just about anything else.

She was in the kitchen fixing something to eat when I arrived, so I poured myself a drink and wandered off in the direction of the bedroom. I heard Bill's car pull up in the driveway just then, but I needed a few minutes alone to try to pull myself together.

I was sure I'd be okay as soon as I'd had a drink and calmed down a little, but I felt my hand shaking as I pulled the door closed behind me. I sat down on the edge of the bed, took a long, bracing drink of the scotch, and began to cry.

A few moments later Cindy came looking for me, and when she saw the shape I was in she called out to Bill, who came immediately. The two of them sat down beside me on the bed, put their arms around me, and let me cry until the worst was over and I could speak calmly again. "What's wrong?" they asked repeatedly as they began probing for the source of the trouble.

But how could I tell them what was wrong when there really *wasn't* anything wrong? How could I make them understand when I didn't even understand it myself?

I just knew that everything had gotten too quiet around me, and that once again all I could hear was the ticking of the clock. The old restlessness was back, and with it the need to keep on running, to keep some sort of forward-moving momentum going in my life. The need was stronger now than ever; something inside me was pushing hard for a change. This time it had to be a big one, and it had to be right away. The only problem was, I didn't have the faintest notion of what it was I wanted to do.

So all night long the three of us talked, and by morning we'd come up with the perfect plan: effective right away I would quit my job, give up my cabin, and move everything I owned up to Anchorage. After four years in the woods, the big city would be an enormous change for me—and if I did it right, one with all sorts of interesting possibilities. I could step up my career in a more sophisticated agency, make new friends, find new challenges, and, best of all, keep the noise level around me at a deafening roar.

It nearly broke my heart to leave my cabin, the Peninsula, and so many of the people I loved, especially Bill, Cindy, and Helen. But some things are meant to be, I suppose, and when they are, all of the pieces just naturally fall into place.

* * * * * * * * * *

Pacific Rim Brokers was a classy little brokerage house with a healthy book of strictly commercial-lines business. The partners, Mark and John, were looking for a third property/casualty agent to handle all their in-house accounts while they expanded their own areas of expertise out on the big construction sites scattered all over the state.

It was exactly what I was looking for. The job carried loads of responsibility, a certain amount of prestige, and, most important, offered me a chance to expand my knowledge of the business far beyond anything I'd attained yet. It would keep me occupied, interested, and moving straight ahead at optimum speed. Therefore, I was delighted to accept their generous offer, and when I reported for work a week later I was sure I was on my way to the top.

I couldn't have picked a better place to work. Mark and John turned out to be two of the wildest, wickedest wits in the business and the three of us settled quickly into an easy, if somewhat crazed, working relationship. They spent most of their time out in the field while I spent most of mine ensconced in my new private office, feeling like a big shot as I dictated long, elaborate letters to our beautiful secretary, Debra.

It was a stretch-to-fit kind of job—the more responsibility I took on, the more I could have—and in no time at all I was completely overextended and up to my ears in work, a state of near ecstasy for an unrepentant overachiever like myself.

Socially, things were shaping up nicely, too. When I first got to town the only person I knew even vaguely was a woman named Jane

Hein, a tall, beautiful representative of the Insurance Services Office in Alaska. We'd met a couple of times in Kenai while she was there on business, and as soon as I got to Anchorage I looked her up. She was single, too, and before long we were spending most of our free time together, chasing men for sport and commiserating over endless cups of coffee about the lack of time there was to do them all justice.

By then the only huge thing missing in my life was Bill. He was still living down in Kenai, and although we talked on the phone every night and visited back and forth on weekends, somehow it just wasn't the same. I missed having my best friend around all the time, and so did he.

There was only one way to solve the problem, and Bill made the move right away. Inside a month he'd landed himself an impressive new job in Anchorage, and by November we were back in business. He and Jane and I solidified ourselves into a single unit almost immediately—an unholy Gang of Three, dedicated to the proposition of making noise, making money, and making ourselves heard individually above the general commotion of our raucous, three-way alliance. They didn't call us the Loud Family for nothing.

So the stage was set. Once again I'd managed to tear my world apart and put it back together, just the way I wanted it, and for one whole year the three of us filled that world with laughter. I only wish I could remember what I was laughing about the day it all began to fall apart.

* * * * * * * * * * *

Mark and John and I were sitting around the office talking one evening after work, when one of them said something especially stupid. This wasn't an unusual occurrence, considering it was late in the day and we'd all been running on adrenaline for hours. But whatever was said struck me as particularly funny and sent me off on one of those laughing jags from which there is simply no recovery. It seemed the harder I tried to stop, the harder I wanted to laugh, and all the two of them could do was sit by helplessly while I roared my way into the stratosphere.

And that's when I felt it happen.

I jumped up out of my seat, ran to the bathroom, and checked to see if I was imagining things. It wasn't much, certainly nothing anyone else could notice, but it was unmistakably there. And it proved the cliche still held true—I'd laughed so hard I'd actually wet my pants!

All that did was set me off again, and for the next five minutes I sat on the toilet, giggling deliciously, completely lost in my mirth. When I finally made it back to the office, John and Mark had decided to call it quits for the day, so we packed up our things and walked together to the parking lot.

I can still remember the looks on their faces as they watched me drive away, wondering, no doubt, what the hell had gotten into me. But by the time I got into bed that night I had all but forgotten the incident, and never gave it another thought until a week later, when the same thing happened again.

Bill and I were at lunch and I'd just taken a big sip of hot coffee when he said something funny, and I felt the coffee burn its way straight down into my lungs. Naturally this set off a huge, embarrassing scene as I coughed and hacked wildly, thrashing around in my seat, desperately trying to clear my lungs. I just about had it under control, too, when I coughed one last time and felt my bladder go into a tight little spasm.

In the bathroom it was the same thing again, only worse. I was beginning to get a little worried, but I took care of things the best way I could and joined Bill back in the restaurant, resolving not to say anything to him until I'd had some time to check it out.

I talked the problem over with Jane that night and felt a lot better when she said she'd had similar episodes before and that they were usually the result of some minor bladder infection. I understood immediately. Lately I hadn't been as careful as I should have been about taking the antiseptic the doctor had prescribed, and I thought maybe I'd picked up some kind of bug. It certainly couldn't be a result of the MS *this* time, I reasoned, since it had produced exactly the opposite effect before—the tests I'd taken had proven that unequivocally.

But since I didn't have any of the other symptoms consistent with a bladder infection, I decided to sit tight for a while and see if it got any worse. If it did, I'd just have to call a urologist and see what he or she had to say.

It wasn't until two weeks later that I realized how serious a problem I really had.

Work was finished for the day and John and I were relaxing in his office, cleaning up a few last-minute details in one of the files. I was settled comfortably in one of the leather armchairs facing his desk, shoes off, coffee cup in hand, when I felt a sudden, strong signal from my bladder. I *really* had to go and I excused myself immediately.

But I wasn't three inches off the chair when suddenly my bladder cramped down hard and I felt a burning stream of urine gush from between my legs. I sat, frozen, unable to move or breathe or even think as the flood spilled down my legs, across the leather chair and dripped slowly onto the soft, cream carpet at my feet.

There wasn't a sound to be heard in the room.

Riveted to my chair by the shock, I could only stare mutely at John. He looked like a man who had just walked into a nightmare, stunned and unbelieving. I felt my breath coming in short gasps as I gripped the armrests of the chair, fighting to regain some composure.

"John," I pleaded quietly, "please go call Bill at his office. Please. Tell him to come right away." It was all I could say, and it was all he could possibly do for me. He closed the door quietly behind him and never opened it again until Bill arrived fifteen minutes later.

The two of them managed to get me bundled up and down to the car, and after a hurried conference with John, Bill climbed behind the wheel and took me home. I don't even like to think about what John had to do in the office that night after we left.

As soon as I was showered and changed, Bill got me settled on the sofa and tried to talk me through what had happened. But I was so embarrassed that all I could do was stare at the ceiling wordlessly while he jabbered on and on, doing his best to figure it all out. I was no help whatsoever and finally, either out of frustration or sheer lunacy, he cut straight to the heart of the problem with one inelegant stroke.

"Aw, the hell with it, JJ," he quipped brightly. "So you whizzed all over Johnny's office? I can think of a *dozen* people who'd pay money to do the very same thing—you just got to do it for free!"

We laughed so hard we both took off running for the bathroom.

First thing the next morning I called and got an appointment with a urologist. Something strange was going on and I had to get it taken care of before I even thought about going back to work. As it was, I didn't know how I was ever going to be able to face John again.

As I climbed out of bed to get dressed, I made a disturbing discovery. My left leg was dragging again and I had to pull it behind me as I made my way down the hall, clutching at the walls for support.

Goddammit—not again! I didn't need this on top of everything else, and as I stood in front of the sink I punched the wall hard, skinning all four knuckles. Good. At least now I had an excuse to cry.

But as I sat down and thought the whole mess through, I realized I was actually close to being right on schedule, and I probably should have been expecting something like this to happen. It had been roughly a year since my last attack, and that seemed to be the pattern I was following. So far, it was all pretty standard stuff.

Oh well, I thought, it looked like I was going to have to tough it through one more time. As soon as I was dressed, I called and made an appointment with Dr. Bowers for later that morning after my appointment with the urologist. It wouldn't hurt to get started on the steroids.

When I got to the urologist's office I explained what had been happening, then gave him a specimen and waited while he checked it out. It didn't look like anything serious, he said, most likely just a little touch of cystitis. It would take a couple of days to do a culture in order to be sure, but in the meantime he gave me a prescription for an antibiotic that he said ought to clear the problem right up.

Could something as simple as a bladder infection really be the cause of what had happened yesterday, I asked? It certainly could, he assured me, and that was why it was important to get started on the medicine right away, before it got any worse. If left untreated these things could get really nasty, especially in an MS patient. Vastly relieved, I thanked him for the help, promised to call in a couple of days for the results of the culture, and took off for my second appointment of the morning.

It was good to see old Bowers again. We'd gotten to be pretty good friends over the years and we chatted easily as he wrote out a prescription for some prednisone.

"You're looking great, kiddo. How long has it been now?" he asked, referring to my diagnosis.

"Six years this month. Not too bad, huh?"

"Not too bad? You're doing *terrific*, and this year's attack looks like it's going to be a mild one. The prednisone should straighten you out right away."

We smiled and shook hands that day, two old friends in cahoots, so sure of ourselves in the fight we were winning.

On the way back to the office I stopped by the pharmacy to fill the prescriptions, and while I was there I picked up another cane. It looked like I'd be doing the MS Shuffle for a while.

* * * * * * * * * * *

Over the course of the next month I got steadily worse. My left leg weakened dramatically, my eyes began to blur and lose focus, and the old familiar MS days began recurring with maddening regularity. Even if I started out the day feeling relatively energetic, by mid-afternoon I'd invariably find myself slumped over my desk, so deeply, bone-weary *tired* that I was sure I'd never recover strength enough to make it out to my car at the end of the day.

And to make everything worse, my bladder went totally out of control. When the results of my urine culture came back clean, showing no infection whatsoever, the doctor was completely stumped. The only other thing he could think of that might be causing the problem was the MS itself. Short of putting me into the hospital for a complete workup and something called "urodynamic studies," he was fresh out of ideas and so was I. Since the thought of lying around in a hospital bed for days on end while waiting for yet more bad news held no appeal whatsoever, I decided I'd hold off a bit and see what happened.

What happened was everything and anything, and in no particular order. Suddenly I'd have to go to the bathroom, and I had to get there right away. I rarely had more than thirty seconds' notice, and if I didn't make it up from my desk, down the hall, and onto the toilet in time, I'd wind up soaked and embarrassed, waiting for a chance to sneak out to my car so I could go home and change before anyone noticed.

There didn't seem to be any rhyme or reason to it at all. Some days

I'd make it through without a care, swilling coffee like a libertine, stopping by the john only once or twice at the most. But the next day I might have just one *mouthful* of coffee in the morning, and then quite literally make ten or eleven frantic trips to the bathroom before the afternoon was over.

As the problem worsened, it became obvious that I could no longer do my job. As my physical condition deteriorated I found that I simply couldn't do what I had to do each day and still keep up appearances at the same time. Oddly enough, it was the *appearance* of normalcy that concerned me the most. It was imperative to me that I go on pretending that nothing was wrong.

But that finally became impossible late one evening in September. It had been a long, tiring day in the office and the only place in the world I wanted to be was safely at home in my bed. John and Mark decided I needed a little TLC, however, and since they could sometimes be as persuasive as a couple of poorly trained pit bulls, I let them lure me out for a late supper at Simon and Seaforts, one of Anchorage's nicer restaurants.

Once we got there I began to relax a little, and since my bladder had been behaving all day I even joined them in a beer before dinner. The meal was fine, the conversation bright and funny, and I was even considering ordering another beer when I began to feel that familiar sensation. I had to get to the bathroom, and fast. My cane was leaning against the wall beside me and as I turned to reach for it, I felt my bladder let go in a convulsive rush, all down the front of my skirt, across the seat, and down onto the floor.

There was only one thing I could do. I yelled as loudly as I could to everyone in sight that I had just spotted a whale in the inlet outside the window. Then quickly, while everyone's attention was diverted, I reached for a full pitcher of beer and "accidentally" spilled its contents directly onto my lap. The chaos that ensued was hilarious. Everyone forgot the whale, preferring instead to marvel at my predicament, and by the time I finally got out of there I'd actually made a couple of new friends.

Once again I'd managed to avert disaster by thinking fast, but this time there was no doubting the fact that my career as a high-powered professional was in serious jeopardy. The stress of the job itself, combined with the constant worry about my bladder, was simply more than I could take.

I lay awake most of that night, confused and unsure of what to do next. But by seven the next morning I'd made my decision; at nine sharp I walked calmly into the office and resigned my position at the firm. So much for the fast track.

* * * * * * * * * *

For weeks afterward I hid out in my apartment, obsessing on my physical condition, just waiting for the next disabling symptom to appear. Even if the disease never progressed any further, I was sure I'd still never be rid of the problems I'd already developed. As I saw it, I had only two options: a) I could quit everything and go home to mom and dad, or b) I could pull myself together and look around for another job.

If I chose the latter, then I'd have to find something much less demanding that would allow me to take it easy and concentrate on getting my body back in shape. I'd been running too fast and too hard for much too long, and the results were beginning to show. More and more now I needed *two* canes to get around.

I don't know what I was thinking back then, why I didn't just pack it in for good and run away to some place safe. It would have been so much easier, and God knows I had every reason in the world to call it quits for a while and take a long, much-needed rest. But I think the reality of what was happening to me was so frightening that the only way I knew to deal with it was to deny it completely. If I allowed myself—even for a moment—to face the truth, then I wouldn't have any choices left. I would *have* to quit. I'd have to give up Alaska, my friends, the life I loved, and everything I'd worked so hard to build. And if all of that happened, then I would finally have to admit to myself that I had an incurable disease, one which could someday destroy my life.

I couldn't afford to let any of that happen just yet, and the best way I knew to prevent it was simply to keep on running. That meant pretending to the rest of the world that I was just like everyone else—normal, healthy, and bursting with energy. It was a lie I was willing to perpetuate for as long as I possibly could. Jane and Bill were the only ones who knew the truth, and since I was sure I could count on them to keep my secret, I set out immediately to look for another job.

Radio was the only other thing I knew how to do, and I saw right away that it would be an ideal solution. If there's one thing hardly anyone worries about in radio, it's appearances. There are exceptions, of course, but mostly it's an anything-goes proposition, and anything-goes is exactly where I was headed.

I didn't care where I went, what it paid, or what it played. If it had a microphone I could hide behind for four hours a day and a bathroom within twenty feet of the studio, then that was home for me. I didn't want to have to work too hard, I didn't want to have to be good, and I didn't want to have to try my best anymore. The only thing that mattered was finding a place where I could hide my face from the world for a while. It was the best plan I could come up with, and in order to make it work all I had to do was find the worst radio station in the world. A place where nobody cared.

That was remarkably easy, considering it was sitting right there in Anchorage all the time. I'd heard all the horror stories about KANC. It seemed like everyone in Alaskan broadcasting had worked there at one time or another and, try as I might, I couldn't find a single soul who had a kind word to say about the place. It sounded perfect.

The lobby was deserted when I arrived for my interview, and despite repeated calls of "Hello" and "Is anyone home?", I was unable to conjure up a body. The only sign of life came from a cheap, tiny loudspeaker on the wall that blared forth the worst country music I'd ever heard. Bad was one thing, I decided, but this was way, *way* too much. Even for me. I was just about to leave when a skinny, waiflike woman emerged from one of the incredibly messy offices adjoining the lobby. She smiled and called out to me to join her, introducing herself as the brand-new owner of the station.

So this was the notorious "Mad Aunt Lucy," the woman who'd bought the world's worst ratio station and was determined to make it work. I had to admit I was impressed. Even stations as bad as that one could cost a bazillion dollars, and anyone with that kind of scratch (not to mention nerve) was someone I felt was at least worth talking to. I hobbled into the office behind her.

We talked for several hours that afternoon and I was surprised to discover that she was a bright, articulate, uncommonly intelligent woman. It was immediately clear to me that she didn't know shit from shinola when it came to putting together a radio station, but her enthusiasm was contagious and before long she had me believing she could really pull it off. She needed me, though, she said. She needed me bad.

That was the worst thing she could have possibly said. The minute anyone says they need me, I *always* wind up going to work for them, and it usually turns into some kind of stupid crusade. Mad Aunt Lucy was a crusader all right, an avowed feminist who was going to show everyone what-for, and if I would come and be her good, strong lady deejay, then we'd shoot for the moon together and somehow build a perfect world where peace was everlasting, no one ever died, and rock 'n' roll was king. That woman could pump more sunshine in one short afternoon than most people see in a lifetime.

But what the hell. I needed something quick, the money was decent, and she really did promise to have the place cleaned up and hire a program director who knew what to do about the music. What more could I ask? The deal was made in no time flat, and that's how I wound up going to work for the worst radio station in the world.

* * * * * * * * * * *

I wish I could say that everything she said that day came true, and that KANC started to improve right away and that I had everything in the world to do with it. The sorry truth is, though, that the station nearly collapsed and died, the result of one disastrous decision after another. Over the next three months we went through at least four program directors I can recall by name, each with a plan more outrageous than the last. People kept quitting, Aunt Lucy kept fretting, and the music just kept getting worse.

On-air, I was demoralized, depressed, and embarrassed even to come to work every day. My voice had taken on such a twang that I sounded like Dolly Parton with a chest cold, and all I wanted to do was to find a way out of the mess I'd gotten myself into.

But I was really stuck. Despite a fresh infusion of prednisone, my legs and virtually everything else kept getting worse. My bladder was all but shot, and it was nothing for me to make seven or eight trips to the bathroom during a single four-hour airshift. Of course, each time I left the studio I had to have a piece of music on that would play long enough to cover me, and before a week was up I'm sure all five of our listeners were heartily sick of listening to the "Orange Blossom Special."

The old MS days were occurring almost continuously by then, and it became a real struggle to get through an entire airshift without falling asleep. I could relax while the music was playing, but every three or four minutes I had to pull myself up to a standing position, shake my head to clear the fog, and say something at least mildly entertaining into the microphone. It was beginning to be more than I could handle.

And emotionally I was in the worst shape ever. I could somehow still make it through the day at work with a smile on my face, but the underpinnings were beginning to crack. As it became more and more difficult to face my empty apartment alone each night, I took to passing the long winter evenings with Jane and Bill, basking in their company as a balm for my wounded soul. They were my escape and my refuge, a solid wall of support I could lean on any time the going got too rough.

But by December it was all but over. My legs had become so weak that crutches were now a full-time proposition, and my bladder had finally gone beyond all semblance of manageability. I finally realized it was time to call it quits the day I peed all over the studio floor and had to pour a full thermos of hot coffee onto my lap to cover up the mess I'd made. As soon as I got off the air that day I drove to Bill's office, wet pants and all, and with tears of shame streaming down my face, fell into his arms and told him I wanted to go home.

From that moment on Bill took over completely, and within forty-eight hours he had me packed and bagged and ready to go. He had taken care of everything, and all that was left for me to do was to break the news to Aunt Lucy.

But she didn't want to hear any of it. When I finally broke down and told her the truth of what had been going on, and all the reasons why I was leaving, she insisted that we merely call it a sabbatical. I would go to Pittsburgh, she said, do what I had to do to take care of things, and then hurry right back to Alaska. The station would be housed in its new studios by then and my job would be waiting for me when I returned. I didn't have the heart or the energy to explain to her that the problem was much more serious than she understood, and that chances were I could *never* come back. So I let it go at that and said goodbye to everyone with a lump in my throat. I'd actually grown kind of fond of all the craziness.

From then until the time my plane took off, I behaved as though nothing was wrong. The idea that I was really and truly leaving Alaska, maybe for good, was more than I could cope with considering the shape I was in, and once again I got through the hard part by pretending it wasn't happening. Somehow I managed to convince myself that what I was doing amounted to little more than a vacation, a chance to get away for a while and take it easy. It had nothing to do with multiple sclerosis, I told myself, or the fact that I could no longer live in the world I had created.

But Bill wasn't nearly so good at pretending, and when we finally kissed goodbye at the airport that night, I was astonished to see that he was crying.

＊ ＊ ＊ ＊ ＊ ＊ ＊ ＊ ＊

The first thing I did when I got home to Pittsburgh was sleep for a month. I was completely worn out, and all I wanted to do was hide away and forget the rest of the world existed. Dad and Annabelle hovered over me like guardian angels, making sure I was well fed and taken care of, and when I finally came out of my coma I was feeling rested, revived, and stronger than I'd been in months. Strong enough, even, to begin the rounds of the doctors.

First up was a urologist, who told me a lot of things I didn't want to hear. I learned that as a result of the progression of the disease, my bladder had gone from a flaccid state to one of almost constant spasm, and that this was the reason for my endless and embarrassing incontinence.

It helped to know the cause, but all I really cared about was what could be done to fix it. I knew such things as catheters existed and I wondered out loud if I might be a candidate for one. Absolutely not, he insisted. The very idea was too dangerous even to consider. The only things I could do were to watch my intake of fluids and to take a drug called Pro-Banthine, which should dry me right up and make my life a whole lot more manageable. Oh yes, he added, I might consider a pair of rubber underpants and a sanitary napkin too, just in case . . .

That was just great, I snapped angrily—rubber drawers and a Kotex for my bladder. What was he going to have me do next, wear a diaper?

I never should have opened my mouth. Diapers *would* be the best all-around solution, he admitted, and if I could bring myself to do it, a box of Pampers might not be a bad idea.

That was it. I told him where he could stuff his Pampers, grabbed the prescription off his desk, and walked out of the office in tears. There had to be a better way.

My next appointment was the one I'd been dreading from the start. The time had come to meet with my original doctor for an examination and a long heart-to-heart about my condition. I hadn't seen him for a couple of years and I wasn't at all sure I wanted to hear what he had to say. But there was no way to avoid it. I needed his help and the only way to get it was to face the facts. And as far as I was concerned, the news couldn't have been worse.

For now, he said, it looked like the disease had shifted from its original, relatively benign course of annual attacks and remissions to a slow but steady pattern of progressive deterioration. Of course I'd figured all that out for myself some time ago, but there was something about hearing the words out loud that made it sound like a death sentence all over again, and I felt my eyes fill with tears as he continued.

He took my hand and held it as he explained how unpredictable the disease could be. I could wake up one morning to find all my symptoms had disappeared completely and forever, or it could just as easily go the other way. There was simply no way of knowing. The wisest thing to do, he urged, was to continue to live my life as fully as I could for as long as I could, and to remember that there was still every chance in the world that I'd never wind up in a wheelchair. In the meantime we would run another IV course of steroids and hope we'd get lucky this time.

We did, and it was while I was in the hospital that I made the decision to return to Alaska. If he meant what he said about living my life for all it was worth, then for me that could only mean one thing. I would spend whatever freedom I had left by the mountains and the sea, in the place I loved above all others. I might not be able to climb those mountains anymore, and maybe I could never sail away again to the far side of the horizon, but if just by being there I could somehow keep that life alive, then that's what I wanted to do. It was the easiest decision I ever made.

I stayed at home for another two months while I worked to build up my strength as much as possible, and by the time I was finally ready to leave I was actually in pretty good shape. I'd gotten a real boost off the steroids this time around and the results were more than promising. My sense of balance had returned, I was back to using just one cane, and best of all my bladder was functioning almost normally. I wasn't taking any chances, though, and tucked away in my luggage was a prescription for Pro-Banthine, six pairs of rubber pants, and—just in case—a big box of super-absorbent Pampers.

The mood at the airport the night I left for Anchorage was upbeat all the way. If my parents had any misgivings about my leaving, they managed to hide them from me, and it seemed like we were all filled with a blazing sense of optimism. Things were going to be just fine this time around. They *had* to be. Everyone had tried so hard.

TEN

— ▪ —

Anchorage
March, 1981

I COULDN'T BELIEVE ALL the changes at the station. The new location was perfect and everything in the building was fresh and clean and professional-looking. Even master control and the production studios were carpeted and soundproofed and filled with all kinds of fancy new equipment I couldn't wait to get my hands on. But what really surprised me was the way the station sounded.

The music I hated so much was gone and in its place was a much brighter, Urban Cowboy type of format. Despite the fact that it was still country, and therefore (to my mind) dreadful, it was a whole lot better than it used to be, and I actually found myself excited at the prospect of taking over my old midday airshift.

But typically, things didn't work out quite the way I had them planned. The Arbitron ratings had been released during my absence, and while the station itself remained firmly in the cellar, I learned that my own personal numbers had come up something like a billionth of a point. As a result, I was to be accorded the honor of filling the station's premier on-air position, the six-to-ten A.M. "drive-time" slot.

While it's true that morning-drive really is radio's showcase spot and most announcers would jump at the chance to fill it, for me the pronouncement was a disaster. The very idea of getting up at four-thirty in the morning in order to be on the air at six sounded more like a punishment than a promotion. And anyhow, all it really meant was that now I'd be filling the number-one spot at the worst radio station in the world. For my money, the distinction was hardly worth the sacrifice.

I begged and pleaded with Aunt Lucy to reconsider, but she wouldn't budge. The deal was non-negotiable, she insisted. I could either take it or not, the choice was up to me. So, since I was in no mood to go looking for another job, I did the only logical thing, and that's how I happened to go down in history as Anchorage's first-ever female "morning man."

It was now my job to wake everyone up in the morning, put my arms around them and let them know they had a brand-new day to screw up. But six A.M. was still six A.M., and I'm afraid I didn't do any of it graciously. Most of my early-morning airshifts started off something like this:

"Good morning boys and girls, it's 6:05, it's raining, and I don't know why in God's name I'm here. You can get up and go to work now if you like, or you can roll over and sleep until Christmas for all I care. It's all the same to me. But since they're paying me to sit here either way, I guess we might as well get started."

Then I'd punch up a song and sit swilling coffee for an hour while I chain-smoked Kools and tried to pry the sleep from my eyes. By seven I was usually okay, but that godawful first hour was miserable and I never did get used to being up and alive that early in the morning. I never got any nicer about it, either. But strange as it sounds, people actually seemed to enjoy the abuse, and little by little the audience began to grow. There's a moral in there somewhere, but I've never been able to figure out what it is.

Once I got settled in and adjusted to the routine, I was surprised to find that except for that first damnable hour, the world of early-morning radio wasn't nearly as bad as I'd feared. And before I knew it, April, May, and June had come and gone with little in the way of trauma.

Happily, everything else stayed relatively calm, too, especially in the area of my health. I still walked like a sailor on a three-day pass, but other than that I was in remarkably good shape. My bladder hadn't been a real problem in months and I don't remember having more than two or three MS days in that whole stretch of time.

Admittedly I was in no position to take anything for granted, but I was beginning to wonder if maybe the doctors hadn't called this one all wrong. As far as I could tell, the progressive phase of the disease seemed to have turned itself around completely, and instead of the slow deterioration everyone had predicted, I appeared to be in the middle of a long and stable remission. The longer it held, the more complacent I became, and before too long Jane and Bill and I were back to our wild and wicked ways.

It's difficult to explain to anyone who's never experienced it, how utterly simple it was for me to slip back into my old, familiar lifestyle, as though nothing had ever been wrong. Certainly the cane was always there as a reminder, but I'd been carrying it for so long it had become the status quo, and in the absence of any other symptoms it was easy to assume once again that the problem had cleared itself up for good.

Part of the reason was the enormous sense of invincibility I still carried around inside me. Like everyone else my age, I was sure that all of the really terrible things in life happened to *other* people, to strangers who were somehow equipped to cope with whatever came their way. None of it had anything to do with me. I was special, after all. People had been telling me that all my life, and everyone knew that special people always came out on top.

So I was going to be just fine, thank you. I was young, strong, confident, and lucky to be surrounded by friends and family who cared. With all of that in my favor, what could possibly go wrong?

* * * * * * * * * *

The morning of July 4 dawned bright and clear, but the instant I awoke I sensed that something was wrong. I was groggier than usual, my legs felt limp and sluggish, and the blankets covering me felt unusually heavy. I struggled to sit up and investigate.

The bed was soaked. The sheets, blankets, and pillows were a sodden, dripping mess, and the nightgown I was wearing was icy-wet and clammy against my skin. But where had the water come from? I pushed back the blankets to see and almost choked at the smell. The odor was sharp and unmistakable, and when I realized what it was, I began to fall apart.

Not today God, please. There's too much going on and I can only cope with one thing at a time.

Eldridge Cleaver was due in the studio that morning and all week long I'd been nervous about the interview. It had been almost fifteen years since the Black Panthers first unleashed their fury on America, but I was a true child of the sixties and the frightening image of their anger and violence was still vivid in my mind. I needed every bit of confidence I could muster, and now everything was ruined.

But still I had to go to work. It was too late to call in sick for a six A.M. show, and besides, no one else was even vaguely prepared to do the interview. So, angry and upset, I got out of bed, peeled off my wet nightgown, and headed for the bathroom and a shower. Afterward, I tried hard not to think about what I was doing as I opened the closet door and reached for a box of Pampers.

The interview went a lot more smoothly than I'd anticipated and was, in fact, somewhat of a letdown. Instead of the fire-breathing revolutionary I'd expected, I found myself face to face with a dignified, soft-spoken gentleman who looked like he could have been anyone's much-loved grandpa.

We talked quietly for an hour or so about rape and murder and the insanity of the sixties, and when he left we shook hands politely, professional to professional. He must have sensed my disappointment, though, because a few minutes later he poked his head back in the studio, smiled, and raised his fist to me in that old defiant gesture. Burn, baby, burn . . . Now, *that* was the Eldridge Cleaver I remembered so well.

He hadn't been gone five minutes when my bladder started acting up again. Disgusted, I jammed the "Orange Blossom Special" into the tape deck, grabbed my cane, and took off in the direction of the bathroom. Thanks to the Pampers I managed to make it in time, but obviously the problem was back again and somehow I was going to have to deal with it.

The Pro-Banthine proved to be far less than perfect almost immediately. It dried up my urinary tract as promised, along with everything else. My eyes and nose burned constantly, my head pounded with a resounding headache, and my mouth got so dry I found it impossible to speak unless I had some form of liquid nearby to sip. And as if all that weren't enough, I learned the hard way that the drug was extremely constipating, exacerbating the already severe difficulties I had in that area. All along I'd been trying to manage the problem with a regimen of laxatives and enemas, and so far I'd been fairly successful.

But all of that would change one cold, rainy Saturday afternoon, in the single most horrifying moment I've ever known.

I was shopping for groceries at Safeway and I'd gotten as far as the frozen food section when I felt a low rumbling from deep inside my abdomen. This was a welcome sign, one that meant I wouldn't have to rely on my usual dose of laxatives that night. With that in mind, I finished shopping quickly and headed for the front of the store.

The line at the checkout counter was unusually long that afternoon, and I was only about halfway to the register when I noticed that the rumbling I felt earlier was getting louder and more insistent. Wisely, I decided to leave the shopping for another day, but as I turned to go I was suddenly doubled over by a powerful, violent cramping in my abdomen. The pain was unlike anything I'd ever felt before, and I clutched at the shopping cart for support as one huge spasm after another tore through my body like shock waves from some massive internal earthquake.

What was happening to me? I fought wildly for control—chest heaving, fists clenched—but it was hopeless. There was no holding back, and I gasped out loud as everything inside me let go.

There was an explosion in my brain, a fracturing of the senses, and in the space of just one second, everything I knew and believed in became a lie.

Oh dear God, I prayed desperately. Please don't let it be true. Please, in the name of all that is sane and rational, don't let this thing be happening!

But it *was* happening, and I stood alone, paralyzed with shame and horror as I felt the unspeakable mess slide down my legs, over my shoes, and out onto the floor of the supermarket.

A sudden, deadly silence fell over the store. People were staring in disbelief, the shock and disgust registering on their faces as they backed away slowly, into the safety of the anonymous crowd.

Please don't leave me alone like this, I pleaded silently, don't make me stand here all alone with no one to help, or I'll die.

I'm sorry God, I'm so sorry, I didn't mean for it to happen. I tried to make it stop but it wouldn't. It just kept coming and coming and now it's all over the floor and it smells, God, and I don't know if I can live through this. Where were you, you bastard? How could you have

let it happen? How could you stand by and do nothing while I plead-
ed and prayed, cried and begged, and then shit on the floor of the
Safeway store? That's right, God, I shit my pants like a baby and you
watched and you didn't lift a finger to help. And now I hate you so
much. Do you hear me God? I HATE YOU!

My mind was racing out of control. I could feel the panic rising in
my throat, a hot, sick terror that swept aside everything but the need
to run. But I was trapped, surrounded on all sides by a frightened
mob. There was no way out, and the silence was growing deeper and
more ominous every second.

Then quietly, like a whispered obscenity, someone in the crowd
began to laugh. Within seconds the others joined in, and as the laughter reached a crescendo I felt myself falling to the floor . . . as everything around me faded to black.

I have no memory whatsoever of leaving the store that day, of getting in my car, or even of driving home. The next thing I remember I
was lying naked in the bathtub, clutching at my stomach and screaming into a towel as the shower poured down on me and washed away
the filth.

But there wasn't enough water in the world to ever make me clean
again, or to wash away the stink of humiliation that would cling to
me forever. My body had betrayed me in the foulest way imaginable
and the loathing and revulsion I felt was indescribable.

I got into bed that night and lay awake until morning, staring
blankly at the ceiling, hurt and more ashamed than I'd ever been in my
life. But I didn't cry and I didn't pray, and I didn't ask God for absolu-
tion. What was the point? *I* wasn't the one who needed to be forgiven.

* * * * * * * * * *

So it was time for another attack, I thought to myself with disgust.
But so what? I'd been through it all before and I'd get through it once
again. I called the doctor right away and he ordered up another big
round of steroids, hoping at least to lessen the severity of the damage
the MS would do. Surprisingly, the ACTH actually helped a little, but
as the attack wore on and on and my stamina decreased, I began re-
moving from my life everything that wasn't absolutely essential.

Work took precedence over everything else, and before long virtually everything I did revolved around those four hours I spent on the air each morning. I started drinking Kaopectate by the quart to make sure I stayed constipated all week long, then on Friday I'd down an enormous amount of laxatives and spend the entire weekend in the bathroom, cleaning myself out for another week. I was tearing myself apart inside, but I didn't care. I never wanted to live through another incident like the one at the Safeway store.

As hard as it was to take, I forced myself to swallow a big dose of Pro-Banthine every morning and then followed it up with five or six aspirin to take care of the headache that was sure to follow. Between the medication, the rubber pants, and the Pampers, I usually managed to stay dry while I was at work, but nothing was guaranteed and I sweated it out every day.

When my vision was bad I left my car at home and took a taxi to work, refusing to put myself or anyone else in jeopardy on the road. If there was something I had to read on the air, I took a copy of it home with me the night before and memorized it, hoping fervently that no one would decide to make any last-minute changes in the wording. I was terrified at the thought of going blind, and refused to acknowledge it was even a possibility.

But what worried me most were my legs, especially the left one. It had become even weaker than before and when I walked anywhere it was slowly, tentatively, like an old woman would. I had to concentrate totally on every step I took, and before long I became one of those people who truly couldn't walk and chew gum at the same time. It was especially rough at work, considering the number of trips I had to make to the bathroom, and by the end of a four-hour airshift I was utterly spent.

When I signed off the air at ten in the morning, it was all I could do to drag myself home and fall into bed. Completely done in, I'd lie there all day long, hoping to recover enough strength just to get up and fix myself something for dinner. After that I'd get back into bed and sleep until four-thirty the next morning when the alarm went off, waking me up so I could get out of bed and struggle to do it all over again.

It was an unbelievably difficult way to live, and sometimes even now I ask myself how I ever did it. Or more precisely, *why*? The only answer I can come up with is that I did it because I had to. As tiring and painful as it was to make it through each day, to take more than fifteen or twenty steps at a time, I did it because the only other alternative was, at that point, unthinkable to me.

But I wasn't pretending anymore. I knew how close I was to losing it all, and for the first time ever I became conscious of the need to fight. There wouldn't be any avenging angels to pull me out of the fire this time around, no medical miracles to save me from the dragon. Whatever time was left would have to be won at the expense of everything else and, no matter what it took, I vowed to carry the fight to the very limits of my strength and ability.

Any fear or self-pity that I might still have harbored inside me was swept aside by a fierce, blinding anger, and it was deep inside that anger that I found what I needed to keep on going. How could I think of quitting now? There was still a world out there I had to live in, and I made up my mind that no matter how bad it got, the face I showed to that world would be smiling.

I would do in private whatever it took to maintain my facade in public. If that meant crawling around the apartment on my hands and knees when I was too fatigued to walk, or waking up mornings in a noxious sea of my own waste, then dammit, that was exactly what I'd do. But I wasn't giving an inch. This attack couldn't last forever, and when it ended I promised myself I'd be standing tall and strong, with my dignity and sense of humor intact. I probably would have made it, too, had I not gone and done something stupid like falling in love with Tony Stone.

* * * * * * * * * *

Aunt Lucy made the big announcement at one of our weekly staff meetings in August. After a long, directionless summer she had finally gotten around to finding another program director for us, something she'd been promising for months. In the interim she'd been doing the job herself, an odd arrangement with predictably laughable results.

It's important to understand how crucial a program director can be to a radio station. It's his/her job to train and direct the announcers, keep the music fresh and current, conceive and carry out on-air contests and promotions, and oversee the day-to-day operations of the station. It's a demanding job, one that requires a lot of radio background, humor, and creativity—qualities Aunt Lucy appeared to have in short supply, if at all.

It was amazing to me how much she'd changed since the first time we'd met. She'd been so open and enthusiastic then—a woman eager to set the world on fire with her nerve and bold determination. But lately she'd become oddly secretive and cynical, making decisions about the station that, in my opinion at least, bordered on the ridiculous.

From that standpoint alone, I was glad to hear we were getting a replacement, but by then I was convinced she was just setting us up for yet another loser. God knows we'd had more than our share already.

But this one wasn't like all the others, she insisted. He was a real pro, a popular radio personality who really knew his stuff. He was a young, bright programming genius and, to hear her tell it, radio's version of the Second Coming. My only response was to yawn loudly and check my watch. I'd heard it all before.

Besides, we'd all grown quite comfortable with our place at the bottom of the Anchorage radio market, and if there was one thing we didn't need, it was some troublemaker who wanted to come in and shake up the solid level of mediocrity we'd all worked so hard to achieve. Somehow it just didn't seem fair. But in the end we decided we'd ride it out and wait to see what the genius had to say.

We were all feeling bored and resentful as we filed into the conference room to meet our new leader on the day he arrived. It was only ten o'clock in the morning, but of course I was wiped out already, and judging by the way the other guys looked, they all felt pretty much the same way. Most of them were sprawled carelessly around the big wooden table, feet up, heads somewhere off in the ozone. As B.J., my old skipper would have said, we were one sorry-looking pack of assholes.

But the moment Tony Stone walked into the room and began to speak, everything suddenly changed. The energy and enthusiasm he radiated were irresistible, and in no time at all we were wide awake and attentive, sitting up straight in our seats, hanging on every word he said. Even Mason Davis, our cynic-in-residence, seemed impressed.

It was hard not to be. For starters, he was wearing a coat and tie, a phenomenon all but unheard of among on-air people, especially here at the Lazy-K Ranch. But that was just the beginning. He looked like a cross between a Beach Boy and Warren Beatty—golden hair, big brown eyes—and every time he flashed that incredible smile of his, it was like someone had turned up the wattage in the room. I took one long look and decided he couldn't have been more perfect if I'd dreamed him up myself. The effect he was having on me was anything but a professional one, and as the presentation went on it was all I could do to tear my eyes away from his face and concentrate on what it was he was saying.

The first order of business, he insisted firmly, was to dump this godforsaken country music format *immediately*. Willie and Waylon and the boys were being put out to pasture for good, and from here on in KANC would be known as Anchorage's "Number One Adult Music Station."

All RIGHT! Rock 'n' roll still lived! None of us could believe it at first—it was like we'd suddenly landed in Oz and from here on in everything was going to be wonderful. Ding dong, the wicked witch was dead! All the other jocks were jumping up and down, yelping like a happy litter of puppies, caught up in the hysteria of the moment. I was so excited I was shaking—this could really be it!

But my euphoria quickly turned to despair as he went on to outline his plan for the big transformation. For the next forty-eight hours straight we were all expected to camp out at the station, where we'd work in shifts to complete the taping of an entirely new rock 'n' roll music library.

Following that, after the new format debuted on Monday morning, each of us would be required to work a *minimum* of eight hours a day at the station. There would be no more dashing out of the studio at the end of a four-hour airshift for this crew. Life as we knew it at the Lazy-K was about to come to a screeching halt. If we expected to become a real radio station, he declared, we were going to have to start acting like one.

It sure looked like the end of the line for me. I was pushing myself to the limit as it was, and I couldn't even imagine trying to keep up with the kind of schedule he was calling for. So as soon as the meeting was over, I asked if I could speak with him privately. I explained my situation briefly, and told him that because of it I was willing to resign from the staff, effective immediately. It broke my heart to have to say it, but there was simply nothing else I could do.

Nonsense, he said, blinding me with another one of those megavolt smiles. Aunt Lucy had already filled him in about me and he didn't see where we had a problem at all. Of *course* it went without saying that I would be excused from the weekend marathon and all the extra weekday hours. The morning show was going to be my one and only responsibility and he would do everything he could to make sure it was the best one on the air.

In the meantime, I should go home and get all the rest I could, since Monday morning looked like it was going to be a real circus. Oh, by the way, he asked casually as I turned to go, would it be okay if he stopped by my apartment later that evening for a while? He wanted to pick my brain a little about the way the station operated.

How could I say no? He was new in town, he was the best-looking thing I'd seen since meeting Bill Werber, and if there was anything to the law of averages he wasn't going to be around for very long. So I gave him directions to my apartment and said I'd expect him around eight. Then I walked out to the parking lot, got in my car, and swore out loud as my bladder emptied all over the seat.

He got to my place a little early that night, but I was ready for him. I'd taken a long nap, a double dose of Pro-Banthine, half a dozen aspirin, and all the Kaopectate I could swallow. By the time he arrived I was showered, diapered, and dressed—utterly determined not to embarrass myself in front of the boss.

He brought a bottle of scotch with him, and as soon as the drinks were poured we settled down on the sofa and proceeded to get to know one another. The conversation developed easily, the way it does when two people sense from the start that they're going to become good friends. He was curious about my illness, so I told him as much as I was comfortable with, then sat back and pretended to listen to the story of his life. But that was just a cover. All I really wanted was an excuse to prolong the evening.

Everything about him appealed to me, from his murderous wit to the easy, careless way he was dressed. There's something downright sexy about a soft woolen jacket and jeans on a man, and the way he wore them made me think of lumberjacks and poets and long winter nights by the fire. It's a combination I've never been able to resist.

I'd never known anyone remotely like him before and I was captivated by his openness and candor, and by the sheer, unstoppable force of his personality. But I was concerned for him, too, and more than a little worried about the plans he had for the station. It went without saying that he had the very best of intentions, but I'd already seen whole battalions of program directors come and go, and I wasn't sure he had what it would take to go head-on with Aunt Lucy and win. Besides, did he really expect to take that ungodly mess of a station and turn it around in the space of one short weekend?

Sure he did. The new format fell into place as scheduled, and on Monday morning we commenced to rock 'n' roll.

The change was almost unbelievable. Overnight we went from being the worst radio station in the world to one with real potential. All we needed was development, and that, make no mistake, was what Brother Stone had come to town to give us. He was the Messiah and we were his True Believers, a band of dedicated disciples privileged to kneel at the foot of the master.

I remember the first time he kissed me. Anchorage was buried under a deep fall of snow and we were parked in a field on the outskirts of town, watching the sun go down over Cook Inlet. As usual, the heater in his little green MG wasn't working and we were bundled up under a pile of blankets, sipping brandy out of paper cups. The sunset was spectacular that night, and neither one of us spoke as the last crimson rays burned across the water and turned the sea into a glowing pool of molten copper.

In spite of the brandy we were shivering, and when he reached over to wrap his scarf around me, his fingers brushed softly against my cheek in a gesture so carelessly intimate that I nearly cried. My breath caught in my throat as I felt his arms circle my shoulders and then he was kissing me, and I was kissing him back wildly. The deal was sealed. I was crazy nuts in love.

But it was hopeless from the start and I knew it. I had no business getting involved with anyone at that point in my life, especially someone like Tony. We had no history together, and certainly no future. As a newcomer to my life he had no way of knowing what it meant to live the way I did, or what it cost me just to make it though each day. As far as he knew, I had a little difficulty walking and that was the extent of the problem. He didn't know about my other life, the ugly, secret one I lived when no one else was looking.

And he never would. I didn't want him or anyone else feeling sorry for me, or telling me how "brave" I was, or what an "inspiration" it was to be around me. And I didn't want to be an exception in his life, either—someone he had to make excuses or apologies for. All I wanted to be was the girl who lived on the air from six to ten each morning. She was strong, feisty, fiercely independent, and more than a match for the likes of Tony Stone.

But that girl hadn't ever really existed. She was someone I'd made up a long time ago in the hospital, the day they told me I had MS. A part of me had stopped living in a very real sense that day when I, purely subconsciously, created another person to live *for* me, one who could face the world boldly, with spunk and spirit, and a courage I never possessed. As long as she was out front, running strong, I was safe. I could hide away and pretend my turn would come some day. And when it did, I'd sprint across the finish line and fall triumphantly into my lover's waiting arms.

But nothing like that had ever been for real, and I was just then beginning to accept what I'd known in my heart to be true all along.

There had never been anyone waiting for me in the distance, no shining knight, no handsome prince. There would never be anyone to love or honor or cherish me, or tell me I looked pretty in the morning, or bring me roses on my birthday. All those things were meant for other people, for people with futures they could share together. None of it was ever meant for me.

Ever since the diagnosis was pronounced I'd been searching for a hero, for that one impossible dream of a man who could wrestle with the dragons, drive away the demons, and somehow save me from the peril of the sword. But there weren't any heroes anymore; there was only Tony Stone, a mere mortal, and the very last chance I would ever have to love someone physically and wholeheartedly.

For almost half a year he and I worked and played together side by side, and through it all I felt as though I'd been given a shot of some powerful, magical potion that allowed me to keep on going, far beyond the limitations I'd set up for myself. Tony had the drive of ten men his size and, crazy as it sounds, it seemed like I actually *walked* better when he was around.

When he made love to me I was beautiful. I could close my eyes and fly away and pretend I was the woman he'd been searching for all his life—I could take him with me to faraway places where princes rode white stallions and fairies slept in fields of stardust. If only I could keep him with me somehow, safe in the land of make-believe, then nothing would ever have to change and tomorrow would always be waiting.

But that was the problem. Tomorrow *was* always waiting, and no matter how hard I fought and scratched to keep it at bay, tomorrow—like the sword—would always be there, waiting to take it all away.

* * * * * * * * * *

All through the fall and early winter I managed to hold everything together, but by December the facade was beginning to crack. The pace I'd set for myself was too much, and when the long months of frantic activity finally caught up with me, it was too late to stop the inevitable.

At first all I noticed was a worsening of my original symptoms. Both legs were noticeably weaker, my vision was cloudy, and once again I found myself making more and more urgent trips to the bathroom. But I'd been through all that before and wasn't especially alarmed. What did frighten me, though, were the strange *new* symptoms that began to appear and then disappear almost daily.

All of a sudden my skin began to burn. It felt as though someone had poured kerosene all over me, and then struck a match to it. It hurt like crazy and I remember sitting up in bed for hours, rubbing my arms and legs with lotion, trying to put out the fire.

And my sense of touch seemed to be all confused, as though my brain had gotten everything backwards. Hot water felt cold and vice versa, and if I stuck myself with something sharp, like a pin, it felt like someone was tickling me with a feather. And worst of all, whenever

Tony touched me his soft hands felt like sandpaper, rasping and scratching against my skin. It was maddening and it was getting worse all the time.

I became exquisitely sensitive to heat and had to be careful any time I was in the bathtub. If the water was too warm and I stayed in too long, my muscles turned to jelly and refused to move until I'd soaked my entire body in frigid water for at least half an hour. I learned to allow myself plenty of time in the bathroom, and just to be on the safe side I began bathing in the evening instead of early in the morning before I went to work. I was learning to adapt, but still I was unprepared for what happened a week or so later.

At first I thought I was having a seizure. I was taking dinner out of the oven when the pot-holder slipped and my fingers accidentally brushed against the hot pan. Suddenly, both of my arms and legs went rigid and began to shake uncontrollably as the pan flew from my hand and sailed across the room, narrowly missing Tony's head. The spasm only lasted a second or two but it was enough to terrify me, and early the next morning I called the doctor and told him what had happened.

He'd been expecting something like this, he said, and went on to explain what the symptoms meant. The spasms, the burning, and the confused sensations were all the result of a short-circuiting in my brain. As the disease ate away at the myelin sheath, my central nervous system had gotten all mixed up and was now sending jumbled, inappropriate signals to all the different parts of my body. But regardless of what was causing them, he said, the symptoms had to be brought under control. Hoping to slow everything down, he prescribed another round of steroids and we waited nervously to see what would happen.

But the effort was in vain. My legs grew weaker, the spasms got stronger, and the fatigue finally threatened to overwhelm me. I was running out of steam, and fast.

I began having nightmares again, terrible, frightful dreams filled with horrifying images of death and mutilation. Hideous creatures prowled through the darkness and waited, panting, in the shadows of my mind. Their mouths were foul with vomit, and the open sores in their skin crawled horribly with fat white maggots. In the darkest part of each night they came for me, into my bed, where they would rape

179

me again and again and again until I awoke screaming in Tony's arms.

He'd hold me tightly then, and beg me to tell him what was wrong. Where did it hurt? What could he do to help? But I couldn't tell him anything about the dreams or why they frightened me so badly. They were all a part of my secret life, the one he knew nothing about. The most I could do was reassure him that nothing was really wrong, and that everything would be fine in the morning.

It wasn't until later, when he was safely asleep, that I opened up my heart and told him everything I wanted him to know. I told him how much I loved him and how I'd always known he didn't love me back, but that it was okay. It was enough that he was there beside me, and if he couldn't stay forever, then please would he stay as long as he could?

I told him all about the life I'd lived and who I was before he knew me. I talked about the places I'd been and all the wonderful things I'd seen, and I tried to make him understand how much it meant to know I would always have the memory of those years to cling to, long after the running stopped and everything else was gone.

But mostly I told him how scared I was, and how tired of the ups and downs and the devastating attacks. The fight had gone on too long, and now with the end so close I wasn't sure I had the strength I needed to make it to the finish. I'd tried too hard for too many years to hold back the clock, running as fast as I could in a race I would never be able to win. But the race was almost over now, and I didn't know how to let it end.

I told him how terrified I was of what was coming—of the day when my legs finally stopped working. Who would I be if I couldn't walk anymore? Would I still be me? Or would I just be a *thing*, a pathetic cripple to be stared at and pitied and then forgotten?

There was so much I wanted to say, and all through the night while he slept I made my confession. When morning finally came I brushed back the hair from his eyes, kissed his cheek softly, and curled up warm and close beside him, safe for just a little while longer.

* * * * * * * * *

At first I thought I was just being paranoid, but it was uncanny— even sort of spooky—the way the station seemed to be falling apart as fast as I was. Tony had done an unbelievable job of turning things around; the music was tight, commercial time and ratings were up, and all us on-air types were sounding hipper and better than ever. But by late December it was obvious to everyone that we simply weren't going to make it.

All the elements for success were in place, but more and more we found ourselves being met with resistance from higher up. A long time ago someone had hung the moniker "Mad Aunt Lucy" on our esteemed owner, and now the reasons why were becoming increasingly clear. From where we sat she appeared to be self-destructing, making one disastrous decision after another, almost as though she were deliberately trying to fail. It was frustrating to say the least, and before too long the tension began to affect everyone. Morale plummeted and we quickly went from being a tight, cohesive band of committed crusaders to a ragtag collection of dispirited second-raters who felt as though they'd been betrayed.

I think the collapse affected me more than it did anyone else, for the simple reason that I tended to identify so strongly with the person I was on the air. That, and the fact that I had little else left in my life by then outside of Tony and the work we did at the station. But by the end of December it didn't matter anymore.

The first time I fell it was because I wasn't watching where I was going. Pooch, my big, lazy cat, was sleeping on the rug by the bed, and when I got up to go to the bathroom I tripped over him, lost my balance, and crashed headlong onto the floor. Luckily I wasn't hurt, but when I tried to get up I found my legs wouldn't bear any weight at all and I fell back clumsily against the dresser. Tony rushed over and tried to help me up onto the bed, but when he lifted me in his arms my bladder opened up and poured all over the floor.

I was so embarrassed all I could do was cry. I'd tried so hard to keep the truth from him and now it had finally caught up with me. My secret was out and I felt hot tears of shame burning down my cheeks as I turned to him and tried to apologize. But he just smiled sadly and held me close while he called the doctor and arranged for a room at the hospital.

For the next five days I slept, wet the bed, and prayed.

Please God, get me out of this in one piece and I'll do anything you ask. I'll go to church twice a day, I'll sing in the choir, I'll even give all my money to charity. Just don't let it end this way. If you take my legs away from me now, I don't think I can make it. I'm not ready yet, God, so please give me just a little more time.

Nurses crept in and out of my room constantly, changing the bed, fiddling with my IV, and doing the thousand little things necessary for my comfort. I did my best to get along with them, but early one morning when the head nurse came in with a wheelchair and said it was time to go downstairs for a mandatory chest x-ray, something inside me snapped.

"Get that thing out of here RIGHT NOW!" I screeched wildly. "Take it away and don't you ever bring it in here again. DO YOU HEAR ME?"

She turned white at the outburst and tried to explain that it was just a routine procedure. *Everybody* rode in a wheelchair to be x-rayed. It was safer that way, she insisted, and standard hospital policy.

I told her I didn't give a fat rat's ass about her hospital *or* its policies, and added that if she didn't get that wheelchair out of my sight immediately, then there was a real good chance she was going to need one herself in short order. It wasn't my proudest moment, but the sight of that wheelchair did something to me and I reacted blindly, out of fear.

Shortly before I was released, Doctor Bowers came in to see me and we had a long heart-to-heart about where I was headed in the future. The steroids had helped some, he said, and my legs were a little stronger, but he didn't know how long it all would last. He said he was worried, too, about the lousy shape my bowels and bladder were in, and he warned me that the fatigue that dogged me constantly was only going to get worse if I didn't slow the pace down some and give my body a chance to rest.

I had to start taking it easy, he insisted, and added that it might be a good time to think about heading back East for some help. There were big rehabilitation centers there, he explained, places where they knew all about MS and the problems associated with it. There was a lot I could learn in a place like that, he stressed, and it wouldn't be a bad idea to have my parents close at hand for a while.

I thanked him for the advice and promised I'd give it a lot of serious thought. But in the meantime, I explained carefully, there were still a few things I wanted to finish, and if he could keep me patched up for just a little while longer I'd tough it out as best I could. I knew he had my best interests at heart, I said gently, but I wasn't quite ready to give it all up yet.

Not yet God, please, I need just a little more time. There's so much I have to think about and so many things I still have to do. If you can slow it down even a little, God, then maybe I can make it. I promise I'll be good and I'll never ask you for anything else ever again, if only you'll help me now.

Several days after I was discharged, Aunt Lucy announced she was scrapping our new format and intended to automate the station, putting all of us out of work. We were dumbfounded. What could she possibly be thinking? We had all worked so hard and poured everything we had into making the station a success, and now that it was actually starting to happen, she was going to pull the plug. I couldn't help wondering why she didn't just shoot us all in the head and get it over with right away.

Her decision meant the end of virtually everything for me. There was nothing left to fight for anymore, no reason to go on beating my head against the wall. Everything was gone now, and soon Tony would be leaving, too, for another place and another life far away.

I remember thinking that if only I could hold on to him tightly enough, then maybe I could make him stay. But holding on to Tony was like trying to carry water in my arms, and the night he kissed me goodbye forever and walked away without a backward glance, I finally understood. I'd never been anything more to him than just another lonesome girl in another lonesome city, and the truth was I'd never really known or loved *him*, either. Like all the others, he was just another hero I'd made up, someone strong enough to help me through the night.

After he was gone I sat on the sofa for a long time, staring into the darkness, wondering what to do next. But just then I couldn't seem to focus on anything. I was drained of all feeling and emotion, and I felt as though I'd been beaten up and left for dead. Now all I wanted was to go far away, to someplace safe where I could lick my wounds and maybe regain a little strength.

But when I tried to get up off the sofa, my legs wouldn't move. There was nothing left, and my only reaction was one of dull surprise.

So this was it. The moment I'd been dreading for so many years was finally at hand, and there was nothing but silence to mark the occasion. No bells went off, no doors slammed shut, and no one came to carry me away. There was just me and the reality of the moment. The sword had fallen. The clock had finally stopped ticking.

I sat quietly for a while until my heart stopped pounding, then with steady hands and a calm voice I called Bill at home and asked him to bring me a wheelchair.

Everyone came to say goodbye. Jane and Bill were there as always, and even Cindy and her new husband, Jesse, made the long trip up from Kenai to be with me on that last day. It's a funny thing about good friends, the way they pull together in times of trouble, and as we sat around the table at the airport bar that evening I remember thinking how lucky I was to have found the very best.

If it hadn't been for all of them I never would have made it through the last several years, and now the thought of saying goodbye was more than I could bear.

The snow was falling softly, and as the big jet circled Anchorage one last time, I looked out and saw the Chugach Mountains far below me, their sharp, snowy peaks shining white in the hazy winter moonlight. It was the sight I loved above all others, and as the plane roared off into the frosty purple night I pressed my face against the window and began to cry.

I'm coming home, Mom, I whispered softly into the darkness. I messed everything up and now I'm coming home.

ELEVEN

Pennsylvania
Summer, 1982

IN MY WILDEST DREAMS I never imagined a rehabilitation center would look like this. I don't know what I was expecting—a snake pit, maybe, a dark and frightening world filled with maimed and broken bodies, a place where hopeless cases came to die when no one else could help them. But what I found instead was a world-class, state-of-the-art facility, one that bore more of a resemblance to a fancy resort hotel than anything else.

The complex itself was immense, covering acres of thickly wooded countryside and overlooking a lazy, bluewater river that meandered by, reflecting back the colors of the trees and wildflowers gathered along its banks. It was pretty spectacular, and a lot to take in at once.

But the thing I remember most clearly about that first trip through the Center was the unprecedented sight of hundreds of people in wheelchairs all going about their business unconcernedly, as though there was nothing even vaguely unusual about the manner in which they were doing it. I wasn't sure how I'd react to a sight like this, but instead of the confusing tangle of emotion I'd expected, all I felt, finally, was an overwhelming sense of relief.

This was where I belonged now. I was home at last with my own kind, safe in a world where everyone was just like me. I didn't have to make excuses anymore, or apologize for the way I looked. Here I was free to be exactly what I'd become—a thirty-year-old multiple sclerosis patient who was bewildered, apprehensive, and more than just a little scared at the thought of starting her life over from scratch. The people here would understand, though, because they were different, too, and they knew what it meant to be less than perfect in a world that held perfection as its standard.

But it wasn't going to be easy and I knew it. I had a lot to learn about life in a wheelchair, and if I meant to make a go of it, then I was going to have to work harder than I'd ever worked before. My battle against the disease was only just beginning and it was here I would find the ammunition I needed to carry on the fight for the rest of my life. With all that in mind I signed the admission papers eagerly, grateful for the chance I'd been given and determined to make the most I possibly could of it.

Patient education was the Center's first priority and mine began immediately. As soon as I was processed in and installed in my bed, a team of nurses arrived with a videocassette machine and a stack of instructional tapes. Surprisingly, some of it was actually interesting.

I learned that Unit Six (where I would be staying) specialized in the treatment of spinal cord injuries (broken necks and backs) and brain and central nervous system diseases, the scope of which included multiple sclerosis, cerebral palsy, Guillain-Barre syndrome, and the like. Once in a while there would be an amputee or stroke patient admitted when space allowed, but most of the Unit's fifty or so residents were of the basic spinal-cord variety.

Patients were separated into two broad categories—paraplegics and quadriplegics. The paras (which now officially included me) were essentially without function from the waist or hips on down, while the quads were usually paralyzed from the chest or even the neck down. Generally speaking, the higher the injury to the spinal cord, the more severe the disability.

But regardless of the classifications, there were certain management problems common to virtually everyone with any kind of spinal cord "involvement," as it was termed, and it was during the discussion of these that I first became aware of the medical profession's great and abiding love for the euphemistic form of expression. Why call a spade a spade when there are so many other ways both to confuse the issue and to protect everyone's Calvinistic sensibilities?

For example, if you should happen to wake up one morning to find the sheets full and your bladder empty, take heart. You haven't peed, or whizzed, or even so much as wet the bed. All you've done is had an "incontinent episode" or, even more politely, "voided." It sounds kind of cute actually, something Princess Di or even Nancy Reagan might do on occasion.

By the same token, you'll be relieved to know that the embarrassing mess in your pants isn't what you think it is at all. It's merely the result of an "involuntary bowel movement," or simply an "involuntary" for short. Either way the result is the same, but who knows? Maybe it smells a little better if you use the proper terminology.

And on the subject of bedsores, it's important to remember that nobody gets them anymore. Ever. Now we develop "decubitus ulcers," "skin breakdowns," or, best of all, "areas." Such a precise little term that one is. "Areas" occur at pressure points—buttocks, hips, knees—any place where bones press against skin and restrict circulation. If the pressure isn't relieved periodically the skin itself begins to break down, and before you know it you've got yourself a nasty, ulcerated little "area" and more grief than you ever dreamed possible. But cheer up—at least it isn't a bedsore.

While I was listening and trying to absorb all the new information, I managed to pee, or rather, "void" twice, and by the time the doctor arrived the bed was soaked and I was on the verge of tears. It certainly wasn't the best way I could think of to make a great first impression.

But he seemed like a good egg and calmly proceeded with his examination as though this sort of thing happened to him all the time, which of course it did. The exam was the most thorough one I'd ever received, lasting well over two hours, and during that time he discussed with me in great detail where I was, medically speaking, and what would happen during the course of my long stay at the center. The disease had shifted from its original attacking/remitting pattern, he said, and had settled firmly into one of steady, debilitating progression. The fact that I was already using a wheelchair wasn't a good sign, he continued, and my best hope was that the progression would be a slow one. To that end, he and everyone at the Center would do everything they could to maximize my chances and see to it that I stayed as fit and as healthy as I possibly could. But the first order of business, he insisted, was to begin to get my bladder into better shape.

He explained to me how dangerous it was to leave it in its present condition, saying that if the bladder wasn't completely emptied regularly, the residual urine left behind would act as a breeding ground for all kinds of pesky germs. This could result in a horrible urinary tract infection, something we didn't even want to *think* about with MS. But there was a way to fix it, he said, and we were going to get started right away.

I was ecstatic at the news and enormously relieved to hear there was a solution to a problem I had long considered unsolvable. That is, I was ecstatic until I found out what the solution actually was. He told me a nurse would be in shortly to catheterize me and then, believe it or not, she was going to teach me how to do it myself! That way—if I took the necessary medications, watched my intake of fluids, and cathed myself every four or five hours—I could keep myself dry, avoid infection, and go through the rest of my life smelling like a rose.

I said it all sounded wonderful in theory, but he was out of his mind if he thought for a minute that I would even consider doing something like that to myself. But he just nodded curtly, scribbled something in my chart, and left the room without a backward glance.

Fascist. The aforementioned nurse arrived moments later carrying everything she needed—sterile gloves, a cleansing solution, a tube of lubricant, and the catheter itself—and immediately got down to business.

Simply put, the procedure involved passing a long, plastic tube through the urethra and up into the bladder itself, a feat she accomplished easily and with remarkable precision. Other than the humiliating position I was forced to assume, there was really little in the way of discomfort and I thought I bore it all with a great deal of dignity and grace. But that was just a temporary condition.

There was something about the thought of forcing a foreign object that size into an opening that small that caused my hands to shake and my face to sweat, and by the time I was ready to begin the air was filled with tension. Suddenly the thought of spending the rest of my life wet and smelly didn't seem like all that bad an idea.

But my pride was at stake here, so I swallowed hard, took a deep breath . . . and screwed the whole thing up.

While the nurse had enjoyed the clear advantage of being able to see what she was doing, I was reduced to operating strictly by touch, and it immediately became evident that this was the source of the problem. I wasn't sure where anything was to begin with, and every time I put the catheter in the wrong place (don't even ask) I had to throw it away and start all over again.

To make a long story short, it wasn't until two hours, three temper tantrums, and eleven catheters later that I finally met with success. By then I'd attracted quite a crowd of nurses, and at the moment of victory the room exploded with the sounds of cheering and applause. I almost felt like standing up and taking a bow.

But I'd done it. And in the doing, I marked a major turning point in my life. For the first time ever, I'd taken control and stolen something back from the disease, something I'd never thought would belong to me again. In addition, I learned that I truly was capable of doing *any-thing*. If I could learn to cath myself—and I'd just done it, hadn't I?—then nothing was beyond me, and there wasn't a person alive who could tell me there was.

It was a giant step forward, and later that evening when I went out to the lounge to meet the other patients for the first time, it was with an empty bladder and a brand-new feeling of self-confidence. Maybe there really *was* hope for me after all.

* * * * * * * * * *

"Nuuurse . . ."

"Nuuuuurse . . ."

"NUUUUUURSE!! . . ."

God, it was annoying. And it was hard to believe all that noise was coming from just two little old men. They were wrapped up in blankets and lying on hospital carts in the corner of the lounge, right beside the nurses' station. Neither one of them seemed to be in any real distress, but still they kept on yelling, louder and louder, in spite of the fact that no one was paying them the slightest bit of attention. I decided everyone in the room must either be deaf, crazy, or comatose. There was simply no other explanation.

Sitting at the big wooden table in front of the nurses' station was a small group of young guys in wheelchairs who were playing poker and laughing uproariously at one of the nurses, who'd just spilled an entire pitcher of prune juice all over herself. The oldest of the group looked to be somewhere in his mid-thirties, and when he spotted me sitting by the doorway he waved and invited me to join the table.

"Hi, I'm Gino!" he announced cheerfully. "You new?"

"Well, I got here early this morning," I answered. "But I've been with the doctor most of the day."

"Oh yeah, Brezhnev. You'll hate him. Matter of fact you'll hate everything about this place once you've been here long enough. Got a smoke?"

Just as I was reaching into my pocket, one of the old-timers let loose with another loud shriek and I jumped, startled, at the sound.

Gino just laughed. "Pay no attention to the Veg-O-Matics," he said offhandedly. "You'll get used to them soon enough."

"Pay no attention to the *what*?" I asked, horrified.

"Those guys," he shrugged. "The strokies. They pull this shit all the time. Gets old after a while, too. You got another smoke for Mikey, here?" he asked, nodding toward the young black man sitting next to him.

I handed him another cigarette and as he lit it up he explained that Mike had broken his neck in a diving accident the previous summer, and as a result was now a quadriplegic, or as Gino so tactfully put it, "worth shit from the neck down."

"It's a real son-of-a-bitch, ain't it Mikey? Tell her it's a real son-of-a-bitch."

Mike allowed as how being a quad could be murder at times, and added that if he didn't get that cigarette *right now*, he was going to tell a certain nurse where a certain sorry-ass dago had hidden a bootleg pint of whiskey. (Booze was strictly forbidden on the Unit and possession of same was grounds for immediate expulsion.)

Gino smiled weakly, placed the cigarette between his buddy's lips, and went on with the introductions.

Eric "Nothing Beats a Great Pair of Legs" Britten was a double amputee who'd lost both of his lower limbs in a freak accident with a bus, the details of which were too gruesome to mention. He was a happy-go-lucky kind of a guy except when he was worrying about his artificial legs, which was almost constantly. And for good reason. Stealing Eric's legs had become the favorite pastime of everyone, nurses and patients alike, and any time he wasn't wearing them they were sure to disappear. As a result he spent most of his day prowling the grounds with a worried look on his face, perpetually in search of the missing appendages.

Sitting next to Eric in a big blue electric wheelchair was Bob Irvin, a CP quad and everyone's favorite character. The CP stood for cerebral palsy, an altogether unpleasant condition, but Bob rarely let it get him down. Despite the fact that his speech was severely affected by the disease, he could swear like a trooper and had no problem whatsoever keeping up with the generally rank level of conversation the group maintained.

The longer I sat there the grimmer the conversation got, and it didn't take long for me to pick up on the concentration camp mind-set of the group. Like any big institution, the Center ran on a set of rigid, inflexible rules, and since the staff was responsible for enforcing them, it was only natural that they would come to be viewed as the enemy. And like good prisoners of war everywhere, the residents of Unit Six were sworn to uphold the principles of liberty and justice for all, and to defend their God-given right to raise a little hell once in a while. To that end, the rules were accorded all the respect the "inmates" felt they deserved (which is to say, none), and patient-staff relations suffered mightily as a result.

While there were rarely any open acts of aggression, the undercurrents of insurrection were evident everywhere; the Unit was known as the "compound," the code name for the doctor was "Brezhnev," and even the nurses were commonly referred to as the "Quadriplegic Control Squad," or QCS. (There were a few wonderful exceptions of course, but you risked serious damage to your reputation if word got around that you were kissing up to the staff.)

The man voted "Most Likely to Kill a Nurse" was the fifth member of the group, a para introduced to me as Gabriel Dante Joseph Smith, the owner of the World's Most Amazing Bowels. "Shitty Smitty," as he was known to one and all, was a legend in the annals of rehab history in that he'd broken all existing records for the number of spontaneous bowel movements, or "involuntaries," recorded in a single month. But he wasn't revered so much for his prodigious output as he was for his unique sense of style, and everyone was eager to tell me the story of the time he actually caused one of the nurses to toss her cookies.

He'd just had one of his innumerable involuntaries and was lying on his side in bed while one of the young nurses labored mightily to clean him up. She was up to her elbows in the job and not really paying attention as Smitty reached into his dresser drawer and pulled out a huge bowl of chocolate pudding which he'd hidden earlier in anticipation of just such an opportunity. He quickly filled his mouth with the gooey, viscous stuff, then turned toward the nurse and, grinning his best demented grin, slowly squeezed the thick, brown pudding out through his teeth.

That was it. She took one look, lost her lunch, and a legend was born.

I was never able to confirm whether the story was true or not, but if it wasn't it should have been. Granted, it was obnoxious and juvenile, but then so was the idea of grown men and women living day in and day out with virtually no control over their most basic bodily functions. The only way to fight a reality like that was with humor, and as far as almost everyone was concerned, the blacker that humor got, the better.

So stroke patients became "Veg-O-Matics," the quads were known as "Talking Heads," and even the head-trauma unit on the second floor was regularly referred to as "Banana Town." Rough? I guess you just had to be there.

* * * * * * * * * *

The work began in earnest the next morning when I was given my daily schedule and told to report to Physical Therapy. "Morning PT," as it was called, consisted mostly of passive "range of motion" exercises. After you've spent any length of time in a wheelchair your muscles tend to tighten up and contract, and these "ranging" exercises were designed to keep everything as loose and as flexible as possible.

All you had to do was lie down on one of the big gray mats and close your eyes while a therapist took each limb in turn and put it through a series of soothing, stretching maneuvers. Once in a while you'd be assigned a real Nazi who'd get carried away and try to pin your ankles back behind your ears, but that was rare and for the most part the whole routine could be quite relaxing.

One patient named Tony Gianelli really knew how to enjoy himself during PT. He was about three hundred years old and senile as a bat, and he could always be counted on for a little entertainment in the morning. I guess when you get to be that old you tend to lose all your inhibitions, or maybe he was just too addled to know the difference. But either way, the minute a therapist got near him, old Tony went into his act. He'd moan and groan pitifully at the start, but within minutes he'd be sound asleep, snoring loudly, with his hands down his pants and a great big happy smile on his face. Considering his age and all, it was really something to see, and it just goes to show there really *is* life after eighty.

Next up was Occupational Therapy. Most of the work done here was from the waist up, with a lot of special emphasis on the hands. Reluctant fingers were encouraged to move again by putting them to work on a variety of tasks such as macrame, decoupage, ceramics, and the like. If you got stuck in OT and didn't like to do crafts, you were sunk. I didn't mind the crafts so much, really—it was just the atmosphere of the place that got to me.

I don't know what it is about occupational therapists as a group that makes it difficult for them to relate to anyone on an adult basis, but the way they talked made me crazy. You know the type: "How are we this lovely morning, Miss James? Would we like to do some finger-weaving today? Or how about making a darling little pot-holder?" It was maddening, and if I'd ever given in to the urge to tell her what it was that "we" *really* wanted to do, then "we" would have been bounced out on our backsides.

Luckily for me I was doing just fine from the waist up, and once everyone was satisfied that I was fully independent in that area, I was permanently excused from OT, much to the relief of everyone concerned.

In addition to morning PT and OT, the Center provided a wide variety of vocational and recreational therapies—homemaking instruction, psychological counseling, and so on, all designed to ease the transition from the able-bodied world to that of the disabled. But all of these miscellaneous programs were just a prelude to the main event of the day, which was Afternoon PT. This was the big one, the reason we were all there to begin with, and if there was *anything* on your body that still moved, you can bet it got a workout there.

The main gym was enormous, and it was filled with dozens upon dozens of patients, therapists, and every mechanical device known to modern rehab medicine—a bizarre study in chrome and sweat. Anywhere you looked, people with every physical disability imaginable were sweating and straining, pushing themselves to the limit in the never-ending quest for "physical restoration."

Off to the right was a big portable platform with a ramp and a built-in set of stairs where the amputees practiced walking on their artificial limbs. Eric Britten could always be found there, stumping around happily, delighted to have his legs firmly attached to his body once again. (We always made sure he got them back in time for PT.)

Both sides of the gym were lined with rows of gleaming, stainless-steel weight machines, and it was there that most of the upper-body conditioning was done. The procedure was simple; you'd park your wheelchair in front of one of the machines, set the brakes, grab the wooden handles, and sit there pulling repetitions until your arms seized up. It was hot, sweaty work, and for my money the most massively boring thing a human being could do. But it was necessary, because if you planned to haul your messed-up carcass *and* a fifty-pound wheelchair around for any length of time, you were going to need all the upper-body strength you could muster.

Most of the rear side of the gym was an area known as "Paraplegic Heaven," and it was here that the bulk of the restorative work was done. Two long sets of parallel bars were set up for the purpose of getting all the paras up and "walking" each day, in an effort to strengthen whatever little bit of muscle might be left.

But before you could even get started, you had to strap yourself firmly into your brand-new, custom-built, stainless-steel-and-leather leg braces and make sure everything was secure. Then, if you had any strength left at all, you were required to hoist yourself up to a standing position and "walk" back and forth endlessly between the bars, while a semi-sadistic therapist put you through your paces. I always felt like one of "Jerry's Kids" when I was in my braces and up on the bars, but damn if it didn't feel good to be standing again, however artificially.

Finally, "Wheelchair Skills" were taught outside the gym in a special area designed for just that purpose. The most functional thing you could learn to do in a wheelchair was something called a "wheelie," a stunt that involved jerking your front wheels up off the ground, and then balancing yourself on the big rear wheels while you performed a variety of maneuvers. These could include anything from spinning wildly in circles just for the sheer fun of it, to something more practical, like bouncing up and down a flight of stairs. Needless to say, these feats were only attempted by the young and strong of heart.

In addition to all the daily scheduled programs, each resident of Unit Six was required to attend a series of lectures on subjects ranging from catheter care to wheelchair "etiquette," and to meet weekly with representatives from the Psychology and Nutritional Departments.

I'm the only person I know of who ever admitted to enjoying the weekly visit with the psychologist. Everyone thought I was crazy (and consequently in *need* of the visit), but I saw it as a chance to sit and talk calmly and quietly with a woman my own age about weightier subjects than were usually discussed around the poker table in the lounge. Besides, she had the keys to the Biofeedback room, and I could always talk her into letting me strap on the electrodes for an hour or so while I cleared out my brain and drifted off into oblivion. She was my buddy, and I considered the hours passed in her company as time well spent.

* * * * * * * * * *

Overall, there was no denying the Center had really made a name for itself in the area of total patient care. It had a well-deserved reputation as a miracle worker, and the job it did in educating newly disabled people and their families could only be described as magnificent.

But there was more to rehabilitation than the purely mechanical functions of physical therapy and wheelchair skills. There was the emotional, human side, too, and it was here that the Center fell far short of my expectations. Most of the work in that area was done by the patients themselves, within the confines of the Unit where we lived together and occasionally made each other miserable.

It might not have been so bad had the Center paid more attention to the need we all had to be alone once in a while, to think our private thoughts and come to terms with the emotional aspects of the new realities we were all now facing. But, in fact, we were widely discouraged from indulging in such solitary pursuits. Instead, we were thrown together at every turn, and made to participate as a group in virtually every aspect of daily life. We ate together, slept together, worked together, and believe it or not, even showered and went to the bathroom together.

As it turned out, I wasn't alone in the difficulties I'd been having with constipation and its direct opposite over the past several years, and I was surprised to learn that the majority of spinal-cord patients experience the same kind of problems to one degree or another (witness Shitty Smitty). I was even more surprised to learn there was actually a solution to the problem, and that it had nothing to do with the use of either Kaopectate *or* mass quantities of laxatives. It was, however, just as uncomfortable.

"Bowel Training," or "BT" for short, was held promptly at six P.M. every Monday, Wednesday, and Friday, come hell or high water. Immediately after dinner we were all ordered to report back to our rooms, where the nurses were waiting and the stage was set for the greatest scatological extravaganza known to humankind.

Beside each bed there now sat a huge, plastic wheelchair, the seat of which had a large round hole cut out of its center. Beneath it on the floor was a big plastic bucket, and sitting next to that was a brown paper bag which contained the following: one disposable Fleet enema; a large tube of lubricant; five or six paper towels; and a handful of latex surgical gloves. (Hint: the gloves were for the nurses.)

The rest is best left to the imagination, but suffice it to say that the hours I spent sitting on that dreadful chair were among the most unpleasant I've ever known. The only consolation lay in knowing that everyone else was going through the same uncomfortable ritual just a few feet away. Since the doors to our rooms were always left wide open for the nurses' convenience, we were able to call out loudly to one another with encouragement, support, and up-to-the-minute progress reports, just like on the Waltons (Any luck yet, John-Boy?). There was no sense whatsoever in being embarrassed, so no one gave it a second thought as we broke down the barriers between us and explored new worlds of togetherness.

Hours later, after the long ordeal was over, we were all herded together into the large communal showers on either end of the Unit. It would have meant a lot in terms of dignity and self-respect if we'd been permitted to use the private, roll-in showers we each had in our rooms, but that would have meant some extra work for the cleaning staff, and was therefore disallowed.

All this forced togetherness could really wear on your nerves, and I'm surprised there weren't more open flare-ups of temper as a result. It was just that there was virtually nowhere you could go to escape the constant presence of other people, since *they* didn't have anywhere else to go either. And you could forget any thoughts you might have of seeking comfort in your room watching TV, or simply talking to friends and family on the telephone, since both were strictly forbidden.

If you wanted to watch TV you did it in the lounge, in your wheelchair, in the company of twenty or thirty other people, all of whom were laughing or talking loudly in your ear. And if you wanted to make a phone call, you waited your turn in line because the Unit provided exactly *one* standard pay telephone, to be shared by all fifty residents.

But that wasn't the worst of it. When your turn at the phone finally came, you had to conduct even your most private conversations publicly, since patients weren't accorded even the simple courtesy of a phone booth. Instead, the telephone hung on a bare wall in the center of the Unit, within earshot of every single resident. We all learned early on that our alleged "right to privacy" had its limitations.

All the restrictions might have made sense if we'd been in the charity ward of some big, public hospital. But the Center was a private facility, and with the price tag running as high as $15,000 per month, *per patient*, it was easy to see why resentment ran so high at times. People had a tendency to feel as though they were paying handsomely to be punished for something that hadn't been their fault in the first place.

197

But it didn't do a bit of good to complain, since Brezhnev ran the Unit with an iron fist and an inflexible turn of mind. His word was law and if you didn't like it, well, you could leave any time—there were always plenty of others who would be delighted to take your place. So how did we deal with it all? We played a lot of poker, broke a lot of rules, and never for a minute stopped bitching about the system.

It's important to draw a clear distinction here between bitching for its own sake and whining as a way of life. One should never be confused with the other, since the intent and result of each was different, and one of them could get you ostracized faster than admitting you'd voted for Ronald Reagan.

Bitching was considered healthy and was widely encouraged in thought and deed, especially among the younger population. If you let more than five or ten minutes go by without expressing, loudly and clearly, your displeasure with the world in general and the Center in particular, people all around you began to worry and your emotional stability was quickly called into question. As a result, the air was always filled with the sounds of cursing and profanity as, singly and collectively, we pledged our allegiance to the flag of the unsubtle protest.

Whining, on the other hand, was strictly taboo, and was simply not tolerated by anyone under the age of fifty. Some of the older patients (who should have known better) never stopped pissing and moaning, but in all the time I spent at the Center I don't remember *ever* hearing a young person whine, or cry, or even seriously complain about their personal woes out loud. Never. Not once. No matter how bad or how boring it got.

Undoubtedly, the hardest part of the day to deal with was the long, empty stretch of time between dinner and lights-out. The Recreation Department was charged with coming up with some type of diversion for us in the evening, and I guess they did try. But man does not live by Bingo alone, as the saying goes, and after BT and a shower, everyone wandered out to the lounge, looking for something to do until the nightly poker game got started.

If we were lucky, a new patient would have been admitted that day and we could all participate in his or her initiation. There were victims of a lot of unusual injuries on the Unit that summer, and we never tired of scaring the wits out of the poor, unsuspecting newcomers.

The "halos" really had an edge here. These were guys with freshly broken necks who'd had them set in metal, vice-like contraptions designed to keep their heads from moving while their vertebrae and spinal cords healed. The device itself rested on the shoulders and encased the head, cage-like, in a series of thick steel rods that were joined at the top by a wide metal band, or halo. This halo orbited the head in a wide circle and was fastened securely by half a dozen long silver screws that passed through the skin and were bolted directly into the skull.

It was a horrible thing to look at, and for that reason alone we always made sure Rob Lauriguet was around at initiation time. He had more fun with his halo than anyone, if such a thing is possible, and he loved to set everyone's teeth on edge with the story of how he'd been injured. (He was working under his car when the jack slipped and the car fell right on top of him, crushing his spine.)

The story itself was hideous enough, but things *really* got bad when Brezhnev arrived with his tool kit to tighten up the screws in Robbie's head. They have a tendency to work themselves loose and have to be adjusted periodically—an uncomfortable but certainly tolerable procedure.

You'd never know it by watching Robbie, though. The minute Brezhnev went to work with his screwdriver, blood began to drip from the holes in Robbie's skull and he'd start shrieking and thrashing about wildly as though the pain was unbearable. Meanwhile, the rest of us were screaming with laughter as the new kid hyperventilated and came close to passing out from the shock. It wasn't the nicest thing we ever did to anyone, but it was easily the most fun.

Like any large group of people thrown together for a prolonged period of time, we quickly developed our own social hierarchy, a class system based almost exclusively on luck and individual degrees of disability. At one end of the spectrum were the quads—specifically the high quads—who were paralyzed from the neck (or, God help them, even higher) down and could do virtually nothing for themselves. The unluckiest member of this group was Dave Frohlich, who'd been shot in the neck by a hunter and who could only operate his wheelchair by blowing into a tube attached to a motor (known as a "sip 'n' puff" chair). When someone like Dave asked you for something, you did it immediately, out of deference to his condition and respect for how tough it must have been for him to ask in the first place.

Next came the low quads, like Bob Morgan. These guys did have some use of their arms and hands, but only in the most restricted sense of the word, and they often required the aid of special devices to accomplish even the simplest tasks. For instance, if Bob wanted to smoke it was necessary to attach a fork to his hand by means of a wide velcro strap. Then a lit cigarette was wedged between the tines and that way, by swinging his arm up towards his face, he was able to smoke independently—independence of course being the key to everything. (Brezhnev *hated* these smoking devices, but the prevailing attitude was that he could go screw himself—no one would even consider giving up this one simple pleasure just to please His Eminence.)

After the low quads came the paras (like me), an infinitely more fortunate group by comparison. Paras could feed themselves, shower themselves, and, best of all, get themselves in and out of bed. This was crucial, because the rule on the Unit was that if you needed any help at all in that area, you went to bed whenever the nurses damn well felt like putting you there. This was often as early as eight o'clock, even on weekends, and was bitterly resented as the ultimate violation of an individual's personal rights. Paras, as least, could stay up until eleven-thirty or even later, if the nurses were decent and Brezhnev didn't catch you.

At the very top of the heap were the amputees, who, as a group, were considered to be some of the luckiest people alive. If that sends a chill up your spine, try to remember that everything is seen in relative terms in a place like the Center, and if you had to be there for any reason at all, the loss of a limb was a relatively minor one. I agree there can't be anything easy about losing a leg or learning to use a prosthesis, but the reality was that these people ultimately would strap one on and *walk* out of the Center, a distinction that made all the difference in the world to the rest of us.

As in any ordered society, rank had its privileges and obligations, and both were taken seriously by every single member of the group. Early on we got together and figured out it would take roughly 3.6 of us to make up one normal body, and armed with that scientific data we set about assigning specific tasks within the group. Gino was

responsible for the nightly poker games and it was up to him to shuffle, deal, and place the cards into little plastic racks for anyone who
couldn't use their hands. Eric was in charge of raiding the vending
machines on an hourly basis, and Tom "Sparky" Donohue (a para
who'd been struck by lightning) was responsible for emptying individual catheter bags and seeing to it that no one ever sprung a leak.

My job involved helping all of the quads to smoke, an effort I put
my whole heart into. It was up to me to light all the cigarettes, place
them in the proper mouths, and then flick off the ashes as they
burned. It could get confusing at times, depending on the number of
quads who were smoking, but I never burned anyone up and I'm
happy to say no one ever suffered nicotine withdrawal on my account.

Once the game got started it would be every man for himself, and
at first the betting was generally wild and reckless. But as the evening
wore on, things would quiet down considerably as a dozen old friends
who knew each other too well began to rehash the same tired conversation they'd had, night after endless night, for longer than anyone
cared to remember.

It took a while for the newness of it all to wear off, but after two or
three weeks I had the routine down pat and one day became just like
any other. The days were boring, the nights interminable, and before
too long the conversation was as familiar to me as it was to everyone
else.

* * * * * * * * * *

It would be difficult to imagine a place with more potential for
human pain and suffering than a rehab center. This was where the
worst cases came, people with bodies so hopelessly damaged it sometimes seemed doubtful they could even survive. That being the case,
the average person might be justified in thinking a visit to such a place
would be a depressing, even terrifying experience.

But they'd be wrong. And no one was more surprised than I was to
discover that suffering and hopelessness had little to do with what
really went on there.

A rehab center was a place for fighting back, not giving up, and all
the self-pity in the world wasn't going to help a bit. Everybody there

was in the same shape you were in, or worse, and no one wanted to hear your sad story—leastwise, they didn't want to hear it more than once. As long as you kept that in mind and did your best to hang on to your sense of humor, it was easy to fit in and find your place among the others.

Once you did, you had the sense of having joined the most exclusive club in the world. The dues were high, but the fact that you were sitting in a wheelchair was proof that you had paid them, and because of that no one ever questioned your right to belong. There was a special, unspoken bond between the members, and more than anything else I think it was this sense of "us" that got us all through the toughest times and kept morale from crashing through the floor. That and the bitching, of course.

But there was one of "us" who couldn't participate in anything at all. She was a young woman about my age, and if you looked closely you could tell she must have been pretty at one time. She had long, pale blonde hair, delicate features, and two of the clearest, bluest eyes you've ever seen. According to her parents, she'd been quite a skier not so long ago, one with real Olympic potential.

But all of that was gone now, destroyed by the disease. Her once-strong arms and legs were thin and wasted, the muscles atrophied, the bones hard and brittle. Her hands were useless, the fingers curled and stiff, and those beautiful blue eyes, now gone blind, stared out blankly from a face devoid of all expression.

Her name was Jenny O'Brien and she had multiple sclerosis.

I'll never forget the first time I saw her. She'd been strapped into an enormous padded wheelchair and she was thrashing about furiously, caught in the grip of a powerful spasm of some kind. Her arms were contracted and drawn up tightly against her chest, her legs jerked uncontrollably, and every time a new spasm ripped through her body, her head snapped forward and she cried out involuntarily. It was an ugly, grunting sound, but it was the only one she could make. She was unable to speak or see or move independently, and as I sat staring at her tortured body, I felt everything inside me give way.

So this is what it comes to, I thought dully. After all the running and all the wasted years spent pushing back the clock, this is how it ends—in a writhing, spastic dance as empty and meaningless as a vacuum.

From the very beginning, a wheelchair had symbolized the end of the line for me, but now I saw it was only the beginning. Looking at Jenny that day I let go of all my illusions and understood at last that there aren't any exceptions in this world. It didn't matter who you were, where you'd been, or even what you'd done with your life. If your number was up, it was up, and there wasn't anything in the world that would change that fact. Not even God.

Jenny wasn't special and neither was I. We were both caught up in the same fiendish nightmare, and there was no way out for either one of us. The only difference was that she had already run her race, while I, perhaps, still had a few more miles left to go.

I tried to imagine what it would be like to live the way she did—to wake up every morning knowing someone else would have to bathe me, feed me, dress me, and do *every personal thing* imaginable for me. To know that I would never again be able to read a book, or watch a sunrise, or even *speak* to anyone I loved. The image it brought to mind was horrifying, and in reaction all I could do was close my eyes and cry. I'd never be able to forget the way she looked that day, and while I knew in my heart there was still every chance in the world that I'd never progress to the point she had, I knew, too, that time and luck were now all that stood between us.

But time and luck meant everything with MS, and so far I hadn't done too badly in comparison with Jenny. I still had my arms and hands, after all, and in the world of the disabled, nothing, absolutely *nothing*, was more important. A wheelchair in and of itself was a nuisance, and sometimes a painful one, but it sure as hell wasn't the end of the world. As long as my upper body remained strong, much of what I considered important in life was still possible, and I made up my mind at that moment to stop feeling sorry for myself and just get on with my life.

* * * * * * * * * *

Discharge day came and went without much in the way of ceremony and I returned to my parents' home in Pittsburgh feeling somewhat disjointed and unfocused. Uncharacteristically, I had no real sense of what I wanted to do at that point, and for the next five or six months I ambled around aimlessly, just waiting for something to come along. My car had been equipped with hand controls during my stay at the Center, so I spent much of my time traveling around the state, visiting friends and relatives I hadn't seen in years.

But by the time the following summer rolled around I was beginning to grow bored and restless, and I decided it was time to think about going back to work somewhere. Nothing in particular sounded very tempting, but at the very least I needed to put *some* sort of structure back into my life, some reason to wake up and get out of bed every morning.

But late in June of 1983, an unfortunate accident occurred. I was sitting in front of the stove, boiling a large pot of water for spaghetti, when somehow my sleeve got caught on the pot's handle. As I reached to untangle it, the pot overturned and I screamed frantically as a full half-gallon of boiling water poured directly onto my lap, searing my thighs, legs, and feet with its blistering heat.

The ambulance ride to the hospital was a blur of blinding pain, and when I arrived at the emergency room I was given a local anesthetic and treated for a series of first, second, and third degree burns extending all the way from my groin to the raw and bleeding tips of my toes.

To make a long story short, I spent what seemed like an eternity flat on my back in bed, immobilized and completely stoned from the narcotics needed to control the pain. When the whole ordeal was over and I was finally able to move again, I was dismayed to find that I'd lost all the ground I had gained at the Center, and more.

All my strength was gone and the stress of the burns had brought on another major attack of the MS. Add to that—incredibly, almost unbelievably—an emergency appendectomy, and my run of bad luck had taken on almost epic proportions. As a result, I had no alternative but to go *back* to the Center and start all over again from scratch. This time it would mean an even longer stay than before, involving months and months of arduous and painful therapy. I was almost physically sick at the prospect.

But I got through it. And thanks to the physical therapists and their relentless prodding, I actually ended up in better shape than I was in after my *first* stay at the Center! From the waist up I was in prime condition—I could do push-ups and lift weights with the best of them, and my arm, back, and shoulder muscles were as strong as a gorilla's. I was absolutely thrilled with the progress I'd made, and so was everyone else.

As my second discharge date approached I began to think seriously about what I planned to do when I got out. Work was a priority, of course, but I still had plenty of options open to me and I wasn't too concerned about finding something interesting.

Surprisingly, it was actually my bladder that still worried me the most. Granted, I'd come a long way in that area, but the need I still had to cath myself regularly made the thought of leading any semblance of a normal life all but impossible. The problem was a huge one for me, and I fretted over it for weeks without coming up with an answer. Finally, I stumbled upon it almost by accident.

Depending on their medical condition and their ability or inability to cath themselves, some of the patients were equipped with a device known as a Foley or "indwelling" catheter. This little wonder was nothing more than a long rubber tube which could remain in the bladder for weeks at a time, obviating the need for regular, intermittent self-catheterization. Of course I'd always known they existed, but up until then I'd never paid them much attention.

But the more I thought about it, the more I realized the idea wasn't such a bad one after all. If I had a Foley, I reasoned, my freedom and independence would increase tenfold. I could drink *whatever* I wanted (including beer!) *whenever* I wanted and never again worry about being incontinent. Best of all, I could finally forget about cathing myself, something I was now doing as often as five or six times a day. It was a simple, efficient way of dealing with the problem, and I couldn't help wondering why I hadn't thought of it before. As soon as I could, I grabbed one of the nurses and asked her to tell me more about the magical little gadget.

She explained that the catheter itself was anchored in the bladder by means of a small, water-filled balloon at its tip. The other end was attached to a piece of surgical tubing that ran down the leg and was, in turn, attached to a small plastic bag worn strapped to the calf. This was where the urine collected, and it was a simple matter to empty it

205

every couple of hours as the need arose. Best of all, she said, the catheter only had to be changed every two weeks or so, and any damn fool could see the advantages of that.

The news couldn't have been more welcome. I told her it sounded exactly like the sort of thing I needed, and asked her to fix me up with one of the rigs as soon as possible. But she just shook her head and rolled her eyes. That was something I'd have to take up with the doctor, she insisted. Foleys were *way* out of her jurisdiction. I couldn't see what the big fuss was all about, but I said I'd ask Brezhnev first thing during rounds the next morning.

I did, and he exploded. Absolutely NOT! he cried, highly agitated. A Foley was entirely out of the question! It was far too dangerous, he insisted, and did I want to spend the rest of my life horribly infected, waiting for my kidneys to turn black and rot away? Was that what I wanted? *Well? Was it?!*

He really was a fascist. And it's also worth mentioning that he wasn't the one paying the bills. Intermittent catheterization can be an obscenely expensive proposition, and according to my calculations I was looking at a price tag of up to $600 a *month*, just to stay dry. While I had a lot of respect for Brezhnev's opinion on matters such as these, the issue was just too important to trust to one man's judgment. After all, it was *my* life we were talking about, not his, and in the long run I was the one who had to live with the consequences. Keeping all that in mind, I gave the subject a great deal of thought and ultimately did what I'd planned on doing all along and installed the Foley. It's a decision I've never regretted, and one that eventually even Brezhnev came to support fully.

Having solved all that, I still faced the problem of deciding on what I planned to do with the rest of my life. I spent months trying out one idea after another, but for some reason nothing sounded right. The longer I spent trying to settle on something, the harder it became to ignore the one thought that kept running through my brain.

I couldn't stop thinking about Alaska and everything I'd left behind up there. The thought nagged at me like a broken record, and I played it over and over again in my mind. I spent hours sorting through old snapshots, and I daydreamed constantly about the people and places I loved and missed so much. It had been almost two years since I'd left, but still I ached with loneliness and the need to wake up each day to the early morning gold of a pure Alaskan sunrise.

But it was absolute foolishness to torture myself with such thoughts. Alaska was an impossibility for me now, and any idea I had about returning was utterly out of the question.

Or was it?

Of course it was. Young women in wheelchairs simply do *not* get on airplanes all by themselves and fly six thousand miles from home to live alone in a place like Alaska. They stay at home with their families where they belong, and they live in nice, safe places, and work at nice, normal jobs, and do their best to make it all come out okay. That was how it was done, and there was absolutely nothing wrong with the plan. Case closed.

It was a good argument, but I wasn't buying a word of it. Why *couldn't* I go back? I was still the same person I was when I left Alaska, the only difference being that now I couldn't walk. But so what? I was accustomed to living in a wheelchair by then, my car was equipped with hand controls, and—thanks to the spectacular job the Center had done—I knew all there was to know about living within my limitations. I'd be safe enough, I reasoned, as long as I was careful and used whatever common sense I still had left. Besides, all my friends were there, and I knew from experience that I could count on them for all the help and support I would ever need.

Sure, there was no way of knowing how long my condition would remain stable, or what the result of another attack might be, but all things considered I was in terrific shape. The Foley catheter was working splendidly and I'd learned how to "manage" my bowels. And above all, the ultimate, most important, most vital thing in the entire world was in place—I still had my arms. I still had my arms. I still had my arms. And that was all that mattered.

By the middle of February I was ready to go. My car and everything I'd need had been shipped ahead to Anchorage and all that remained was to say goodbye to my parents at the airport.

This time they were a little shaky. It must have taken an enormous amount of courage to let me go once again—this time in a wheelchair—and if they'd asked me to stay I probably would have, simply out of respect. But to their eternal credit, that's one thing they've never asked me to do.

The takeoff was a smooth one and as the plane climbed up through thirty thousand feet, I closed my eyes and did my best to ignore the burning sense of numbness that was creeping slowly up my left arm.

TWELVE

Anchorage, Alaska
February, 1984

ANCHORAGE HAD BEEN CAUGHT in the grip of a wild arctic blizzard all day and by the time I arrived at midnight, the entire city was buried under a deep blanket of snow. Winter had always been my favorite time of year, and as Bill and I made our way to his home through the silent city I kept my eyes on the mountains and the vast black canopy of the sky, afraid that if I blinked or even looked away for a second it would all disappear forever. Once again I was overcome by the realization that no matter how well I thought I'd remembered it, the *reality* of Alaska would always far surpass anything I could conjure up in my mind. I was overjoyed to be back.

Thanks entirely to the willing help and abundant generosity of Jane and Bill, I was able to quickly reclaim most of what I'd left behind. Within a matter of weeks I found a place to live, landed a terrific job at the big, multinational brokerage house where Bill had become a highly paid vice president, and put together a circle of friends, old and new, who were caring, supportive, and always eager to lend a hand whenever I found myself in a jam. It was almost as though I'd never left.

As the winter wore on we gradually settled into a relaxed routine that centered primarily around work and seemingly endless games of Trivial Pursuit. I still have fond memories of marathon games that stretched on and on, far into the wee hours of the morning, and I remember now how warm and secure I felt with all my friends gathered around me. They were confined, too, not by their bodies but by the weather, and as long as it kept on snowing I had all the fun and companionship I could handle.

But with the coming of spring and summer all of that began to change. The days grew longer and warmer, and soon everyone was involved in typical Alaskan activities like hiking, fishing, and camping, none of which I could readily participate in. Of course I was always invited and I *could* have gone along, I suppose, but it would have meant an extraordinary amount of work and inconvenience for everyone else, and that would have defeated the entire purpose of the trip. So while everyone else was off enjoying the long summer days, I could usually be found alone at home, with little more to do than worry about my left arm and hand, both of which seemed to be growing a little bit weaker every day.

The numbness I'd first noticed during the flight to Anchorage had been slight, and when it disappeared a few days later I'd forgotten all about it, assuming it to be nothing more than excitement over the trip. But now the numbness was back again, and I knew from experience that no amount of wishing, hoping, or denial was going to make it go away. The remission was still holding, but I was under no illusions anymore that it would last indefinitely. The time I'd spent in the rehab center surrounded by people like Jenny O'Brien had proved to me that no one was exempt from pain and suffering; the worst in life could always come to pass, even to the best and strongest of us.

Whatever lay ahead would be mine alone to deal with, and I wanted to face it the way I always had—an hour and a day at a time. In the meantime I resolved yet again to keep moving forward, and somehow I found what it took to open myself up completely to all of the possibilities still left to me. It got a little scary at times, but for the rest of that wonderful year I worked hard, played hard, and once—for just a brief and shining moment—I even managed to fly.

My mom arrived in July for her long-awaited annual visit, and by way of a surprise I'd arranged for a midnight hot-air balloon ride to celebrate the occasion. Initially I wasn't even sure I'd be able to go along, but our pilot, Ted Sthal, assured me the wheelchair wouldn't be a problem at all. There was plenty of room in the basket, he said, and the added weight wouldn't make that much of a difference. Good old Annabelle was beside herself with excitement as we drove out the Old Seward Highway to the launch site, and I remember thinking that if for some reason we didn't make it through the flight, at least she'd die a happy woman. It seemed the least I could do for her under the circumstances.

Everyone was waiting for us when we arrived. Jane had volunteered to join the chase team on the ground and several other friends were there with their video cameras, hoping to make a record of the great event for posterity. Ted and his crew of four were hard at work in the open field behind us and had already begun the slow process of filling the enormous balloon with superheated air.

There's something about the sight of a hot-air balloon that is irresistible to most people. I'm not sure what it is—maybe it's the bright colors, or just the sheer size of the thing that captures the imagination—but it's impossible to look away once you've caught sight of one of the serene giants floating silently overhead.

There must have been a lot of dreamers out that night, because the field was full of onlookers by the time we got into the basket and prepared to take off. There was a flurry of activity as safety lines and pressure gauges were checked, and while the ground crew shouted last-minute instructions to everyone around us, Mom and I smiled and waved at the crowd, eager to leave them all behind and get on with the business of flying.

At a signal from Ted the ground lines were released and we all held our breath excitedly, waiting for the ascent to begin. But like the first wobbly seconds after a rocket is launched, nothing happened. The basket hovered just inches off the ground—almost, but not quite, airborne—and I remember the disappointment I felt at the thought that we weren't going to fly after all.

Then, suddenly, there was an enormous boom as Ted fired the propane jets, and like a silent, ghostly monolith the unwieldy craft shook off her earthly ties and rose proudly into the sky. We were off! The crowd below us was cheering excitedly, and as the basket cleared the rooftops I turned my face toward the sky, waiting for the first exhilarating rush of flight.

But it never came. There was no wild sensation of takeoff, no noisy explosion of power and thrust. The lifting-off was gentle, like an idea taking shape, and in the time it takes to remember your name we were there, high above the earth, looking out over the world like giddy explorers on a quest for the magical land of Oz. At midnight in July the skies over Anchorage are flushed with the pastel colors of twilight, and we floated soundlessly through wide, shimmering sweeps of pink and blue and violet so intense they colored the very clouds and made everything around us seem dreamlike and surreal.

Below us, the city looked like a toy, something built to scale for a child of three. From five hundred feet up we could still make out individual buildings and cars, and it was fun to watch Jane's Jeep and the other chase cars scurrying around on the ground, trying to stay within striking range of us in case we touched down unexpectedly. Once in a while, just for the fun of it, Ted would fly so low that the bottom of the basket grazed the treetops, allowing us to pick pine cones off the very highest branches.

But the best part of the flight for me was when we flew so high that the city no longer existed. Thousands of feet up, all that mattered were the mountains and the sky and the awesome silver reaches of the sea. The kingdom of the clouds is a silent one and no one spoke above a whisper as we drifted gently over the rugged peaks of the Chugach Range and looked down on the secret, far sides of the mountains. Slowly the years fell away and I felt wild and free and invincible again, and I remembered quite clearly why I'd come to Alaska in the first place.

For the better part of two hours we stayed aloft, lost in time and space, unwilling to admit we couldn't stay forever. And when the time finally came for us to return to earth, we did so only with the greatest reluctance. The world seemed like an intrusion all of a sudden, a noisy, noxious interruption, unfit for human habitation.

Annabelle was thrilled with the ride, and the rest of her visit was spent in a flurry of activity, each of us eager to do as much as we could in the short time we had together. I didn't mention anything to her about my arm and hand, but I sensed she knew something was wrong; when we finally said goodbye at the airport two weeks later, there were tears in her eyes and a worried look on her face.

* * * * * * * * * *

At that time in Anchorage there were several groups and programs in place that were dedicated to making a wide range of outdoor activities available and accessible to the disabled population. These activities ranged anywhere from wheelchair hiking and camping to more ambitious pursuits such as skiing, horseback-riding, and even open-water kayaking. The idea was to have fun while promoting physical fitness, self-reliance, and independence, and most of the programs enjoyed excellent reputations for providing all three.

Late in August I was invited to join one of these groups on a white-water raft trip down the Chickaloon River, a favorite ride among sportsmen in the area. I'd done my share of rafting before and I knew how much fun it could be, as long as care was taken to follow safety regulations and avoid any unnecessary risks—white water is no place to be if you don't know what you're doing. While the Chickaloon wasn't a world-class river by anyone's standards, it could be rough in spots, and at first I was concerned about the idea of a disabled person going along on a ride with so much potential for danger.

But Linda, one of the able-bodied group members, assured me that the guides we'd be using were real pros and that they had tons of experience on the Chickaloon *and* with disabled people. There was no cause for worry, she insisted, since we'd be in good, safe hands and the trip would be very, very wonderful for everyone concerned.

She sounded knowledgeable and sincere, so like the optimistic fool I've always been, I took her at her word and agreed to go along. Bright and early Saturday morning I drove the eighty-some odd miles north of Anchorage to our destination, and joined up with the rest of the group.

We numbered eight that day including me, four able-bodied helpers (Linda, Derek, Jason, and Steve), our guides Rick and Gretchen, and one other disabled person, a young, extremely spastic quadriplegic named Jay Garber. Jay had a severe case of cerebral palsy and couldn't voluntarily move any part of his body from the neck down. His arms and legs were pulled up against his body like twisted, brittle matchsticks, he was unable to speak intelligibly, and every time someone touched him or even bumped gently up against him, he went into a series of hard, violent spasms that threatened to throw him out of his wheelchair.

Since leaving the rehab center I couldn't remember having seen a body in such bad shape, and I remember thinking that the idea of taking him along that day was an insane one at best. But Linda assured me again that they really *did* know what they were doing, and that everyone, Jay included, would do just fine and we'd all enjoy a splendid afternoon on the river.

Beyond all that, my first real hint of trouble didn't come until we arrived at the end of the long trail leading to our launch site and I got a good look at the river itself. It was swollen and colored a cold, deadly gray, a mammoth stream fed by late-season glacial runoff, heavy with silt and bad temper. Rivers only look like that when they're running hard, their speed and volume greater than the channels that contain them, and the Chickaloon that day was as mean-looking a river as I'd ever seen. The noise it made was deafening, and we had to shout at one another in order to be heard above it as it roared its way downstream. I didn't like the look of things at all.

I also didn't like our guides, Rick and Gretchen. They were the sort of people I've always resented on principle—members of the Outdoor Elite, effete snobs who lived on trail mix and granola bars and who looked down their noses at anyone who didn't share their commitment to the great outdoors. But since I was about to place my life in their hands, I held my tongue and watched without comment as they went about their business.

The two large rubber rafts were inflated quickly and carried to the edge of the riverbank where they were lowered down a steep drop of about six feet into the water. Immediately the current grabbed ahold of each, and if it hadn't been for the thick ropes lashed to two sturdy logs, both would have been swept away instantly by the river's irresistible pull.

It was right then that I realized these people were crazy. Only a group of lunatics would consider risking their lives under conditions such as these, let alone the lives of two disabled people who were entirely at their mercy. But before I had time to react, Gretchen took hold of my wheelchair and pushed it to the edge of the cliff, then hollered "Bombs Away!" as she tipped it forward and dumped me into the arms of the two men waiting below. Jay followed immediately afterward and the two of us stared at each other mutely as Rick and Derek stowed us side by side in one of the rafts, then strapped us into the bulky orange life jackets that were required wearing for anyone on the river.

While the two of them were making last-minute adjustments to the tow-ropes and safety lines, Gretchen, Jason, Steve, and Linda jumped into the second raft and got themselves ready to go. A minute later the tie lines were released and both rafts were swept, spinning crazily, out to the center of the stream. At that point there was no turning back, and I remember thinking that all we could do then was hold on tight and hope the river gods would be merciful.

For the first quarter-mile or so we were okay. Rick, who was piloting our raft, seemed to be in control and we were all able to relax a little and look around us at the spectacular scenery as it flew by on the left and right. We were going a lot faster than I would have liked, but as long as the raft remained upright and we avoided some of the more serious turbulence in the center of the stream, I was willing to overlook the rough start and give the alleged "pros" the benefit of the doubt.

But disaster struck almost immediately as we rounded the first big bend in the river. By then our raft was far ahead of the other one, so we were first through the canyon and, consequently, the first to run into trouble.

Straight ahead, no more than a hundred yards away in the middle of the river, rose an enormous gray block of stone, surrounded on all sides by tons of angry, boiling white water. My first instinct was to panic, but I quickly realized that there was plenty of river on either side of the rock—more than enough room for us to get safely around, as long as Rick stayed firmly in control and didn't do anything foolish.

But instead of taking some form of evasive action like any rational person would, he seemed, incredibly, to be heading straight for the center of the stream! The raft was out of control, moving faster and faster, and the gap was closing rapidly. Collision was imminent.

At the moment of impact, everything went into slow motion. I saw the front end of the raft rise up slowly against the boulder and I remember thinking how odd it was that we were stalled in the middle of this wild river, and wondering how long we'd have to wait there before someone came to rescue us.

People were screaming all around me but I couldn't hear a thing. It was as though I'd been wrapped in a thick layer of insulation that cut off all sound. Sight was the only sense that registered, and what I saw next was a scene I'll never forget.

The entire right side of the raft had succumbed to the fury of the river and was in danger of collapsing altogether, leaving Jay only inches away from the raging water. Terrified, I reached out and grabbed for his arm, hoping to pull him to safety, but I was too late. The side of the raft buckled under the pressure of the water, and the last thing I saw of him before he was sucked beneath the surface was the look of sheer, blind terror in his eyes.

I grabbed for the safety line and hung on with every ounce of strength I had, but a split second later the entire raft capsized and I felt the stinging bite of the water as it closed over my head and dragged me down into its freezing depths.

I was caught in an underwater whirlpool, a powerful black maelstrom that pushed me deeper and deeper as I struggled furiously to regain the surface. My brain was screaming for air and I clawed frantically for a grip on something, *anything*, to help me hold on.

Seconds later, with every molecule of oxygen gone from my bloodstream, reflex action took over and I opened my mouth, breathed in deeply, and fell asleep, overcome by the darkness all around me.

But miraculously I hadn't died, and when I finally regained consciousness I found myself alone in the river, far from the overturned raft, caught in the raw fury of the rapids. Like a piece of flotsam I was swept helplessly downstream as the numbingly cold water drained all the strength I had left from my body. Incredibly, though, I didn't feel the cold at all. Instead, the icy river raging around me felt as warm and soothing as bath water, and the blazing sun overhead was like a furnace, burning hot against my skin.

Clearly I was in shock, a dangerous condition under any circumstances, and one which could become life-threatening very quickly. But in this one instance it probably saved my life, since it kept me calm and relaxed and not inclined to fight when Jason jumped into the river to save me. He had been riding in the second raft with the others when the accident happened, unable to do anything except watch helplessly. But when they spotted my orange life jacket bobbing on the surface half a mile away, they raced downstream to catch me before the river swept me beyond their reach.

The water had calmed a little by the time Jason got to me, and as soon as he was sure I wouldn't panic and put him in any danger, he pulled my arm up over his shoulder, grabbed for the strap on my life jacket and began kicking desperately for shore. Halfway there, the trance I'd fallen into began to wear off and I succumbed to the aching cold of the water. By the time he pulled me from the river I was a shocky mass of hypothermic jelly—frozen to the core, shivering, and nearly unconscious.

The others were all waiting on shore when we got there and as soon as I was safely out of the water, they lay me down on the ground and began stripping off my wet clothes. It didn't matter a bit to any of us that I was lying naked in front of a group of total strangers. All that mattered was getting me warm again.

As soon as I could speak I asked about Jay, fearful of the answer since I was sure there was no way he could have survived the ordeal. But Gretchen assured me he was alive. They'd gotten to him in time and other than being seriously chilled, he hadn't sustained any permanent injuries. Even so, it was imperative that we all get some place warm, and get there quickly.

I was overcome by the blessed sense of relief I felt at finally being bundled into the front seat of my car with the heater turned on full-blast, and it wasn't until an hour or so later that a delayed, stress-induced reaction set in and I began to realize the full import of what had actually happened. I'd come closer to dying this time than I ever wanted to again, and for what? To prove a point? To show everyone how tough I was in my wheelchair? It was a stupid, dangerous stunt to have attempted and I was furious with myself for having placed myself in such a position.

But I couldn't believe what I was hearing from the others, from my able-bodied, so-called "friends." They were talking excitedly among themselves, laughing and joking about what a thrilling ride it had been, and how no river trip was complete unless someone went for a "swim!"

It was unprecedented. These fools had placed in serious jeopardy the lives of two disabled people and now all they could talk about was how much *fun* it had been! They seemed to have no conception at all of what they'd done, and when I learned later that I'd been lied to and that this was Rick's *first* experience as a guide on the Chickaloon, I made up mind to see an attorney as soon as we got back to Anchorage.

I did and we eventually settled out of court. But that wasn't the end of it. I don't know if it was the stress associated with the whole affair or just my long remission coming slowly to an end, but I never quite bounced back to where I'd been before the river trip.

By mid-September I began waking up each morning tired and achy, and more than once my boss was surprised to find me slumped over an open file, sound asleep at my desk. To add to my difficulties, my left arm and hand gradually weakened to the point where I couldn't type more than five or six pages at a time without my fingers curling up painfully and falling from the keyboard into my lap.

The days dragged by with little improvement, and by the last weekend of the month I was conscious of the need to get out of Anchorage for a while, to someplace quiet where I could think out loud and try to get back in touch with myself.

I drove all the way to Homer that Saturday morning, a 250-mile trip, and spent most of the afternoon sitting in my wheelchair by the harbor, soaking up the sights and sounds and smells of the place the way I had so many summers ago. All alone I sat on the dock in front of the harbormaster's office and watched as the fishing boats came home, their bows riding low in the water under the weight of a full day's catch.

I thought a lot about the *Mariah* that day, remembering how splendid it felt to stand on her bowsprit with the sun on my face and the wind in my hair, watching as those great white sails filled with the breeze and bore us grandly out to sea. I'd been so happy then, so strong and confident. But that was a long, long time ago and so much had changed since that time.

I remembered reading a story once about a young woman whose husband had died suddenly one cold winter night, leaving her alone and desolate, grieving for a future she would never be allowed to know. Then, months later, one spring morning as she was cleaning out the attic, she came across a battered old beach ball from many summers past which, incredibly, still contained his breath. As she took it from the shelf and held it in her arms, she remembered how it had been when he was with her, when their lives together were just beginning.

Slowly, reverently, she opened the valve and pressed it to her lips, taking in just a little of his breath. As she did, she was filled with the memory of his love, and for a while at least it was as though he had never gone away. He was *with* her there, up in the attic, where she could hold him close and keep him safe forever.

For more than a year she shared the part of him he'd left behind. Whenever the grief and the loneliness became too great to bear, she returned alone to the attic and drew from him the strength and the peace she needed to go on. As long as she had that part of him to cling to he would never have to die. And because that was true, she was careful never to breathe too deeply.

But the day finally came when all the air was gone and the beach ball lay limp and empty in her hands. Suddenly there was nothing left to breathe, no part of him remained. It was only then that she understood the true nature of his love and the gift he'd left behind. She said goodbye to him then and left the attic quietly, knowing she'd never return. That part of her life was over. It was time for her to move on.

In a way, Alaska had become *my* beach ball, a dream I'd held onto, long past the time when it was healthy or even reasonable. I'd turned it into something sacred, a shrine to the memory of all the things my life had once stood for.

But sitting as I was in my now-forever wheelchair, I finally realized that the marvels and wonders that had enchanted my spirit and touched my heart so deeply were all denied to me now. There would be no more long, wild summers spent exploring the glories of this last frontier, no more winters passed in the quiet company of good friends.

The adventure was finished. The beach ball was empty and it was time for *me* to say goodbye.

The phone was ringing when I got back to my apartment that night, and I was tickled to find that my brother was on the other end of the line. He was calling from Honolulu to brag about the beachfront penthouse he would be housesitting for a friend all that winter.

Yeah, yeah, yeah. I listened with half an ear as he described in extravagant detail the splendors of Hawaii and his life there as a staff sergeant in the Air Force. For the better part of twenty minutes he yammered on and on, but it wasn't until his voice took on a certain edge that I finally caught on to the real reason for his call.

"JJ, you abysmal *jerk*," he sputtered, totally frustrated. "Can't you understand a word I'm saying? I want you to come over and spend the winter with me. Here! In Honolulu!"

He really meant it and in the space of fifteen seconds I'd made up my mind. It had been four years since we'd seen one another, and although we'd managed to stay in touch through telephone calls and letters, it would be fun to go and spend some time in *his* world for a change.

And the fact that his world just happened to be in a tropical paradise only sweetened the deal as far as I was concerned. A complete change of scenery might do wonders for me, and at the very least it would help ease the transition back to Pittsburgh and what passes for civilization in the so-called "real world."

The weekend before I left Alaska, Jane and I took a long, last trip down the Peninsula to Kenai. There were so many people to say goodbye to and I wanted one last look at everything that had meant so much to me. I wouldn't be coming back again, and it was important that the memories I carried away with me be strong enough to last for the rest of my life.

We stopped for coffee at the lodge in Cooper Landing, and as we sat looking out over the lake I thought about my first winter there and all the people who'd come and gone since then. The original lodge had since burned down and been rebuilt, but my old log cabin was still there, up on the hill, and Jane had a good laugh over the story I told her about my first night there and how I almost burned *it* down.

When we got down to Kenai we made a special trip out to the homestead to say goodbye to Crazy Helen Keppel. She was well into her late seventies by then but still as feisty as ever, full of piss and vinegar. Jane was flabbergasted by Helen's house, so while she took the grand tour I rolled my wheelchair out into the woods where my cabin still stood, for one last look around.

Everything was just as I remembered it and I was suddenly overcome with emotion, lost in the memory of a time long gone by. The years spent here in this tiny place were among the best I'd ever known, and just being there again was enough to bring on a flood of memories.

As I thought about all the people who had shared my life and all the places I'd never see again, my eyes filled with tears and I wept. There would be other disappointments in my life, and losses on a far greater scale, but somehow I sensed that none would hurt as badly as this.

Our last stop was at Cindy's house, and it was well after midnight when we arrived. Everyone was tired and ready for bed, but Cindy and I had too much to talk about, and deep into the night we sat in the kitchen with a bottle of scotch and some old photo albums, remembering together our years on the run.

We had a million memories between us and all night long we shared them, laughing hilariously over some of the people and places we'd encountered along the way. There were serious moments, too, when we realized that our time together was short and that we'd already done everything together that we were ever going to do. I told her then how much I loved her and how much her friendship had meant. I didn't know if I'd ever have the chance to say those things again, and I wanted her to know.

When we left Kenai and Cindy the next morning, I was almost sick with the longing to stay. I was closing the door forever on the best part of my life, and no matter where I lived or what I did for the rest of my days, this place would always be my spiritual home.

But it was over now, and as we drove back to Anchorage I memorized every bend in the road, knowing someday it would be important.

THIRTEEN

Hawaii
October, 1984

AS SOON AS I rolled off the plane at Honolulu International I knew I was going to like this place.

Half a dozen fat green parrots screeched and squawked and strutted their stuff overhead, while the voice on the loudspeaker called passengers to final destinations with names like Kahoolawe, Lahaina, and Nawiliwili. Billions of wild, exotic flowers were blooming in the sunshine, palm trees sprouted everywhere like overgrown polyps, and right there in the middle of it all stood Richard The Weasel with an armful of leis, grinning like an idiot.

I was beside myself with excitement at the thought of actually being in Hawaii with my brother, but the fact that he hadn't, as yet, actually seen me sitting in a wheelchair had me a little worried about how he'd react emotionally.

I guess I should have known better.

He hollered when he spotted me and began jumping up and down and pushing his way through the crowd. Thousands of tourists in "authentic" Hawaiian shirts and muu-muus were darting around frantically in search of suitcases and children, and all of them were wearing the same travel-dazed expression—kind of like ferrets on speed.

At last he was standing in front of me and I reached out for a hug, but my stomach tensed when I saw the look on his face. Oh God, I thought, he's taking this even harder than I'd feared. He stood staring, first at the wheelchair, then at me. His eyes grew moist, the corners of his mouth began to tremble, and before I could say a word to comfort him he fell to the floor at my feet, laughing uncontrollably. I sat, stunned, while he had his little seizure, and when he finally pulled himself together, all he could manage through tears of laughter was, "Boy are *you* going to be a pain in the ass at the beach!"

Up yours, little brother.

It took us over an hour to get out of the terminal because I had to stop and drool over every coconut, conch shell, and cheap piece of tourist trash on display, as though I'd discovered buried treasure. Happily, RTW was good natured about it all, and even treated me to the mandatory Mai Tai at the airport bar while I looked around for Tom Selleck. It was close to three by the time we got his pickup loaded and swung onto H-1 for the trip into Honolulu. As we crested the entrance ramp I rolled down the windows and turned up the stereo. Then I closed my eyes and let the wind and the music wash over me in a warm rush. God, it felt great.

"I don't believe it!" he bellowed over the roar of the traffic. "You spend all that money to come to Hawaii, and then you sit there with your damned eyes closed. What the hell's wrong with you?"

"Shut up," I said pointedly, "and just tell me when we get there."

"Get where?"

"To the ocean. Just shut up and tell me when we get to the ocean."

"JJ, for Christ's sake, we're on an island. There's ocean *everywhere!* Just open your eyes!"

So I did, and there it was; the honest-to-God, wall-to-wall, full-of-purple-fish Pacific, right where the map said it would be. It was even more beautiful than I'd imagined and all I could do was stare. To this day, RTW swears we really did pass Aloha Tower and Fisherman's Wharf and all that famous stuff on the way into town, but I was lost to the world . . . this was going to be terrific.

RTW had taken some time off in honor of my arrival and was nice enough to indulge the "haole" in me for a few days. Haole (pronounced howlie) is island slang for tourist—specifically white tourist —but I didn't care. I wanted to see it all.

First up was the standard tour of Waikiki, a glitzy, overgrown souvenir shop that will stand forever as an American monument to bad taste. Hordes of sweating tourists had descended on Kalakaua Avenue in a spending frenzy, and were greedily stuffing puka shells and hula dolls into giant plastic beach bags in a desperate attempt to use up the last of the traveler's checks before they left for home. It was all too much for a beginner like me and I was feeling a little nauseated by the time we left.

We took off for the Dole pineapple fields, then Pearl Harbor, the Kodak Hula Show, and even the mandatory afternoon at the so-called Polynesian "Cultural" Center. By Saturday I was all pineappled out and therefore delighted when RTW announced that we would pick up his buddy, Danny Garofolo, and head out to Hanauma Bay for a day at the beach.

The weather was perfect, the beach was crowded, and I couldn't wait to get in the water. While the boys unloaded the pickup I worked my way down to the beach to have a look around. Having just spent eight winters in Alaska, I was convinced that ice and snow were the worst obstacles a wheelchair could ever face, and so I guess I underestimated the treachery of a sandy beach. How tough could it be?

I gave it all I had and with a mighty shove, struck out in the direction of the water. The chair took off like a shot and made it exactly six inches before all four wheels buried themselves up to their axles in the soft white sand. Damn. I couldn't budge, and now people were beginning to stare. I reared back and popped a wheelie, determined to bust myself loose and show these people how it's done. The front wheels jerked up out of the sand just like I'd planned, but instead of moving forward, the rear wheels dug themselves in even deeper, and the next thing I knew the wheelchair had flipped over backwards.

Oh God. I was as helpless as an upside-down turtle, lying flat-out on my back with my head in the sand and my feet flopping around like flippers in the air. I felt like a fool to say the very least, and when I finally worked up the nerve to open my eyes and look around, I saw RTW and Danny running toward me with looks of pure disgust on their faces.

"I *told* you she was going to be pain in the ass! Let's just leave her here and go swimming."

"Oh hell, Rich. She'll just start hollering and then we'll *really* be embarrassed. C'mon, we'd better get her up."

There was murder in my heart as they picked me up and put me back in the chair, but I had to laugh at their equally lame efforts to make any headway in the sand. Finally, out of sheer frustration, they picked up the wheelchair, with me in it, and we began threading our way through the wild maze of blankets and half-naked sunbathers.

We trekked boldly across the sand while hundreds of onlookers smiled patronizingly and whispered quietly to one another, "Oh, how sweet, they've brought her to the beach for some sun." The crowd soon turned ugly, though, and I heard someone scream "OH MY GOD, THEY'RE GOING TO KILL HER!" as the boys plucked me out of my wheelchair and threw me headlong into the ocean. We escaped incident only by donning masks and snorkels and making tracks toward the reef at the mouth of the bay.

Even without the use of my legs I could still outswim most people, but I really had to work to keep up with these two. As we snorkeled the length of the reef I lost all sense of time and space in my enchantment at what I was seeing. Hanauma Bay is a protected marine preserve and the sheer number and variety of tropical fish there was staggering. Huge pink and blue parrotfish nibbled at the rose-colored coral while thousands of technicolored angelfish sailed by in perfect formation. Big green puffer fish bobbed all along the reef like little hot-air balloons, careful to avoid the sharp spines of the sea urchins that were stuck to the coral like big bristly warts.

I felt as though I was in heaven and easily could have stayed there forever. But the tide was going out and when RTW signaled it was time to leave, we turned around and headed straight for shore. By the time we made it back I was exhausted from fighting the current and was relieved when the guys each grabbed an arm and a leg and hauled me bodily out of the ocean. They left me sitting alone in the sand at the water's edge and headed for the pickup to bring us back some sandwiches and beer. Typically, I was daydreaming and not really paying attention when the surf started rolling in.

It was nothing to get excited about, just a little everyday beach surf that any six-year-old would have enjoyed. But sitting as I was without a pair of functional legs for ballast, things got real scary, real fast. The first wave knocked me over backwards, pinning my head and chest to the sand under about a foot of water. I was stunned, but I managed to get my head clear and was struggling to sit up when the next wave caught my legs and threw them up over my head. Before I could right myself, it had dragged me, somersaulting, down the beach, closer and closer to where the heavy surf was breaking.

The water was getting deeper and I was starting to panic. I opened my mouth to scream for help when a third wave hit me squarely in the face, blinding me and forcing gallons of seawater down my throat. I could hear people laughing and applauding in the distance and I realized, horrified, that they thought I was having fun! I knew then that I was in serious trouble, but all I could think about were the headlines in the next day's newspaper:

THOUSANDS CHEER AS PARAPLEGIC DROWNS!

What a horrible, stupid way to die. Later RTW and Danny would swear they didn't know things were critical until they saw their $70 mask and snorkel snatched from my hand and swept out to sea—at which time they hastened to pull me free of the surf. You had to admire their heroics, I guess, if not their sense of priorities.

All during the scenic drive home along the windward coastline, the boys were busy jabbering and pointing out the various places where they'd almost died during their own little "adventures" on the island. The rocky cliffs and crashing surf really were spectacular, but I couldn't seem to erase the wonder of that one beautiful reef from my mind. There had to be a way to get back down there with some scuba gear and really do some exploring. At first the idea seemed ridiculous, but the more I thought about it . . .

When I brought the subject up over dinner that night, I was surprised at the level of enthusiasm the two of them worked up as we began to discuss the possibilities. Considering the fiasco of that afternoon, we all agreed that a beach dive was out of the question—the surf would be deadly with a full set of scuba gear on. The only alternative was to dive from a boat directly into deep water, and that would mean finding a dive shop that operated a boat and was willing to take on a disabled diver—not a very likely combination. But I said I'd make a few calls the next day, just to see what we were up against.

So, early the next morning, armed with a telephone and a copy of the Yellow Pages, I went to work. After several calls I was discouraged to learn that few places had ever worked with a disabled diver and that fewer still were even willing to try. An hour later, after talking with every dive shop on the island, I was left with exactly two possibilities—Aloha Dive Shop in Koko Marina and Craig's Diving Emporium in Waikiki. Surprisingly, both were enthusiastic, and both had actually had some experience with wheelchair divers. Since Craig's shop was just a couple of blocks away on Ala Moana, I called them back and we arranged to make an experimental dive the next morning.

I spent the entire afternoon at the pool that day, waiting for The Weasel to get home from work so I could break the good news to him. He said it all sounded great (he knew I'd done my fair share of diving before), but he was quick to remind me that he was scheduled to work the next day and therefore I would be on my own. Of course he was sure everything would go just fine, but would I consider drawing up some sort of will that evening? Just in case?

Paranoia intact, I went to bed that night alternating between dread and hysteria at the prospect of the next day's adventure.

* * * * * * * * * *

"I'm not wearing that wetsuit."

"You *have* to wear a wetsuit."

"There's no way in hell. In case no one's noticed, it's pushing ninety out there today, so the chances of frostbite are slim to none. And besides, which one of you apes is going to help me put the damned thing on?"

So much for the hard line. Craig Eslep, the owner, and his two employees, Scott and Phil, just looked at one another and grinned. They were all master divers and the idea of a sassy little firebrand in a wheelchair mouthing off about what she would and would *not* do must have struck them as awfully funny. But half an hour later—diving credentials verified, equipment fitted, and money paid—I was as ready as I was ever going to be. We left the shop and headed across the street toward a big blue van parked at the curb. Phil jumped in and started the engine, and before I had time to worry about how I was going to get inside, Craig and Scott had picked me up and deposited me on the front seat. They tossed my wheelchair in the back of the van, and we were off to collect the rest of the day's divers.

By then I was starting to get a little nervous. Scuba diving can be a tricky proposition for anyone, able-bodied or otherwise. It's a sport that requires a lot of training and practice and a good amount of physical strength and coordination. When something goes wrong underwater things can get scary in a big hurry, and if you happen to be a hundred feet below the surface at the time, you'd damn well better know what you're doing. And that's what had me worried.

It had been five years since my last dive in Alaska, and I wasn't in great physical shape by anyone's standards. Four years in a wheelchair had taken their toll: my legs were useless, my left arm was heavy and numb, I'd put on weight, and my circulation was way below what it should have been. And to top it all off, today would be a series of firsts for me—my first open-ocean dive, my first dive as a paraplegic, and my first dive without a buddy I knew and trusted. It's no wonder that by then even *I* was questioning my motives and wondering what in the name of sanity I was doing there.

I'd learned to dive one summer in Kenai, but all the diving I'd done there was in a few small lakes along the Peninsula, mostly just for training purposes. Diving the lakes of Alaska was great, and as any diver will tell you, half the fun is just getting in the water and blowing bubbles. But to tell you the truth, there really isn't much to see in a lake. Not compared to those Jacques Cousteau specials, anyhow.

I knew that the real action was to be found under the big water, in the open ocean, but the Alaskan waters of Cook Inlet could be deadly cold and treacherous. Not having the resources or experience to attempt all that, I stuck to tamer underwater pursuits and spent the rest of my time daydreaming about warm water and purple fish. After a few more years, though, as I became more and more dependent on a wheelchair, I resignedly added diving to the list of things I would never do again.

But that was all behind me now, and today I would either sink or swim, to coin a phrase.

We turned onto Kalakaua Avenue and headed east toward the Hyatt Regency to pick up the rest of that day's group. Four big men were waiting in front of the hotel, and I judged by the size of their duffel bags that they were all completely self-contained—meaning they'd brought all their own gear with them and wouldn't be needing any rental equipment. This was a bad omen for me, because ownership of a full set of (very expensive) diving gear generally indicates a certain level of competency as a diver, and if these guys were as good as they looked, I was going to feel like a real clown in the water.

Everyone got settled in the van and Phil doubled back toward Ala Wai Yacht Harbor where the dive boat was waiting. Once we'd all introduced ourselves, the conversation naturally turned to past dive trips as everyone sized each other up. I didn't say much, but the more I listened, the more intimidated I felt. What we had here were four crackerjack divers, three professional instructors, and me, the legless wonder. I was pretty sure old King Neptune was trying to tell me something.

The harbor reeked of money. Or maybe it was just the stench of the rotting water. All harbors have a smell about them, and this one was a wonder. Diesel fuel and long-dead fish and the flotsam and jetsam of a thousand faraway places hung in the air, an aromatic travelogue of far-flung ports of call. Sloops and schooners, ketches and yawls were lined up bowsprit to bowsprit along the endless, pristine docks.

These were deadly serious boats. Yacht club burgees from all over the world slapped against their halyards and I even recognized a couple of Gold Platers—famous world-class racing yachts designed and built to do nothing but haul ass. Oh, to be killer rich and afloat.

Everyone climbed out of the van and began unloading their bags while I waited for Craig to bring my chair around. Instead, he picked me up bodily and carried me across the parking lot, down three or four steps, and out to the boat at the end of the dock. I got myself settled on the aft deck while the others climbed aboard and found a place to sit.

After stowing my wheelchair in the bow, Scott cast off the lines and soon we were all chattering happily as we made our way out of the harbor. So far no one had mentioned the obvious, and since I couldn't think of a graceful way to bring up the subject, I didn't say anything either.

It took about ten minutes to reach our dive site, half a mile or so off the end of Magic Island, and while Phil tossed out the anchor and secured the lines, the other divers began putting on their gear. While they were suiting up, Craig assigned dive-buddies and gave the standard lecture on diving safety, water conditions, and local marine life. Buddies checked buddies to make sure weight belts were fastened securely and regulators were functioning properly. Then, one by one, each did a backward roll off the side of the boat. In a minute, all four were bobbing on the surface, making last-minute adjustments to their equipment.

Now the moment of truth was at hand and I was a mess. My hands were shaking, my face was numb, and I wanted desperately to throw up. If only I could throw up. Why oh why, I wondered crazily, do I get myself into these kinds of messes? Was I there because I really wanted to dive that badly, or did I just want to do something outrageous to prove to myself that I still could? Who knew. But it didn't matter anyhow. The important thing just then was to get in the water and get the whole damned thing over with.

While Scott got busy hooking up my equipment, I put my mask and snorkel on and made sure they fit. When everything was ready, Craig and Phil crossed over to where I was sitting, picked me up in their arms, and, with a kiss for luck, dumped me over the side of the boat.

The water was cool and crystal clear, and when I broke the surface Craig was waiting right beside me with my gear. The buoyancy compensator, or B.C., was inflated and I slipped into it with surprising ease. As I adjusted the chest and waist straps I glanced over at the other divers. All I could see were four pairs of eyes staring out, bewildered, from behind their masks, and it occurred to me for the first time that none of these guys had any idea of what was going on.

Oh well, it was too late to explain anything then, and since everyone appeared to be ready, we all turned and swam together toward the anchor chain at the bow. This was it. I grabbed ahold of the chain, dumped the air out of my B.C., and with one last prayer for luck slipped beneath the surface.

We were only diving to forty feet that day, a relatively shallow dive, but it took several minutes to reach the bottom because we had to stop every few feet and clear our ears against the mounting pressure of the water. We worked our way slowly down the chain, and at thirty feet I let go and did a free-fall to the ocean floor, landing with a soft thunk on the white, sandy bottom.

The ten pounds of lead on my weight belt would have held me there forever, but in order to move around freely I had to reach neutral buoyancy, a state of almost perfect weightlessness. This is achieved by pumping small amounts of air from the tank into the B.C. —too much and I'd begin to rise to the surface, too little and I'd sink to the bottom again. I fooled around with it for a few minutes and when I finally got neutral the miracle happened . . .

For the first time in four years I was in a vertical position, completely without assistance, and when I found that a mere flick of my wrist would send me soaring in any direction I chose, I went totally berserk. For the next ten minutes I bounced in slow motion from coral head to coral head, like some kind of drunken astronaut playing on the surface of the moon. I did cartwheels, handsprings, somersaults, and even invented a few new moves that a porpoise would have envied. It was like being let out of jail, and I will never, *ever* forget the feeling.

Just when I thought it couldn't get any better, I heard someone banging on a tank and I spun around to see Craig sitting alone on the bottom, surrounded by thousands of the most beautiful creatures I'd ever seen. He'd brought along a bag of frozen peas and was sitting there calmly as tropical fish of every size and description swam up and nibbled them right out of his hand!

Feeling like Alice in Wonderland, I swam into the kaleidoscope and settled down beside him. He gave me a handful of peas and I watched, enchanted, as a big purple surgeonfish swam up and, with a soft kiss, took a pea from the tip of my finger. He was followed in short order by all his friends—butterflies, angels, tangs, and triggerfish all lined up for supper while little cleaner wrasse nibbled gently at the hairs on my arms and face.

So, I thought to myself, awestruck . . . this is what it's like at the end of the rainbow.

When we ran out of peas, the fish fanned out and became our escorts as we swam slowly from reef to reef. One in particular, a big green spotted puffer fish, attached himself to me. He was about a foot long—it's hard to tell underwater—and with his square, boxy body and big round google eyes he was so homely he was almost cute. He stayed right beside me all day and whenever he got aggravated about something he'd start gulping water until he blew himself up to twice his normal size. He looked really silly that big, and we made a game of batting him around like a volleyball until he got bored and swam away.

I named him Ulysses and began to think of him as a friend. It was uncanny, but on subsequent dives I'd make to the same site Ulysses would always be there, waiting to welcome me and show me around his neighborhood.

Craig led the way across a big reef and down into what appeared to be a submerged crater, and we all set out to do some exploring while he poked around the entrance to a small cave. I was sitting on a ledge, nose to nose with a spiny lobster, when I heard a loud banging noise again. I turned, wondering what sort of treat was in store for us this time. But all I could see was a big black cloud where Craig used to be.

As the cloud slowly dissipated it became obvious he was holding something, but I couldn't make out what it was. I edged closer, cautiously. He turned toward me and, horrified, I saw that a huge octopus had wrapped its tentacles around his chest and arms! The adrenaline kicked in, I blew about a thousand pounds of air into my B.C., and shot like a rocket to the surface.

Of all the dumb things you can do while diving, that was the dumbest of all. And easily the most embarrassing. While I was bouncing around on the surface like an overinflated zeppelin, everyone else was forty feet below, elbow-to-elbow with Craig and his big eight-legged prize. Shamefaced, I worked my way back down to the group and Craig signaled for me to come closer. The catch-of-the-day was still sitting calmly on his arm, oblivious to all the excitement around him. Closer examination revealed he wasn't all that huge—three feet from tentacle to tentacle, tops—but he sure was ugly. His big, bulbous head and grasping arms were a muddy greenish-gray and underneath, row after row of fat sucker discs gleamed a dull white. I swallowed my revulsion and reached out to touch.

Surprisingly, he didn't feel slimy at all. Instead, his skin felt like soft leather under my fingers and it rippled where I stroked. Craig laid the length of his arm against mine and I watched, mesmerized, as first one tentacle, then another reached out tentatively toward me. I stayed absolutely still, my heart pounding, while he slithered over and wrapped himself around my upper arm. I could feel the suckers latch onto my skin one by one as he crawled. Yecch.

But oddly enough, it wasn't too uncomfortable, and I decided that as long as he was being nice I would be nice, too. I knew that buried somewhere in all that flubber was a sharp beak, called a radula, and I didn't want him even to *think* about using it. The others were crowded all around me, amazed no doubt at my courage and daring, and with a smug sense of *noblesse oblige*, I condescended to reach out and allow everyone to pet and fondle my new best friend.

I thought all this was pretty cool and I was actually starting to relax and enjoy myself a little when I felt a cold, rubbery arm circle up around my neck. Oh God. Another was crawling across my chest and a third was reaching for my face mask.

Get him off! I had to get him off! I screamed into my regulator and, panicky, started ripping octopus from skin in a frenzy. As soon as I got one tentacle loose and was grabbing for another, the first reattached itself somewhere else until I couldn't tell where I left off and octopus began. Sick with fear, I spun toward Craig, my eyes pleading silently for help.

I'd done it again.

He was doubled over, shoulders heaving in a paroxysm of laughter, and it was a full two minutes before he could pull himself together enough to remove the hideous thing and set us both free. Even Ulysses looked disgusted. Later Craig would apologize, saying the sight of a fully grown woman with a frightened octopus clinging to her head was just too much, and surely I could understand.

Yeah. Right.

Our pressure gauges showed we were getting low on air, so we regrouped, and with Ulysses leading the way we turned and headed back toward the boat. As we worked our way up to the surface I began to feel withdrawal symptoms, and for the first time in my life I understood how an addict must feel. I would have stolen money to keep on diving if that's what it took—anything, just to get back down there again.

Scott reached over the gunwale and pulled me into the boat, and as soon as I got my diving mask off all hell broke loose. The four divers from the hotel were falling all over themselves trying to get to me.

"I can't believe what just happened!" one of them shouted. "We never dreamed you'd actually be *diving* with us!"

"Hell no!" bellowed another. "We all figured you were just along for the ride. But that was incredible! Where did you learn to dive like that?"

And it went on and on. They weren't any more surprised than I was, and I certainly hadn't counted on this kind of reaction. But it felt great to know that after that day four people would go home with a whole different perspective on the disabled. Not bad for one day's work.

Meanwhile, Craig was being unusually quiet and I noticed him staring at me with a peculiar expression on his face. I asked him what was wrong and he said, grinning, "If you could only see yourself . . ."

See myself? What did he mean? I pulled a mirror out of my bag to see what he was talking about and almost fainted at the sight of dozens of tiny purple bruises all over my face, arms, and neck.

Octopus hickeys! Alone on a boat with seven men in the middle of the ocean, and the best I could do was this. It was one for the record books. We were all still laughing when we arrived back at the harbor and began hosing down the gear. Everyone was full of good cheer and there were hugs and smiles all around when we finally said goodbye at the shop.

* * * * * * * * *

As the hot winter months passed by, my days settled into a delightful routine of diving, eating, sleeping, and then diving yet some more. The hours I spent underwater mounted quickly, and by the end of December I'd completely lost track of the number of dives I'd made to various sites around the island—all without mishap, each more beautiful than the one before.

But gradually I began to notice that the dives were becoming harder and harder to complete. My left arm was rapidly growing weaker, and underwater I was forced to work feverishly with my right arm to compensate. By the time I was pulled back into the boat at the end of a dive I was completely worn out, and when I finally got home all I could do was lie in bed for the rest of the afternoon, hoping to regain enough strength for the next day's dive.

I didn't have to be hit over the head this time to know what was happening, and before I fell apart completely I began making plans to return to Pittsburgh.

It wasn't easy. I'd become so attached to it all—to the island, the ocean, and most of all to my brother. How I would miss that stupid grin and sick sense of humor. And who knew when we'd see one another again?

On my last day in Hawaii, Craig and the others treated me to a final farewell dive at Hanauma Bay—at seventy feet the deepest and most beautiful one ever. But this time it was different. This time Craig actually had to take me by the hand and guide me slowly and carefully across the reefs. It hurt terribly to be that dependent on someone else, especially underwater, but it was necessary since I could no longer get around myself with only one arm and no legs to propel me.

Other than that the dive was spectacular, and was easily the nicest thing anyone could ever have done. They'd all been wonderful to me and I said goodbye to the whole bunch of them with a lump in my throat.

When I got back to the apartment, Rich had everything packed and loaded in the pickup, but kindly allowed me time for a long last look out my bedroom window. I had come to regard that view of the ocean as my birthright and wasn't entirely convinced I could live without it.

My flight didn't leave until midnight, but I wanted to allow plenty of time for Mai Tais and last minute reminiscing at the airport. We sat for a long while in the bar that night, talking quietly over our drinks, mostly killing time until the plane was ready for boarding.

By the time he'd stowed my wheelchair and carried me to my seat on the plane, we had run out of tears and words to say. So with a hug, a kiss, and a big bouquet of flowers he was gone, and my time on the island was ended.

Everything was ended. I buried my face in the mass of white gardenias and wept, feeling lonelier and sorrier for myself than I ever had before. The adventure was over now, and I was going home for good.

FOURTEEN

Pittsburgh
1993

L OOKING BACK NOW IT'S hard to believe that almost nine years have passed since the day I left Hawaii in 1985 and came back home to live with my parents in Pittsburgh. There were parties celebrating my return, half a dozen radio interviews, and even a long, "inspiring" newspaper story done on me, chronicling some of my wilder exploits in various corners of the world.

For a while there I was actually considered something of a local hero—a fearless adventurer who'd broken through all the barriers and had "made it" in a world that had always been considered the exclusive province of men.

And to some degree, I guess I had. But my motives had never been as clear and deliberate as all that, and I never hesitated to say so to anyone who would listen. Despite everything that was said and assumed about me, the truth was that the strength I'd needed to keep on fighting had come, ironically enough, from the very fight *itself*, from the nonstop ups and downs, attacks and remissions, and the thousand other indignities that regularly brought me to my knees in frustration.

Only God and I knew how much the struggle had cost me already in terms of pain and personal loss. But any sense of pride I still had left came from knowing that I *had* fought the good fight without becoming a martyr to it, and that I'd done everything I possibly could to make certain that not a minute of my time had been wasted.

But in the doing I'd used up the last of my reserves of strength and energy. I was thirty-three when I finally came home to stay, but in many ways I felt closer to ninety-three. I was physically drained, unspeakably tired, and scared beyond words at the thought of what might yet come to pass. I'd learned from long experience that once a part of my body was touched by the disease, it was only a matter of time before the damage was permanent and irreversible. Given that, there was virtually no chance now that I wouldn't lose my left arm and hand completely—a loss so profound it was beyond anything I was capable of imagining.

* * * * * * * * * *

After all the fuss and to-do over my homecoming had finally settled down, I felt a deep need to be left to myself for awhile until I could come to grips with my new situation and accept the fact that my life would never again be the same. But more than anything else, I just needed some time alone to sit in my room and think.

Mostly I thought about Jenny O'Brien. She was the young MS patient I'd encountered at the rehab center, and the image of her strapped into her wheelchair, spastic and writhing, haunted me continually. And because it was impossible not to, I began to draw comparisons, terrifying comparisons, between her condition and mine.

To begin with, I was starting to look like her. After so many years in a wheelchair, the muscles in my legs had begun to atrophy and were beginning to take on the brittle, stick-like appearance so common among the long-term disabled. I was still vain enough to be bothered by the way they looked and I stopped wearing skirts and shorts altogether in an effort to hide them—not so much from the rest of the world as from myself. They were just another reminder that my condition was a paralyzing, irreversible one, a fact I'd tried for so many years to ignore.

In addition, the generally mild spasms I'd experienced occasionally had grown increasingly intense and uncontrollable. I could be sitting quietly, reading or watching TV, when suddenly my entire body would stiffen and begin to shake violently, like an epileptic caught in the grip of a grand mal attack. Sometimes a spasm would be so severe that I'd actually be thrown from my wheelchair to the floor, where I'd lie crying until someone came along and picked me up. It was frightening, dangerous, and when it happened in public, embarrassing beyond belief.

Over the next year or so my physical condition continued to deteriorate rapidly, and nothing the doctors tried had any effect on me whatsoever. Then, remarkably, in October of 1986 I got lucky again and was referred to a prominent neurologist at Presbyterian University Hospital in Pittsburgh—a world-class medical facility where great advances were being made in the area of MS research and treatment.

It was pure serendipity. I'd finally found a doctor who really seemed to care more about my medical future than he did about my medical past. He was smart, handsome, and funny, too, and unlike so many other highly trained specialists, he treated me with dignity and respect. He understood the fact that *I* was the one with the disease, and recognized that what I had to say about it might actually have some merit. In short, he treated me as a person and not as just another "case."

At the time I met him he was experimenting with something new for MS—an intense program of cancer chemotherapy that had proven somewhat effective in slowing down the disease process in the few patients who had tried it. Naturally, I wanted to hear more.

It was a miserable procedure, he warned me, one with all sorts of potentially dangerous side-effects, such as a (slight) risk of bladder cancer or even some form of leukemia ten or fifteen years down the road. On top of all that, he cautioned, the drug would likely make me ill—very, *very* ill. He suggested I talk it over with my family carefully before making any kind of final decision.

"Oh by the way," he grinned devilishly as I turned in my wheelchair to go, "you might start looking for some sort of wig pretty soon, since in about a month you'll likely be as bald as a billiard ball. Heh, heh." Leave it to him. He always managed to save the worst for last and thoroughly enjoyed himself in the process.

The drug was administered intravenously over twelve consecutive days, and by the last six or seven I was sick beyond belief. I'd been cautioned, I know, but even so I was in no way prepared to feel as horrible as I did for as long as I did. It wasn't the nausea or even the perpetual vomiting that bothered me the most—it was the sheer, relentless pain that nearly did me in. Every bone and muscle in my body cried out for relief, my skin burned constantly, and I felt like I'd come down with six cases of malaria at once.

239

By the last two days all I could do was lie in bed, panting, so desperately ill I didn't know or even care whether I was dead or alive. It was the most excruciating thing I've ever put myself through and I remember to this day the relief that swept through my body the day they finally told me I could go home. But since my immune system was by then so severely compromised, I had to be kept in total isolation at home for at least a month. It was a strange and lonely time for me. Blood had to be drawn twice daily at first, and no one but my family and the nurses were allowed to be in the house with me during that whole long period of time. And whenever one of them came near me they had to be scrubbed, gowned, gloved, and masked. There was no question this was pretty serious stuff.

The morning the isolation ban was lifted I awoke to find my pillow covered with small clumps of hair that had fallen out while I slept. It was a jarring sight, but one I'd planned for all along, thanks to the doctor's earlier warning. Determined to avoid the pointless emotionality that would come from pulling out fistfuls of my own hair day after day, I immediately asked for a pair of scissors and, with my mother's help, sheared off every last wisp of hair still clinging to my head.

I caught all kinds of hell from a lot of people when they found out what I'd done, but I figured it was none of their business to begin with. Vanity was one thing, but in light of what was at stake here, the loss of my hair meant absolutely nothing to me. Besides, the wig I'd bought looked twice as good as my own hair ever had.

But now to proceed to the obvious question: Did the chemotherapy work? From my perspective now, the answer would have to be a limited but otherwise unqualified "yes." While I saw little actual *improvement* physically, it's crucial to remember one very important thing: before the procedure began, my left arm and hand were in such bad shape that within the space of just six or seven months, the loss of function would be complete and irreversible. At least that had been the process so far. However, for the following five *years* (with regular monthly booster doses of the drug), I was able to hold onto whatever function still remained. And overall, the progress of the disease seemed to slow down to a crawl.

As always, though, because of the quirkiness of MS and the odd courses it sometimes takes, it's impossible to know for sure whether the chemo had anything at all to do with what happened. It *might* have, but it could just as easily have been purely anecdotal. Either way, my run of good luck gradually came to an end, leaving only the hated physical pain behind.

Over the past several years I'd begun experiencing increasingly intense bouts of pain throughout various parts of my body. But any time I asked for help, all I got was a patronizing pat on the head and the standard, never-varying lecture. Doctor after doctor insisted stubbornly that pain, especially the kind I was describing, was *never* associated with MS. I was made to feel like a fool—or worse, like a drug-seeking junkie.

Maybe I *was* crazy, as they all seemed to think, but on especially bad days my body hurt like hell in triplicate. My bones—mostly the spine and major joints—felt like they'd been pounded on with a jackhammer, my muscles ached unbearably, and my skin burned as though it had been dipped in lye.

However, my new doctor, unlike all the others, *did* believe what I was saying and was perfectly willing to help out with a wide variety of medications. But it wasn't until early in 1991, during one of my countless hospitalizations, that even he realized the full import of what it was I'd been experiencing.

It had been a bad night, and by late the following morning the pain had escalated beyond all reason. When he arrived on rounds and found me sobbing and screaming into my pillow, he immediately picked up the telephone and called in a member of the Acute Pain Team, something I'd never even known existed.

Dr. Dawn Marcus, a neurological pain expert, arrived twenty minutes later and took over. She explained that I wasn't crazy at all, and that the pain I was feeling was *very* real, but that it was a somewhat rare phenomenon. Studies had been done recently, she went on to say, which showed that a very small percentage of all MS patients *did* experience some intense pain as the disease progressed and that unfortunately, I was among the unluckiest of that unlucky group.

She went on to explain that due to the nature of MS and the severity of my pain, the most effective means of controlling it would be through a combination of physical therapy, stress-reduction techniques, and a closely monitored protocol of strong, long-term narcotics. It took us a while to find the right mix of everything, and although I know now that I'll never be totally free of the pain, what Dr. Marcus has done for me means more than I can ever say. By taking away the worst, most unendurable aspects of the pain, she's given me back my will to live and the ability and desire to go on. And because she has, I'll continue to work as hard as I can with the therapists, take my morphine faithfully, and stop fantasizing about having my legs amputated in order to get rid of the pain once and for all.

Later that same year the indwelling Foley catheter I'd been wearing for so long finally went sour on me, resulting in constant, highly dangerous urinary tract infections. And the day I was biopsied for bladder cancer (result: negative) was the day I decided to have a much-dreaded operation done.

A urostomy, briefly put, is a long and intricate surgical procedure wherein a four-inch piece of intestine is removed and connected directly to the kidneys via the tiny tubes (ureters) that normally run from the kidneys to the bladder. Once that's been done, the bladder itself is removed and the piece of intestine, with ureters attached, is pulled through a hole cut in the abdomen, then sutured firmly into place. And from that moment on, the act of urination becomes safe and automatic as the urine flows through the piece of intestine, or "stoma," directly into a plastic bag glued firmly to the abdomen.

The recovery process was a long and painful one, but once I'd gotten through the hard part, both physically and emotionally, the sheer relief of finally being rid of my bladder and all its attendant problems ultimately made the whole ordeal worth it. Before long now a colostomy will become necessary too, and when it does I'll grit my teeth and go through it all once again, simply because I'll have to. I won't have any choice.

* * * * * * * * * *

Despite all the frantic efforts of physical therapists, nurses, and doctors, by Christmas of 1991 my arm and hand had succumbed to the disease completely. This ushered me into an entirely new level of disability, completely different from anything I'd ever known before —even on a purely mechanical level.

For the past ten years I'd enjoyed the relative ease and comfort of what was commonly known as an "ultra-light" manual wheelchair— a stripped-down, streamlined, almost sexy-looking sports chair weighing all of twenty-eight pounds. Designed primarily for athletes and otherwise active paraplegics, these ultra-lights were comfortable, highly maneuverable, and, most important of all, small and unobtrusive—little more than a seat on wheels.

But with the loss of just one arm my ultra-light days came to an end, and the day they delivered my first electric wheelchair I broke down and cried like a baby.

To my eyes it was hideous—a gleaming, 150-pound monster of chrome and black vinyl that looked and moved like a tank. There was nothing the least bit subtle about it, and any time I ventured into the outside world I felt as though all anyone noticed was the wheelchair. It was almost as though *I* had vanished completely.

But the chair itself quickly paled to insignificance compared to some of the other aspects of life associated with a now-severe disability. Simple, day-to-day tasks—things taken for granted by most people—can assume nightmarish proportions for someone unable to, say, brush their own teeth without help. And simply getting through the day in one piece can require the assistance of several people.

My parents of course are with me twenty-four hours a day, preparing meals, running errands, and doing the hundreds of little things necessary for my well-being and comfort. But since both of them are heart patients and unable to do any heavy lifting or moving, several different agencies have stepped in and provided aides and assistants to help out in those critical areas.

Barbara, one of the truly funniest people I've ever known, arrives early in the morning and goes about getting me ready for the day. Her chores include changing my diaper and emptying my urine bag— unpleasant jobs she does laughingly and without the slightest bit of embarrassment. Next she bathes me and helps with my personal care, then lifts me bodily into my wheelchair. Once she's made sure I'm positioned correctly, with splints and braces securely in place, she scurries around seeing to it that everything I'll need for the day is available and easily within my reach.

After she's gone I do the best I can to stay as busy and productive as possible. Mostly I pound away on my computer—a slow, difficult process with only one functional hand—determined at all costs to keep my brand-new writing career alive and kicking, no matter what.

Occasionally, when I'm up to it, one of my other assistants will take me out for an afternoon of shopping, to the movies, or even sometimes to dinner—anything to break the monotony. Other times when I'm feeling especially lousy or don't have the will or the energy to work, I'll sit reading quietly or talking with friends on the phone until Bob, my evening aide, arrives after dinner to put me back to bed.

He does all the things Barbara does in the morning, only in reverse, with the added tasks of showering me and checking every square inch of my body for any signs of bedsores or, rather, "areas" that might be developing. He, too, does these things without the least bit of shame or embarrassment, qualities I've always considered endearing in a man.

But once he's lifted me into bed and made sure that I'm comfortable and positioned correctly, he leaves for home—and the longest, most difficult part of my "day" begins. Way back in the good old days I could spend unlimited amounts of time in my wheelchair—as much as twenty-four hours at a clip, if I wanted to—without ever giving it a second thought. But now, mostly due to pain and fatigue, the longest I can manage to sit up at a time is only eight or nine hours at the most. Sometimes even less.

That being the case, I'm faced with the daily prospect of spending fifteen, sometimes sixteen, hours in bed alone with little to do to pass the time. When lying in one position begins to hurt too much, I'll call my mom or dad in and ask them to move my arms and legs around a bit, or simply to sit and massage the parts of me that hurt the most.

Once in a while a friend will stop by for a visit, and occasionally on a Friday or Saturday my neighbor and best nine-year-old friend, Emily Wellman, will come and spend the night with me. We've been best friends for a long time now, and we always have a great time together. We eat pizza, watch a lot of movies, and, best of all, stay up late giggling and acting goofy.

I do the best I can to fill the long and solitary hours, but mostly I just lie there like a "big old lump of mashed potatoes" (as my little niece Deborah would say), wondering all the while why I haven't yet lost my mind.

I've often been asked how I did it—how I managed to live for so many years under the peril of the sword without giving in to the release of a complete emotional breakdown, or at the very least a chronic, self-indulgent depression. Where did I find what it took to push so hard and get myself out of bed each morning, fully aware that the day ahead might be the last one I'd ever know as a normally functioning human being?

The answer is, I don't know. I've asked myself those same questions a thousand times over and have yet to come up with an answer that makes sense. I do know that courage, bravery, or some innate sense of heroics had nothing at all to do with the choices I made. Those are qualities which, for some reason, are *always* attributed to the disabled, as though simply by virtue of our "suffering" we're all somehow automatic candidates for sainthood.

But not me. Not by a long shot. Courage, bravery, and the like are qualities I know I don't possess, and I spend a lot of my time putting the lie to the myth of the Relentlessly Smiling Quadriplegic. On the contrary, it was probably fear more than anything else that was the motivating force behind everything I did. It's important to remember that from early adulthood on, every single day of my life was colored with the threat of an incurable and paralyzing disease. That sort of reality is a heavy load for someone so young to carry alone, and it's bound to have a big impact on the way one looks at life overall.

So if my values were different from society's in general, there was a reason for it. I was often called flighty, irresponsible, and worse by people who had no way of knowing that I measured time by a different standard than they did. If I never stayed with a single job for longer than a year, it was because I didn't have the time most people did to devote to a career or long-term goals. It wasn't that I didn't care about those things, or that I was incapable of trying. It's just the way it was.

If I ran away to Alaska and lived a life that most people considered insane, it was because I was looking for a way to see, taste, and feel every bit of the world I could before the curtain rang down and closed off that world to me for good.

And if I never once loved a man who loved me back, it was because I was so afraid of saying goodbye.

There are those who would argue I made the decision too soon— that by resolving early on never to marry, I cut myself off from any chance I might have had to share my life with someone before it was too late. "Take a chance," friends of mine urged constantly. "You can't be sure of what will happen in the future and besides, if a man *really* loved you, he'd be happy to take care of you later on, if it came to that."

But they were missing the point. It wasn't some poor man I was worried about—it was *me*. If there was one thing I valued above all else it was my independence, and I couldn't imagine anything worse than being on the receiving end of someone's love with no way on earth to reciprocate or carry my fair share of the relationship. Far from being a high-minded act of selflessness or virtue, it was easily the most *selfish* decision I've ever made, and one I'd make again given the same circumstances.

Even so, that part of my life hasn't been easy and I admit it freely. I was only twenty-nine years old when I made love to Tony Stone for the last time and put away forever all thoughts of intimacy with a man. That was thirteen years ago, but my body has simply become too repugnant to me even to think about sharing it with another person. There have been too many steroids, too many operations, too much incontinence, and above all, far too much shame. Over the years my body has become nothing but a burden to me, a shriveled, immobilized "thing" racked with often unbearable pain, incapable of giving or receiving pleasure.

It's an irrelevancy anyhow, and it no longer has anything at all to do with the person I've become. The part of me that matters now exists solely in my mind and in my heart, both of which have grown enormously to compensate. Curiously, I've found I actually have more to give to others now than at any other time in my life. Not in physical or material terms certainly, but emotionally, in terms of friendship, love, and support.

I've grown up considerably over the past five or six years. I've matured in a lot of ways and have come to understand and appreciate what's really important in my life—things such as family, friends, others who are a lot less fortunate than I've been, and above all, the love for and of a child. My niece and nephew, Deborah and Matthew Brooks, have become the happiest, richest part of my life and they, along with my buddy Emily, have taught me what it means to love someone purely and unconditionally, without any thought at all of what might be in it for me. It's a lesson I've learned joyfully, an enduring one that will last me for a lifetime.

But Emily's growing up now, and with Matt and Deborah living in Oregon I still have all those long and empty hours to fill somehow. TV, books, and music can only take me so far, and increasingly I find myself escaping into the world of imagination I've created inside my mind.

One of my favorite devices for passing the long hours alone is a game I call "What If?". Whenever I feel the need to get away for a while, I'll post a hypothetical question to myself, such as, "What if I won fifty million dollars in the lottery?" Then I'll shut out the rest of the world and spend the next twenty-four hours disposing of the windfall down to the very last cent.

Other times I'll ask myself what I'd do if I could live anywhere in the world I wanted to. Once I've decided, I'll begin building a dream house in my mind, brick by brick, then furnish it down to the last roll of toilet paper in the bathroom. Sometimes I'll dream up a few exciting neighbors, too, and create an entire bustling neighborhood for myself.

There's another game I play—my very favorite—called "Tom Selleck and Other Hallucinations I Haven't Had." This one is a lot more involved than the others and goes a long way toward helping me stay sane. Most of the time I'm pretty good at keeping a lid on the rougher emotions like anger, frustration, and depression, but there are times when it gets to be too much, and I run away into my make-believe universe of daydreams and imaginary lovers.

Inside that universe there lives one perfect man I've created all for myself. I'm closer to him than to any other person in the world, and I know everything there is to know about him. I know how he likes his eggs cooked, where he keeps the aspirin, what his favorite movies are, how much starch to put in his shirts, and even who to call when he's sick. When you spend as much time with someone as I've spent with him, you get to know those kinds of things. And we've been together for quite a long time now.

We've sailed around the world together a thousand times and made love on every island beach from Fiji to Fatu Hiva. We've hiked the Himalayas, run naked on the Serengeti, and danced all night to the wild island drums of Jamaica. The world belongs to us when we're together and I know that as long as my friend is there beside me, holding my hand, then nothing bad can ever happen again.

He's the one person in the world I can say *anything* to and never worry that he'll misunderstand. He knows the best and worst of who I am, and he understands the frightened, damaged child who lives inside me, hiding in the shadows, fearful of my anger.

Sometimes that anger is so great, the rage and bitterness so overpowering, that I'm afraid if I ever let it out, it would fill up the universe with so much poison that nothing healthy could ever grow there again. When the fear of it overwhelms me and I begin to scream, he holds me in his arms and lets me cry until everything is washed clean again, and all that matters is that he's there.

Sometimes I get carried away with my imagination, I know, but there's one game I *don't* play anymore, a game I used to call "What Would I Do If They Found a Cure Tomorrow?". For more than a decade, that was my favorite pastime and I took great pleasure in imagining how it would be if suddenly I could walk again and do all the things I used to do.

Almost always, Alaska was the destination I'd choose, and I'd spend countless hours imagining what it would be like to live there for the rest of my life, safe with my friends and family in the land I love so desperately. Sometimes the fantasy was so intense that I could actually feel the cold Arctic breeze against my skin and smell the sea in the distance, its salty spray calling me back to the place where I once belonged.

But I don't do that anymore. Twenty years is too long a time to go on kidding myself, pretending there's a happy ending to all of this, dreaming dreams that can't come true. It's like praying to God for help, night after night, year after year, only to wake up each morning in worse shape than I was the night before. After a while the prayers become nothing more than a rhetorical cry for mercy.

Have I lost hope altogether for a cure in my lifetime? To be honest, I don't even think about it anymore. I've chased my share of rainbows, running all over the world in search of one miracle or another, and now it's someone else's turn. Let the others run to Germany and Israel and God knows where else, looking for answers to questions that haven't been asked. I'll stay right here where I am and wait to see what happens, too tired anymore to follow.

Rest is what I need now, a thousand-year's sleep, a respite from the turbulence in my mind. The future was a place I spent most of my life running away from, but it's gaining on me now and the closer it gets, the more frightened I become. My other arm has begun to weaken recently and when I think ahead to all the things that might imply, my eyes fill with tears and something deep inside me collapses.

I'm not the first person to look down the road and see no end, and I know I won't be the last. The road is well marked now by those who have gone before, fellow travelers who journeyed alone in the darkness and who found a way to leave something behind, a light to guide the way. And I will too. I don't know how, or sometimes even why, but there has to be a way to make it all count for something, to say to the world that I was here and that it mattered.

But for right now all I can think about is yesterday—a hazy, soft remembering of a time when anything was possible. The sweetest days I've ever known are anchored there, in those seven golden years, steeped in dreams and gentle memories of a time I can't forget.

I go there often in my thoughts now, back to the summers in Alaska, remembering how it was when the days were easy and the nights were long and warm. Mornings were somehow clearer then, the sky streaked with shades of blue and gold, and I couldn't wait to wake up each day to see what the world would bring my way.

I think about Homer and the summers spent on the water there, fishing for halibut, pretending I knew what I was doing. I remember sailing all day on Kachemak Bay, arms aching from pulling nets and crab pots, happy just to be alive, and wishing the day would never end.

I remember the Salty Dawg, too, standing ankle-deep in sawdust, drinking pitcher after pitcher of beer while I studied the names of long-forgotten sailors scribbled on the battered life rings that hung on every wall. More than anything, I wanted to earn the right to place my name there someday, too.

But most of all I think about the winters. I'll never forget how the snow smelled in the morning when the air was still and everything was fresh and clean. Or how it felt to snuggle down in my sleeping bag each night, safe and warm in my cabin while the freezing arctic winds howled past my door. There are just some things the senses won't let go of and because that's so, wintertime in Alaska will be mine to keep for as long as I live. My only wish is that I could go there one last time, just to see and smell and taste it all again.

But that's a pleasure left for others now, for anyone lucky enough or smart enough to know that freedom, with all its joy and heart-break, is all that really matters in the end. Those are the people, the independent spirits I'm counting on to finish the race for me—to run to the far, wild corners of the earth and bring back the stories that make it all worthwhile.

So if you ever find yourself in Homer, Alaska, please stop by the Salty Dawg Saloon and say hello for me. But before you sit down at the bar, look on the wall to the left of the front door. The life ring from the *Willie Allen* hangs there now and if you look closely, you can see where they let me sign my name.